Economic Instruments of Security Policy

ECONOMIC INSTRUMENTS OF SECURITY POLICY

Influencing Choices of Leaders

Second Edition

Gary M. Shiffman and James J. Jochum

ECONOMIC INSTRUMENTS OF SECURITY POLICY
Copyright © Gary M. Shiffman and James J. Jochum, 2006, 2011.

All rights reserved.

First edition published in the United Kingdom in 2006 by
PALGRAVE MACMILLAN, Houndmills,
Basingstoke, Hampshire RG21 6XS.

Second edition published in the United States in 2011 by
PALGRAVE MACMILLAN®—a division of St. Martin's Press LLC,
175 Fifth Avenue, New York, NY 10010.

Where this book is distributed in the UK, Europe and the rest of the world,
this is by Palgrave Macmillan, a division of Macmillan Publishers Limited,
registered in England, company number 785998, of Houndmills,
Basingstoke, Hampshire RG21 6XS.

Palgrave Macmillan is the global academic imprint of the above companies
and has companies and representatives throughout the world.

Palgrave® and Macmillan® are registered trademarks in the United States,
the United Kingdom, Europe and other countries.

ISBN: 978–0–230–11062–5

Library of Congress Cataloging-in-Publication Data

Shiffman, Gary M.
    Economic instruments of security policy : influencing choices of
    leaders / Gary M. Shiffman, James J. Jochum. — 2nd ed.
       p. cm.
    ISBN 978–0–230–11062–5
       1. International economic relations—Political aspects. 2. National
    security—Economic aspects. 3. Terrorism—Prevention—Case studies.
    I. Jochum, James Joseph, 1965– II. Title.

HF1359.S54285 2010
327.1'11—dc22   2010023354

A catalogue record of the book is available from the British Library.

Design by Newgen Imaging Systems (P) Ltd., Chennai, India.

Second edition: January 2011

10 9 8 7 6 5 4 3 2 1

Printed in the United States of America.

CONTENTS

Foreword to the Second Edition

Since the publication of *Economic Instruments of Security Policy*, the global economic landscape has experienced a monumental shift. Like never before, today's headlines are filled with references to sovereign debt, monetary policy, exchange rates, and debates about the role of the U.S. economy in the world. Topics likely considered "arcane" or "academic" in nature by the students of yesterday are now debated regularly within governments around the world. The principles discussed in *Economic Instruments* have come alive through real-life events, which enlighten the student but also create havoc in global financial markets by leading to rising unemployment, an unprecedented loss of private wealth, and sovereign defaults.

While the economic backdrop to the book has changed since its publication, the threats to global and national security discussed in the book remain real and urgent. At this writing, the world's major powers continue to grapple with how to prevent states like Iran from developing nuclear weapons and which instruments are best able to prevent states from failing and becoming havens for further terrorist activities. In short, the threats to our peace, stability, and prosperity were not put out of business by the Great Recession. The question which gave rise to this second edition of *Economic Instruments* is whether the financial tools available to fight these threats remain relevant and useful in this new economic environment.

Case studies, which formed the core of *Economic Instruments*, have been enhanced and updated to reflect emerging issues that challenge today's policy makers. Many of these case studies come directly from the personal experience of the authors. Toward this end, James Jochum joins this second edition as coauthor. In addition to being an adjunct professor of security and economics at Georgetown University and American University, Professor Jochum has played a significant role in developing and implementing many of the financial tools discussed herein. The reader of the second edition will benefit from our combined experience as both senior government policy makers and teachers of the next generation.

A principal theme of *Economic Instruments* is that the policy maker can craft more effective policies if one pays heed to the immutable laws of human nature. The Great Recession—as with all crises—revealed the best and worst of human nature. The effective policy maker will take the lessons learned from recent events and incorporate them into new policies to mitigate the threats of the future. The second edition of *Economic Instruments* provides the policy maker with the necessary tools to do so.

ACKNOWLEDGMENTS

Jim Jochum wishes to acknowledge: my wife Rita, daughter Elena, and parents Gary and Donna Jochum, for their consistent support of my twisting, turning career. My great bosses, who taught me the ways of Washington and much more: Senator Chuck Grassley, Senator Phil Gramm, and Secretary Don Evans. I fear that I took more from you than I gave in return. My colleagues in academia who had the faith in me to allow me into a classroom and begin the process that led to this book: in particular, my coauthor Dr. Gary Shiffman, Dr. Rick Cupitt, Dr. Maria Cowles, Dr. Dan Byman, and Dr. Shoon Murray. My friends and colleagues who have contributed to my courses at Georgetown and American University and to this book in innumerable ways: Grant Aldonas, Matt Borman, Marguerite Trossevin, Andrew Shore, Tim Keeler, Clay Lowery, and Karan Bhatia. To the civil servants at the Department of Commerce's Export Administration and Import Administration, thank you for your patience (with me), expertise, public service, and professionalism. I truly enjoyed the time I spent with you. My business partners at Jochum, Shore & Trossevin PC who graciously allowed me the time to work on this project, including Reza Karamloo who contributed directly to the content of this book. Lauren Lotko, for her intellectual contribution, attention to detail, and her diligence in keeping us on schedule. Our great editors at Palgrave Macmillan for their support and assistance. Frankie the French Bulldog, my constant and faithful companion during the writing of this book.

Gary Shiffman thanks all of those acknowledged in the first addition, the Georgetown University Center for Peace and Security Studies graduate students who taught him so much over the past seven years, coauthor Jim Jochum, and our research assistants Lauren Lotko and Holly Ghali. And thanks to my family for continued support, you are awesome.

INTRODUCTION

"It is all about money—you economists are right," a friend and respected national security expert once quietly remarked. But who said economics was all about money? People often believe economics and national security intersect when discussing wealth, the velocity of the money supply, or derivative valuation in financial markets. While economists often work with these issues, the science of economics deals with people: people making choices, and the incentives and constraints that shape those choices. Think of the many decisions you make during the day: how many of those decisions are about money? Are you choosing to read this book because of money? Are you interested in security policies because of money? For most students we teach, the career choice to enter the security field applies to the mission and importance of security. Whether addressing the marketplace for goods and services, or political choices with global security consequences, individuals make the decisions. The individual seeks to maximize something—sometimes political power, sometimes money.

Economics, when applied to national security, remains a science of decision-making—an individual maximizing something (wealth, power, etc.) while facing resource and institutional constraints (democratic or autocratic checks on power, etc.). The United States did not decide to walk out on the Soviet Union at the 1986 Reykjavik Summit; Ronald Reagan walked away. Saddam Hussein, the individual leader of the political entity called Iraq, made the choice to invade Kuwait in 1990. Commander-in-Chief Bill Clinton decided to launch cruise missiles toward Sudan, Bosnia, and Iraq. George W. Bush chose to invade Iraq, and Barack Obama surged U.S. troops into Afghanistan in his first year in office. In statecraft, the stakes are not always this high, but individual people face choices and make decisions. *Economic instruments* employs economic analysis to understand how people make decisions related to national security. Through this micro approach—looking at the individual—we get meaningful analysis of the macro challenges and trends that define the great security debates of the day.

Institutions, such as the form and function of government, cultural norms, and religious practices, place constraints on the decisions of national security decision makers. Beyond individual decision making by leaders, this book analyzes the economic tools of national security by dissecting the decision-making process within institutional constraints provided by political systems. In our work in Washington, D.C., both inside and outside government, we have had the opportunity to identify specific, recurring influences on decision making in a democracy. We have also studied the patterns of decision making in autocracies—dictatorships—whose closed economies and political systems exhibit distinctly different, complex structures. Such systems include totalitarians, tyrants, and individual despots; they also include military juntas and benevolent monarchs. And like democracies, autocratic institutions impose limits on the behaviors of leaders.

Applying economic analysis—individuals maximizing something within resource and institutional constraints—to national security policy making yields economic tools of security policy. By pinpointing the constraints, alternatives, and goals of a security decision maker, we can understand, and then predict, the economic instruments that will change behavior. Policy makers can then craft and evaluate appropriate initiatives and responses to advance their own goals.

This book presents the aforementioned ideas in two parts. Part I of the book describes the theoretical tools for building economic instruments of security policy. No knowledge of economics is required to understand the intuition of this section, but economists will appreciate the full technical details. In addition, the first section ends with a summary of economic principles for national security policy. Part II of the book describes numerous economic instruments employed by policy makers today and contains a number of case studies. To have meaning for policy makers, the analytical method we develop in part I must stand up to real-world situations. We use actual events to explain the theories throughout most of this book.

We begin each chapter with a diagram that posits the ensuing discussion in the overall framework for applying economic instruments to national security policy making. The building blocks for this framework are shown in figure I.1.

At the base is the economic actor—human nature. Chapter 1 deconstructs the inherent characteristics of all people; this nature forms the foundation of economics. Only by understanding the person behind the curtain can you understand Oz. If we want to sway the man at the controls, we must direct our policies at the person.

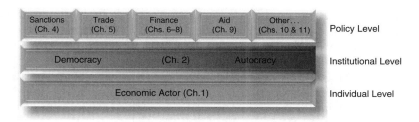

| Sanctions (Ch. 4) | Trade (Ch. 5) | Finance (Chs. 6–8) | Aid (Ch. 9) | Other… (Chs. 10 & 11) | Policy Level |

| Democracy | (Ch. 2) | Autocracy | Institutional Level |

| Economic Actor (Ch. 1) | Individual Level |

Figure I.1

The institutions within which the actors face constraints comprise the middle section. Institutions within a democracy, or within a dictatorship, can vary greatly, and there is a myriad of government institutions in the gray area between the extremes. So keep in mind that as we refer to either democracy or dictatorship, the types of each can also vary greatly. By taking an in-depth look at different types of dictatorships, chapter 2 demonstrates that institutional differences matter when crafting economic and security policies.

The third chapter ends the first part of the book by summarizing certain aspects of the individual and institutional levels of economic analysis, providing the reader with a basic tool kit for thinking about the rest of the chapters.

We begin part II by testing the analytic method we developed in the first three chapters against a specific case study on sanctions using a theoretical model, data, and empirical regression analysis. Specifically, we will examine a detailed case study of Fidel Castro's decisions while running Cuba in the context of U.S. unilateral sanctions targeting him from 1994 to 1999, to test our understanding of how to craft policies aimed at autocracies. No knowledge of regression is necessary to appreciate this in-depth application of an economic instrument—sanctions—to security policy making. Chapter 5 looks at the institutional functioning of a free market democracy, takes the United States as a case study, and examines the policies and politics of trade as a tool of security policy. Chapters 6, 7, and 8 address international finance and tools, such as monetary policy, exchange rates, and sovereign debt. Chapter 9 examines the link between poverty and national security to better inform aid and foreign assistance programs to advance security policies. Chapter 10 looks at recent, evolving economic tools against terrorists and terrorist organizations. The final chapter looks to international law for tools to apply economic pressures to decision makers to influence behavior important to national security.

The authors hope that readers will uncover fresh insights into the nexus of security policy making and economics as a rigorous academic discipline. New capabilities for shaping the world of the future by influencing the actions of leaders emerge as we combine real-world experience with the insights provided by economic analysis. We invite the reader to learn from our experiences by reading ahead.

PART I

The Individual

Every individual shares a fundamental and basic nature with people throughout the world and throughout history. Basic human nature does not change with culture, religion, or nationality, and it does not change over time. By studying human nature, we can understand something about every person. What we understand we can model; and what we model we can attempt to predict. If we can predict the behavior of a person given certain variables, then we can craft policies designed to maximize our objectives. To craft national security policies, we begin with the decision maker. To shape the world, we must first understand basic human nature.

CHAPTER 1

States Don't Make Decisions; People Do

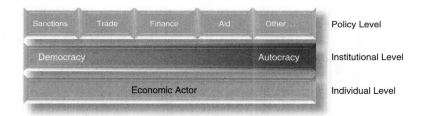

Figure 1.1

Fundamentally, as the building blocks diagram in figure 1.1 illustrates, human decision making resides at the base of our analysis. To be sure, there exists a complex web of institutions and incentives that may affect the outcome of a policy. The president works with the legislative and judicial branches of government in a U.S.-style democracy. The president also works with the private sector, interest groups, and the diplomatic community. The dictator works within his own system, perhaps affording him some advantages but also imposing limits upon his power. For example, the dictator must earn the loyalty of his generals and secret police leaders. Each person involved in this world—each actor—faces limited resources and must make decisions. Statecraft, the art of leading a country, happens at this precise point. One can influence the actions of a country by influencing the leaders. By influencing the actions of the country, we achieve our goal. Sound policy starts with an understanding of the individual.

We begin with a theory of human nature. From this, we will build toward a theory of statecraft. If we assume that within each person resides the same basic and unmalleable nature, we will have one variable identified that will apply to every country in the world. In particular, we will focus on one observable manifestation of human nature: the propensity to trade. Individuals trade to maximize our welfare, and we make decisions based on varying conditions of scarcity.

At the core of men, women, and children, no matter where or when in history they have lived, resides the same propensity: "to truck, barter, and trade one thing for another." From this assertion made by Adam Smith in 1759 emerged what we call economic science—a science of decision making.

People do not need to understand economic science in order to know that they trade and that they maximize. Apples fell from trees before Newton described gravity; the reality of gravity requires no theory in order to operate. But a scientist wishing to test hypotheses related to gravity needs to know the theory. Similarly the policy analyst must have a theory in order to test hypotheses of policy making. And while it is true that you may have learned to play billiards years before your first physics class, you learned by trial and error, and maybe you lost a few dollars.

Enumerating a catalogue of policies and the debate that surrounds the use of each would prove modestly interesting but ultimately not very helpful to policy makers. The value of studying these policies comes, instead, from understanding how to enact meaningful policies and evaluate their effectiveness. We first need to know who the players are and under what circumstances they are making decisions in order to intelligently assess sanctions, trade, finance, and aid, among many other tools of foreign policy.

Imagine a world with only two countries, A and B. They are not at war and, in fact, cooperate on many issues. They also compete economically. I am the democratically elected head of state leading country A, and you are the totalitarian dictator ruling country B (see figure 1.2). How can I get you to do something or stop you from doing something? What tools do I have to influence this sphere that comprises our two countries?

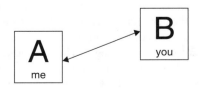

Figure 1.2

I can employ violence. I can invade, launch cruise missiles, or place an armada off the coast threatening military action. However, the people of democracy A are not ready for war. The costs, as they perceive them, would exceed the benefits in the long run. What options do I have to influence your policy decisions short of military action? And how can you avoid susceptibility, also short of war?

Policy making traditionally requires learning about the country: relative wealth, fiscal health, monetary soundness, any current account and capital account deficits, degree of openness to trade, and financial flows. In addition, and more importantly, analysts and policy makers must understand how decisions are made within each country. What are the governing structures? If country A is a democracy and country B is an autocracy, our policies will be different than if both countries are democracies or both are tyrannies.

Beyond traditional economic analysis, or what may be called the wealth variables of policy making, we will start our discussion of economics and national security policy making with a microeconomic view: individuals making decisions in conditions of scarcity.

ADAM SMITH AND TWENTY-FIRST CENTURY NATIONAL SECURITY

It may seem counterintuitive, but to address the security threats of today, we will begin with literature written before 1776. How can Adam Smith teach us to form effective policies directed at twenty-first century dictators? Smith's fundamental principles light the way. How Vladimir Putin makes decisions today and how Henry VIII made decisions 500 years ago remain the same in the most fundamental way—because basic human nature remains constant. The recognition of this unmalleable characteristic of human nature provides us with an opportunity to understand and predict the behavior of all leaders.

Adam Smith wrote and lectured on moral philosophy, not economics or political science; yet his philosophy includes economic and political themes. In this chapter we will investigate Smith's moral philosophy to illuminate his theory of nature, which includes the individual and the individual's desire for approbation. Specific application of Smith's works concludes this chapter.

Human nature, according to Adam Smith, is characterized by a person's desire for survival of self and kin; this desire displays itself in several different traits. While Smith was not completely original in his thinking, he codified in a succinct body of work the study of human nature in a framework suitable for social, political, and economic application. Adam Smith's discourses on human nature can be directly extended to national security.

The life works of Adam Smith consist of three significant extant collections. His *Lectures on Jurisprudence* address natural laws and the objective embodiment of "virtue." In the second, *The Theory of Moral Sentiments*, Smith primarily discusses how men judge themselves and their neighbors, as well as the psychology of benevolence, justice, and prudence. His third and most well known, *An Inquiry into the Nature and Causes of the Wealth of Nations*, sets forth Smith's theory of self-interest and moral judgment.

Nature is the bedrock of Smith's conceptions: his "natural philosophy." Smith expresses his philosophy with phrases like "natural system of perfect liberty and justice" and "system of natural liberty."[1] Nature, by its presence in both definitions, indicates its prominent place in Smith's social philosophy. Nature, the "passionate pursuit of interest," actuates the desire for preservation and approbation; these are the factors that comprise a person's fundamental nature.[2]

> Self-preservation, and the propagation of the species, are the great ends which Nature seems to have proposed in the formation of all animals. Mankind is endowed with: a desire of those ends, and an aversion to the contrary; a love of life, and a dread of dissolution; a desire of the continuance and perpetuity of the species, and an aversion to the thoughts of its entire extinction. But though we are in this manner endowed with a very strong desire of those ends, it has not been entrusted to the slow and uncertain determinations of our reason, to find out the proper means of bringing them about. Nature has directed us to the greater part of these by original and immediate instincts.[3]

Think of the modern-day dictator and politician—a person who is endowed by nature with a desire for self-preservation and aversion to extinction. This just makes sense and comports with what we observe.

While Smith, the philosopher, explored the abstract, he openly conceded the mechanics of "man's nature" to be "a mere matter of philosophical curiosity."[4] Stated more concisely, while the mechanics—the driving force—of morality may be compelling, the nature—the implementation—of morals provides useful practical knowledge.

Reason and passion, according to Smith, constitute human nature and guide the pursuit of self-preservation and approbation. The predominant characteristic of nature applies to all living creatures and constitutes a person's "supervening appetite." Being manifest as an appetite, the means of self-preservation come to a person just as an appetite for physical sustenance causes a person to eat. Survival is not constructed, nor is a person capable of survival through reason alone; survival is nature acting in a person, beyond self-reason. Smith's explanation of this point describes a person who might be selfish, narcissistic, and competitive to the exclusion of compromise. While this may explain some situations at some times, overall the world presents a much greater degree of order. Without contradicting the dominance of passion, Smith describes cooperation through the idea of virtue.

Virtue is a measure of the degree to which an action supports the natural goal of survival; virtue is a measure of "nature's" ability to work within, through, or upon a being. A person's actions, according to Smith, are judged in relation to the amount of virtue the action possesses at the time it is committed.[5]

Smith does not identify the proper end or goal of life; in fact, he is careful not to do so. This is consistent with his other works. Were he to say that everyone should work toward a similar goal, then individuals would not be encouraged to exercise their competitive advantages in pursuing objectives to which they may be more suited than others. The application to the social good is clear. Man is disposed toward preservation of himself and those around him. Any actions that advance this cause provide an internal sense of virtue. The virtue is both internal and social, since social virtue benefits society.

Pairing passion and morality appears to run counter to the ethics of today, as it equally would have in Smith's day. This link, therefore, requires clarification through an explanation of right and wrong, the desire for approbation, and the conduct of the moral person. The assertion might seem less contradictory in consideration of the fact that a person acts virtuously when every other person, provided he is sane and disinterested, would approve of his actions. He attains approval when his actions benefit society. Virtue, therefore, defines "right" and its opposite defines "wrong."

> Every faculty in one man is the measure by which he judges of the like faculty in another. I judge of your sight by my sight, of your ear by my ear, of your reason by my reason, of your resentment by my resentment, of your love by my love. I neither have, nor can have, any other way of judging about them.[6]

Following self-preservation, approbation constitutes Smith's second prominent tenet. If survival represents the selfish impulse, the desire for approbation explains the compassionate impulse. Approbation connects self-interest, which causes a person to act, with the personal concept of good and bad, providing clues for why a person is motivated in one direction or another. We desire approbation. It is a good.

Smith's methodology, and that employed throughout this book, requires no abstract morality or theology; Smith defines virtue upon the conception of man's nature, his will toward conservation, and the sympathetic reaction of his fellow man.

The explanation of Smith's framework to this point has described human nature in terms of survival and, through an "internal spectator," morality. We now turn to the second prong of his philosophy, which describes the manifestation of natural morality in terms of a need for approval from others.

Adam Smith explicitly asserts that man acts virtuously because he has an "impartial spectator" watching his every action; this spectator presides at all times because he is the "man within the breast."[7] The internal man provides a final analysis of virtue. The "man in the breast" represents fellow man at every instant. The internal spectator scrutinizes man, provided he is sane and rational.

Pursuit of survival without temperament by approbation would stoke an anarchic world. Approbation, however, imposes limits. The conflicts arising from balancing the needs of many cannot always be overcome. Proximity becomes the determinant factor when needs compete. Human nature, therefore, focuses on approbation in relation to proximity. It is also a function of human understanding, either intellectually or innately, that survival is more easily accomplished within a group and, therefore, cooperation is conducive to self-preservation. Smith observes, "every man is first and principally recommended to his own care; and every man is certainly, in every respect fitter and abler to take care of himself than of any other person, it is fit and right that it should be so."[8]

Economists do not postulate that people are totally selfish, contrary to popular culture. Gordon Gekko in the movie *Wall Street* passionately indicts "greed" as the evil that motivates markets. Surely an individual maximizes; he wants the most for himself. But he also wants the most for his family and community. He prioritizes: his family's well-being matters more to him than yours or mine. Visualize concentric circles around every person. The closer the circles are to us, the more we want for the people in those circles.

The need for approbation, however, mitigates the raw selfishness theory more than anything else. Person A may want more chocolate ice cream, but will not steal it from another person for fear of losing respect from his or her family and community. The loss would be a scarlet letter of sorts. Shame motivates people just as reward does because people seek respect; approbation explains why there is more order in the world than if greed alone were to motivate people. Keep this in mind when we turn to dictators and democratic leaders.

The concepts of maximizing and approbation contribute to the unlocking and shaping of behavior. Smith's works in their entirety probe human decision making in conditions of scarcity. They comprise the basis for economic science. But when people think of economics today, they often associate the science with GDP calculations, job growth numbers, and interest rate decisions being made by the central bank. In the United States, the Federal Open Market Committee of the Federal Reserve, and economic indicators leap to mind. Certainly these are aspects of economics, but the scientific study dating to Smith guides us to what some readers may simply understand as "microeconomics." If someone talks to you about micro- versus macroeconomics, think of macroeconomics as aggregated issues such as GDP and monetary policies, and think of microeconomics as the scientific study of how a person makes a decision in a condition of scarcity.

This discipline can be applied to many things. Throughout this book, we will use the foundation of economic science discussed in this chapter to analyze the national security decisions made by individual policy makers.

Maximizing, Rationality, and the Bounds of Institutions

Individuals seek to maximize something—money, power, happiness—whatever motivates them. But we encounter scarcity throughout the world. As the comedian Steven Wright dryly points out, "You cannot have everything. Where would you put it?" We've covered the basics of human nature, at least as it is understood by economists. We now move to the limits, or constraints. To go from nature to decisions, we need to understand why people make decisions. Scarcity motivates decisions, a fact that figures prominently in our analysis.

Since you cannot have everything, you make choices. Consider the diamond and water paradox. Diamonds are not necessary to life. In fact, most people around the world live their lives without ever owning a diamond. Water, however, sustains life itself; people cannot live without water. Clearly, water is more valuable than diamonds. But turn on the faucet in any building and water flows freely. At my home, I pay a modest amount on a quarterly basis for unlimited water. Diamonds, however, rank among the most expensive items people buy. Water is invaluable for life itself, yet inexpensive; diamonds are unnecessary and yet expensive. The solution to this paradox boils down to scarcity. Where water is readily available, it is free. Diamonds, however, are scarce and, therefore, expensive.

Alter the conditions of scarcity and the dynamics change. A truck driver with a jug of water comes upon a dying man who has just crossed a desert. The driver can extract extraordinary amounts of money for a few sips (we acknowledge, a cold-hearted example). The dying man would surely give up a diamond ring on his finger in exchange for a jug of water—with no other water available and his survival at risk.

Scarcity is a powerful determinant of human behavior. Prices reflect scarcity. The price of water at a water fountain in a library differs from the price in a desert. Prices facilitate the relationship between supply and demand. We want the price of a commodity to fluctuate freely so that neither a shortage nor a glut appears: the market clears. When prices are free to fluctuate, they signal supply and demand and bring about an economically efficient outcome. Elected presidents and tyrants face scarcity and make choices, as well. Human cognition and institutional constraints influence the way these choices are made.

Imagine the simplest economy: one person choosing between two commodities. In this example, think of Robinson Crusoe on an island producing and consuming either bananas or fish, and that is all. He cannot trade, since he lives alone on the island; he cannot save, so what he produces he also consumes. The diagram in figure 1.3 shows the maximum productive capacity of the economy, known as the Production Possibility Frontier (PPF). If he spent all of his time harvesting bananas, he could produce the maximum number, say twenty, along the y axis, and would have no fish. If he only fished, he would have twenty fish, but no bananas. And he could substitute production of fish for bananas and produce some combination of both bananas and fish. The real economy presents countless choices, even to one person on an island, but for the sake of drawing in two dimensions, we show the PPF here as a choice between two commodities.

Crusoe's preferences are revealed by his behavior—we know he prefers a combination of bananas and fish because he produces and

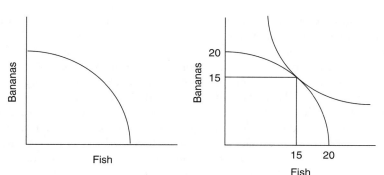

Figure 1.3

consumes a combination. We draw this revealed preference with a line called a utility curve (U). He cannot produce more than permitted by the constraints of his economy, the PPF. So he maximizes his consumption at the tangent of the PPF denoted by the utility curve.

This basic diagram shows the idea of preferences and constraints, and will be used throughout this book in evolved forms to demonstrate the basic economic articulation of fundamental human nature. We can model individual decision making using the ideas of constrained maximization. This applies to you, me, the president of the United States, the kleptocratic leader of a Marxist government, the leader of al Qaeda, and the leaders of the Taliban.

Rationality in Human Cognition

We are moving toward an understanding of leaders and policies. People make decisions in conditions of scarcity, but predictive models make heroic assumptions: sanity and rationality. That is, in order to predict the behavior of an individual, we must understand the unchangeable nature of mankind, appreciate scarcity and the need for decisions, the role of prices, and assume that the individual is both sane and rational. We assume that sane and rational people make decisions that accrue benefits in their own self-interest.

Before we get to how the world works and how we can advance security, we will explore how these assumptions can fail. This understanding will take us to the frontiers of understanding the science of decision making and, therefore, better inform our policy recommendations.

First, economists, incorporating knowledge from other academic disciplines, have acknowledged that we may not understand what it means to be rational. The Nobel Prize in Economic Sciences (the Bank of Sweden Prize in Economic Sciences in Memory of Alfred Nobel) has, in recent times, recognized scholars who challenge the classical assumptions: rationality, perfect information, and no transactions costs. The 2002 Nobel Prize in Economic Sciences was awarded to Daniel Kahneman, a psychologist who questioned these assumptions about human behavior. The laureate joined forces with economist Amos Tversky to develop a prolific body of academic literature.[9] In decades of work, the two argue that the theoretical actor in an elegant economic model is "psychologically unrealistic." Economists have begun to learn from psychology, sociology, and other disciplines that shed light on human choices.

Kahneman distinguishes cognition into two systems: intuition and reasoning. Intuition is fast, effortless, and emotional; reasoning is slow, effortful, serial, flexible, and emotionally neutral. A person makes decisions using one of the two systems. For familiar questions, intuitive answers come quickly. For the less familiar, one must often apply reason and take time to review facts, rules, and the like prior to making a decision.

Kahneman argues that decisions that appear irrational may not be based upon faulty reasoning, but instead upon intuition and reasoning that is not careful. The example of the cold-pressor makes the point. A person immerses one hand in cold water for a short session of sixty seconds, and then immerses one hand for a longer session of ninety seconds. In the short session, the temperature is set at 14 degrees Celsius. In the long session, the first sixty seconds are identical, the water is 14 degrees. For the additional thirty seconds, however, the water is warmed by one degree to 15 degrees Celsius. The water remains painfully cold, just one degree less cold.

When later asked which experience they preferred, a large majority of subjects indicated a preference for the long session. They also indicated that they were unaware of the exact time difference, only that the long session was a little bit longer. The last thirty seconds of the long session, however, felt better than the last thirty seconds of the short session. One may argue these people gave irrational answers: preferring the ninety seconds of pain over sixty seconds of pain. The point of the experiment, however, argues that based upon the characteristics of the intuitive process, it appears that the majority of decisions in this study reflected intuitive rather than reasoned responses. Kahneman and his collaborators therefore claim that while man may be rational, one must differentiate between decisions based upon intuitive processes and those based upon reasoning. When a decision seems irrational, such as preferring ninety seconds of pain rather than sixty seconds of pain, they may simply be based upon the intuitive process.

The power of the intuitive process is the focus of Malcolm Gladwell's bestseller *Blink: The Power of Thinking Without Thinking*. With a series of anecdotes and scientific explanations drawing from the fields of neuroscience and psychology, Gladwell argues that intuitive decisions can be as accurate as decisions made by cautious and thorough deliberations; that it is possible to learn when to listen to intuitive decisions and when to be wary of snap judgments; and that intuitive decision making can be educated and controlled.

Gladwell illustrates this argument at the beginning of the book with the story of an ancient Greek statue. A very rare sixth century B.C. marble statue known as a *kouros* came to market in 1983. There are only a couple hundred *kouroi* in existence, and this one was almost perfectly preserved. The J. Paul Getty Museum in Los Angeles agreed to buy the statue from an art dealer for nearly $10 million, but only after a thorough investigative process by art experts and scientists to verify the authenticity of the artwork. There was considerable fanfare regarding the purchase, and the *New York Times* marked the opening display of the statue with a front-page story. But as art historians and curators were taken to view the *kouros*, they responded in dismay. One historian claimed to feel a wave of "intuitive repulsion" just by looking at the statue. Ultimately, after further research, the Getty's case for the statue's authenticity began to unravel. That which took the Getty's lawyers and scientists fourteen months of painstaking investigation, some of the world's foremost experts in Greek sculpture determined almost instantly through intuition.

We can also see intuitive decisions made in the context of security policy. For example, when President George W. Bush declared in June 2001 that President Vladimir Putin seemed to have a good soul, he did so based upon intuition. Although it may not be possible for us to assess if Bush's statement is true or false, we do know that it was not based upon thorough analysis, but rather a feeling following a ninety-minute meeting. The implications of intuition in decision making, in the context of global power politics, can be significant.

Institutional Constraints

Institutions also play a significant role in explaining decision making. Douglass C. North's 1993 Nobel Prize in Economic Sciences recognized his work that challenged the economic model's assumption of zero transactions costs. In the theoretical model, people exchange voluntarily, and both parties in an exchange are therefore better off. But if transactions include friction, then an industry will arise to facilitate transactions.[10]

Think of purchasing a new car. A lot of people make money on the transaction—not just the people who manufacture the car. I need someone to tell me about the car, help me pick options, fill out paperwork, get a loan processed, explain the service contract, and deliver the car to the dealership. The manufacturers at the factory and the purchasers of cars never meet; they do not take part in a direct exchange. The transaction costs are considerable in purchasing a car, and so an industry—the automobile dealers—exists to facilitate that transaction.

The institutions of the auto industry arise to provide efficiencies so that I can buy a car without having to go to Detroit and Tokyo to compare auto manufacturers and then purchase my car. It is fair to ask to whom they are more efficient. Are Ford and Toyota equally served on any given day by the auto marketplace? What if I wanted to start a car company, would the institutions serve me? Is the purpose of the auto industry to bring about a social good? No. People involved seek to maximize their profits while also keeping and earning respect and approval. Their actions will, however, provide social good in many ways. For example, a dealer that provides services to a customer reduces the hassle of purchasing a car. Although the dealer acts pursuant to his own self-interest, the dealership owner informs consumers and provides competitive prices in the process of providing automobiles to the mass marketplace.

Think also about government as an institution in a marketplace. As Douglass North said in his Nobel acceptance speech:

> Institutions are not necessarily or even usually created to be socially efficient; rather they, or at least the formal rules, are created to serve the interests of those with the bargaining power to create new rules. In a world of zero transactions costs, bargaining strength does not affect the efficiency of outcomes; but in a world of positive transaction costs it does.[11]

Institutions arise from human interaction and input. In the presence of transactions costs, those with the resources to pay these costs, in a manner of speaking, can expend resources to influence the rules. So while a social good may, in fact, emerge from the institutional guidelines, they are subject to influence. Trade regimes, international security arrangements, and financial regulations all face this rule of influence. So much important policy could come from understanding this factor of institution building.

Institutions, once in place, serve to constrain the behavior of all. A dictator must live by many, if not all, the rules of government he sets up. At some point, even the appearance of compliance with his own rules seems logical to prolong his rule and his rules. As North writes,

> Institutions are the humanly devised constraints that structure human interaction. They are made up of formal constraints (e.g., rules, laws, constitutions), informal constraints (e.g., norms of behavior, conventions, self-imposed codes of conduct), and their enforcement characteristics. Together they define the incentive structure of societies and specifically economies.[12]

We know from economic science that people will act to maximize. Institutions matter, says North. "Institutions form the incentive structure of a society and the political and economic institutions, in consequence, are the underlying determinant of economic performance."[13]

How does this inform national security policy? Assembling the foundational pieces, we can model "economic man" based upon over 200 years of study and a healthy understanding of the limits of this science. So far, in examining how the world works, we operate from the premise that all leaders have goals, they seek to maximize, they desire approbation, they command limited resources, and they must work within institutions and with and among other individuals. We will move on to model the decision maker in democracy and dictatorship, and apply policies such as sanctions, trade, finance, and aid to see how they work and why.

Throughout this book, decision-making discussions center on an individual as opposed to aggregating decisions of groups of people. Human nature is constant across the globe and throughout time. Aggregating decisions—people from the United States like hamburgers and people from Japan like sushi—can only lead to errors and trouble. For help in applying theory to real people in the real world, we look again to North:

> Individuals must not only have objectives, but also know the correct way to achieve them. But how do the players know the correct way to achieve their objectives? The instrumental rationality answer is

that, even though the actors may initially have diverse and erroneous models, the informational feedback process and arbitraging actors will correct initially incorrect models, punish deviant behavior, and lead surviving players to correct models.[14]

EXPERIMENTATION IN ECONOMIC SCIENCE

A third frontier in the study of economic science is experimentation (bounds of rationality and institutions were the first two discussed), which takes the model off the paper and exposes it to real decision makers. Man's unchanging basic nature of operating with constraints and within institutions can be modeled. Models do not take into account all details of the world; there would be no point in this. A good model simplifies the world in a predictive and accurate manner. Vernon L. Smith shared the Nobel Prize in Economic Sciences in 2002 for a life's work developing the field known as experimental economics. In this discipline, real people are given real incentives under simulated circumstances to test theoretical models. Testing the bounds of rationality and the incentives provided by institutions— testing the behavior of an actual person in a given circumstance— brings economic science closest to the real world of people.

In 2009, Elinor Ostrom became the first woman to receive the Noble Prize in Economic Sciences, which she shared with Oliver E. Williamson. If Vernon L. Smith is considered the father of experimental economics, Elinor Ostrom may well be the mother of fieldwork in economic science. Following the announcement that Ostrom was awarded the Nobel Prize, Smith wrote of the newest laureate, "She blends field and laboratory empirical methods, economic and game theory...and she constantly challenges her own understanding by looking at new potentially contrary evidence and designing new experiments." In short, by combining theory, experiment, and fieldwork, Ostrom "listens carefully to data, and avoids muckraking."[15]

In the following chapters, we will take a similarly rigorous approach that "avoids muckraking." We have articulated a theory of the economic actor in this chapter, which we will use to create a specific theory of the autocratic economic actor in the next chapter. After summarizing these theories at the end of part I, we begin part II by applying these theories to Fidel Castro's Cuba. Finally, our fieldwork, so to speak, will take the economic actor out of theory and experimentation and into real-world case studies of the use of particular tools of security.

For the pragmatist, the applicability of economics to the real world of people represents good news. Practitioners of policy making and analysis have at their disposal a rigorous academic discipline. More than 225 years of study, intuitive critiques, and tests on real people have proven the relevance of economic science outside academe. Adam Smith's fundamental nature of man, the limits to rationality, and the constraints of institutions advance the analytical tools available to today's policy makers. The policy maker can see the world through a new prism—which is really an old prism. Economic analysis is not just aggregated data and discussion of gross domestic product. Rather, it can serve as the basis for formulating policy options that will achieve a desired outcome.

CHAPTER 2

The Economics of Autocracies

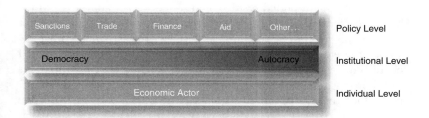

					Policy Level
Sanctions	Trade	Finance	Aid	Other...	
Democracy				Autocracy	Institutional Level
		Economic Actor			Individual Level

Figure 2.1

All leaders share some common nature and face conditions of scarcity. While all leaders also face institutional constraints, each faces different types of such constraints. We must understand institutions and the constraints they impose on decision makers to direct policies at leaders.

Autocrats of one form or another have ruled nations and people throughout most of human history. Looking around the world today, democracy comfortably resides in Europe and North America, but this has only been true for a few hundred years. Most of Latin America's democracies are young. Asia and the Near East have only scattered democracies, and these date back at most half of a century.

In spite of its long history, little has been written on the economics of autocracy. For example, a search of the entire JSTOR database of major journals of economics covering over 100 years reveals only seven articles with the word "autocracy" in the title. On the other hand, a search for the word "democracy" in the title reveals hundreds of articles.[1]

A grasp of autocrats requires stepping beyond the different stages of democratic development and the transition from command to market economies. To begin with the obvious, not all dictatorships are the same. Dictatorships, like democracies, differ from place to place. Deconstructing the incentives facing a specific dictator improves our ability to understand how best to influence them. For example, what if the policies of Western democracies toward a totalitarian regime have no impact on a specific dictator's economy? It is assumed—even taken for granted—that through trade and engagement, or conversely sanctions and embargoes, a country such as the United States can have an impact on another country's internal policies. Take, for example, Iran and North Korea. Although both are autocratic, Iran and North Korea require different policy approaches. Consider the following set of questions: Did multilateral sanctions on Iraq in the 1990s bring about any of the intended results? Did sanctions on Haiti ever work? Should the United States trade with the Communist-led government of the People's Republic of China and not with Castro-led Cuba?

For now we will focus on two themes in this large and charged debate. First we address the incentives facing a dictator. How does a totalitarian dictator view economic development within his economy? Does the answer to this question give us a tool to influence his behavior? As we model a dictator, we can understand what makes him tick—that is, why he will choose option A and not option B. When we have this knowledge, we can begin to craft policies likely to change his behavior. Second, we address policies impacting constraints in the general public, referring to how policies adopted by one country impacts the people of a second country. Again, if we can create an incentive for people in a target country to react in a certain way, we may be able to influence the policies of the government's leaders. Economic insights into these important questions may better inform the current thinking on trade, economic development, policy debates over economic sanctions, and the choices made by a totalitarian ruler and his personal optimum level of national economic performance.

Some Are Ranchers and Some Are Wolves

As recently as 1987, Gordon Tullock outlined what he called an opening in the discussion on dictatorship: "not that this book will be a last word on the study of autocracy, but that it will be the first."[2] In *Autocracy*, Tullock describes the dictator at the time he is in power. This stands in contrast to much of the work on autocracy, which instead addresses the transition of regimes: dictators coming into power and dictators losing power.

A dictator can be overthrown in three ways: by a coup perpetrated by high officials in his own regime, by foreign intervention, or by a genuine popular uprising. Given these threats, a dictator will behave in such a way as to minimize his susceptibility to being overthrown.

The important principle from Tullock's discussion, and one developed in subsequent literature, is that, as David Hume described, a ruler can rule people using security forces and armies, but he cannot rule the security forces and armies by that same power. This is similar to the "dictator's dilemma" described by Ronald Wintrobe.[3] In short, a dictator's trump card in maintaining power is to persuade people around him that "If it comes to an effort to overthrow me, I will win."

The dictator mitigates the risk of losing power if people remain convinced that the dictator will win in any conflict that challenges his power. If, however, those close to the dictator believe that a key member of the elite will successfully overthrow the dictator, then the loyalties of the elite will quickly shift. The salient question, then, is who will win in a threat to the dictator's power? The dictator has a strong incentive to ensure that all remain convinced that he can defeat any challenges.

Tullock suggests ways a dictator might do so. The dictator must always appear strong and prevent the formation of groups and coalitions that could undermine him. He must deter and prevent communications among potential conspirators; "take stringent enforcement of the law against treason"; and prevent others from maintaining positions of power. Rather than rely on individuals, he should use collegial control—such as boards, commissions, and cabinet positions—to hold power. It helps to sustain "a lot of pompous ceremony surrounding the dictator." And the dictator's decision must carry the day.

Mancur Olson, another distinguished voice in the study of autocracy, launched his own scientific line of inquiry into the dynamics of dictatorship. He observes, in the opening of his seminal article contrasting dictatorship with forms of democracy, that monarchists may be right. With power centered on one person, an economy can thrive in the absence of democracy. To explain this observation, Olson proposes a new theory of dictatorship and democracy for how they affect economic development.

Olson asserts that society requires "peaceful order" and "other public goods." Therefore, for society, anarchic violence cannot be rational. The constant plunder and fear of plunder would limit production, because rational people would expect that any wealth they created would be quickly taken from them. They would consequently not produce or accumulate wealth, and the economy would not grow.

Olson concludes that there are "colossal gains" to a dictator from the provision of domestic tranquility along with public goods.[4]

It is often observed historically that domestic tranquility can, in fact, arise among groups of people. For small groups, where coordination costs are low and externalities can be addressed, this order can occur voluntarily, as, for example, among hunter-gatherer bands. Olson treats the subject thoroughly in his writings.[5]

For large populations, however, no voluntary solution exists, according to Olson. To understand how large societies might evolve from anarchy, it is helpful to think of warlords—what he terms "stationary bandits." Warlords regularly steal from their subjects, but they simultaneously provide protection from occasional, irregular plundering by roving bandits. Known and anticipated theft is preferable to theft that is unknown and unpredictable. Therefore, although warlords are not legitimate powers in traditional political, economic, or social spheres, their monopoly power can direct societies away from anarchy to order.

Regular and known theft by a stationary bandit can be thought of as a tax. Moreover, by taking only a portion of society's production— the tax—and leaving the remainder to the producers, a rational bandit (or autocrat) ensures a future stream of income. Society can also rationally plan and produce, free of much uncertainty and certain of reward, albeit reduced.

The Olson perspective discerns why the wealth of the autocrat is proportionate to the production of the population. This powerful truth leads to the somewhat counterintuitive conclusion that a rational autocrat spends resources on public goods, but only when "the provision of these goods increases taxable income sufficiently."[6]

For example, assuming the autocrat keeps 50 percent of any increase in national income, he will receive 50 percent of any increase in national income arising from the provision of any additional public good. If he were to build a road from a river into a village center at a cost of $100, and this road increased national income by $600, then he would net $200 ($300 in incremental tax revenues, less the $100 cost). However, if he built a road at a cost of $100 and it increased national income by only $198, he would lose $1 ($99 in tax revenues, less the $100 cost). This autocrat, therefore, will provide public goods until the point at which the provision of the last good increases national income by twice the cost, or the inverse of his share. Stated another way, he will provide $100 of public goods unless the marginal increase on his investment produces less than a $200 increase in national income.[7]

Within this framework, the wealth-maximizing autocrat will tend to enlarge his personal surplus (tax revenues in addition to other benefits and exactions) through the exercise of his monopoly power, and he will not behave as a predator. The economically successful warlord is "not like the wolf that preys on the elk, but more like the rancher who makes sure that his cattle are protected and given water."[8] The autocrat, likewise, will benefit from nurturing the economy and taxing at an efficient rate.

Formally, the dictator chooses an optimal rate of taxation that maximizes his personal surplus (Π). In order to provide for public order and provide other public goods (G) as well as maximize his personal net surplus (Π), for a given tax rate (t), an increase in public goods leads to an increase in national income (I) and a resulting increase in net surplus.

$$\bar{t} : \uparrow G \Rightarrow \uparrow I \Rightarrow \uparrow \Pi$$

And for a given level of public expenditures (G), an increase in the tax rate (t) will decrease national income (I) and therefore decrease net surplus (Π).

$$\bar{G} : \uparrow t \Rightarrow \downarrow I \Rightarrow \downarrow \Pi$$

Note that increasing the marginal tax rate eventually distorts the incentives to produce. The rational and self-interested autocrat, therefore, will choose the tax rate that maximizes net surplus. He will also spend on public goods, but only to the point at which the marginal expenditure generates benefits equal to or greater than his expenditure. In so doing, he also ensures a gain to society equal to the inverse of his share of the national income.

Of critical importance to this understanding of the rational autocrat is the time horizon. The classic problem of autocracy is succession. The government reflects the leader's preferences and constraints, which means that the subjects will not know the rules by which the next government will operate. A person may produce more than they consume with security while the dictator's rule is assured. If rulers are routinely removed, followed by periods of anarchy and loss of property, then the incentives for production are distorted.

Autocrats who expect to rule only a short period of time will reflect similarly distorted incentives. If the ruler expects to hold power for only one year, for example, he may expropriate any assets whose plundered value exceeds the annual tax yield. In short, he will confiscate property, abrogate contracts, and ignore the long-term consequences of his decisions on the economy.

If, however, a consensus exists within the domain of the ruled over who will succeed the current ruler, then the cost of uncertainty will decrease. In this way monarchy, with a rational and self-interested ruler and a clear line of succession, can, in fact, provide the long-term stability required for a thriving economy.

As previously stated, all dictatorships are not alike. History of thought on dictatorships for this book goes back as far as Hannah Arendt, who defines totalitarianism as a regime that aspires to total domination.[9] Carl Friedrich and Zbigniew Brzezinski define totalitarianism as a syndrome consisting of six interrelated characteristics:

- official ideology
- a single party
- a terrorist police force
- monopoly of mass communications
- monopoly of armaments
- state control of the economy[10]

Jeane Kirkpatrick distinguishes between two types of dictatorships: totalitarian (such as Nazi Germany and modern Iran) and traditional autocracies (such as Samoza of Nicaragua, the Shah of Iran, and Marcos of the Philippines). In Kirkpatrick's typology, underpinning both traditional and totalitarian dictatorships is repression or coercion of the citizenry. The main difference between the two is the level of repression.[11]

Ronald Wintrobe advances Mancur Olson's work by addressing varying types of autocracies.[12] He compares totalitarianism with tinpot rulers, tyrannies, and *timocracies*. According to Wintrobe, who draws upon Arendt, Friedrich and Brzezinski, and Kirkpatrick, a tinpot gets involved in repression "only to the modest extent necessary to stay in office, and uses its rewards of monopoly of political power to maximize personal wealth or consumption."

Wintrobe defines tyranny as "a regime in which repression is high but which lacks or abjures the instruments of mass communication and control that make totalitarianism possible." He also offers that "timocracy (borrowed from Plato's *The Republic*) refers to a benevolent dictatorship in which the dictator genuinely cares for his or her people."

Wintrobe advances the literature of autocracy by identifying four general types of dictatorship common in the literature. Of particular value to our analysis is his conclusion that each style of leadership consists of different combinations of two tools of power: loyalty and repression.

Repression restricts freedoms, and includes bans on speech and press freedoms, and limits rights to organize civil, religious, and political organizations. Loyalty is usually sparked through payment premiums, either monetary or in the form of improved quality of life, to those in elite positions. Figure 2.2 provides Wintrobe's typology for understanding the varying combinations of loyalty and repression.

A totalitarian regime combines high degrees of repression with high degrees of loyalty among the elites. Today's totalitarians include Cuba's Raúl Castro, North Korea's Kim Jong Il, and Libya's Col. Muammar al Qadhafi. Tyrants maximize repression, usually minimizing investment into systems to promote loyalty. Think of Burma's ruling military junta, and kleptocracies like the Republic of Congo (Brazzaville) and Equatorial Guinea. Tinpots manage to remain in power with low levels of both loyalty and repression. These leaders usually do not stay in power as long as a tyrant, since they do not invest in the mechanisms to hold on to power; they usually try to strike it rich quickly and get out before getting killed. The *timocrat* manages to retain high degrees of loyalty with low amounts of repression. We consider Singapore's much-respected Lee Kwan Yew as a timocrat. He ruled as an autocrat, but spent a great deal of money on winning the support of the people he ruled.

We build on Wintrobe's typology of dictatorships by adding constraints to the diagram in figure 2.2. Referring back to figure 1.3 and the constraints characterized by the production possibilities frontier (PPF), we will draw the possible production constraints of a dictator in figure 2.3.

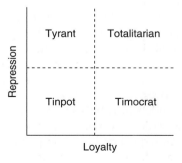

Figure 2.2

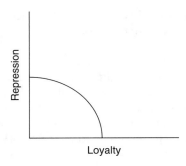

Figure 2.3

Nothing is free, including the cost for dictators to maintain power. Specifically, dictators must purchase loyalty and repression. The price of more loyalty is the forgone repression and, conversely, the price of more repression is the forgone loyalty, holding all other expenditures constant. Facing conditions of scarcity, a dictator will have to choose expenditures on loyalty and repression. The possible combinations are limited by the dictator's resource level—wealth, as well as his institutional constraints. For example, a dictator with few resources will be limited to a smaller amount of repression and loyalty than one with wealth. The possible combinations, shown on the curve in figure 2.3, limit the autocrat's ability to produce loyalty and repression.

On the other hand, an autocrat with greater resources can purchase more of each and may, therefore, choose to rule as a tyrant, totalitarian or timocrat. Institutional constraints limit options beyond wealth. For a given amount of wealth, a leader may be forced to produce more repression to maintain a hold on power (see figure 2.4). Conversely, a leader may produce more loyalty, because of an inability to produce repression (see figure 2.5).

We combine these two ideas of incentives and constraints to understand a dictator's decision making. In figure 2.6, the preferences take the shape of the utility curves, and the constraints are the PPF. Formulating effective security policy means influencing options so that the decision you want them to make will be better, for them, than all their alternatives.

Tullock, Olson, and Wintrobe have contributed substantially to the literature, but we still know relatively little about the dynamics at play within functioning dictatorships—despite the fact that they have been the predominant form of government throughout world history. Policy choices under dictatorships, however—like those under

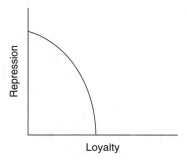

Figure 2.4

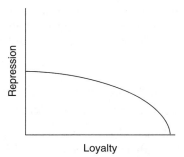

Figure 2.5

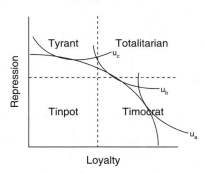

Figure 2.6

democracies—can be modeled and understood in a systematic way. Both political structures consist of rational and utility-maximizing individuals. Man's nature is universal and not malleable and, therefore, transcends borders and institutional regimes. So growth and development, as well as wealth and poverty, can be studied in terms common to any country: institutions, freedoms, and physical and human capital.

If we are going to understand security policies and how to maximize their effectiveness, we need to understand the mechanics of how they work. People make the decisions, and people maximize subject to the constraints described earlier and their particular preferences. They also face constraints arising from the institutions in which they operate. Human nature is universal around the world. The world can also be divided into two broad political institutions: dictatorship and democracy. Within dictatorship, there are many different variations, for example, Wintrobe's typology of totalitarian, tyrant, tinpot, and timocrat. What can we do with this knowledge? In the next section we will begin to build a model to simplify and explain a dictator's behavior. By doing so, we will make progress on maximizing our policymaking skills to enhance security.

PREDICTING THE DICTATOR: A THEORETICAL MODEL

To change a dictator's behavior for the benefit of our national security, we can model the dictator's behavior and test our policies for effectiveness and efficiency. This chapter assumes a model of a dictator with specific and defined attributes. We begin with a plausible totalitarian dictator, but keep open the option to exercise the model by changing these attributes later. Although the technical aspects of the model may be of special interest to academics, the narrative provides sufficient information for readers with limited experience in microeconomic modeling.

Generalized Dictator X: An Extreme Totalitarian Defined

The initial model makes six assumptions about the dictator.

- He has total control over government operations, fiscal and monetary policies, and taxation.
- He has total control over trade and foreign investment.
- He has an infinite time horizon in that he desires to remain in power throughout his lifetime, and for his state or revolution to continue forever.
- He came to power without the consent of the people he rules.

- The costs of maintaining power include the costs of repression and loyalty, as described in Wintrobe's typology: internal security and maintenance of a police state, as well as a system of benefits to engender loyalty among senior members of the security forces and other elites in domestic society.
- He desires to maximize his net income, which can be considered synonymous with government surplus: government revenues (from taxation, tariffs, joint ventures, international aid, and graft) minus the costs of running the country and staying in power.

Other factors can simplify the description of this dictator and his environment: the economy can be characterized as in a general state of poverty; domestic investment is assumed to be zero; and civil society is effectively absent. "Civil society" refers to civilian organizations pertaining to and among the public—not military or officially government-affiliated. Examples would be political parties or interest groups advocating for human rights, freedom of press, health care, or education.

These assumptions differ from Olson's in the following ways. Lacking legitimacy, dictator X uses force and the threat of force to maintain power. Olson seems to assume, beginning with a state of anarchy, that people will choose controlled theft over erratic theft and uncertainty, and therefore chose the dictator. We agree that controlled theft will be preferable to erratic theft; but, in addition, the model in this chapter simply assumes that the subjects prefer less theft to more theft, and therefore will desire to undermine the dictator in proportion to the amount of theft in which he engages.[13] Olson's model fails to address the uncertainty arising from the totalitarian's lack of legitimacy and, therefore, does not include security costs. The dynamics when security costs are added, however, are fascinating.

Here, the model assumes that the dictator's only threats arise from insurrection and overthrow; this totalitarian need not fear elections. He can direct expenditures and outlays among ministries, consistent with his absolute control over the economy. The dictator does not engage in production; he chooses the amount of government outlays and rate of taxation. As in Olson's model, the economy's wealth is, de facto, the dictator's wealth. He spends this wealth on public services (G) (roads, public works, and so on) that can increase national income at a cost (C), and on security services (S) (army, police, and security forces) that increase his likelihood of staying in power and, better yet, staying alive. His security costs increase as the wealth gap between the dictator and his subjects decreases, because both his loyalty among the elites and his coercive power over the people arise from his monopoly power over the sources of wealth. He pays these expenses, (C) and (S), from tax revenues that take two forms: a proportional income tax on domestic earnings and a tax on foreign direct investment (FDI) levied through mandatory partnership with the government. Property rights within the country are ill defined and, therefore, domestic savings and investment are negligible and assumed to be zero.

The Basic Model

Reminder: the model is provided for the economist or student experienced in microeconomic modeling. The intuition of the model should be apparent by reading this section without studying the complex system of equations.

We begin with the basic structure of incentives for this stylized dictator and then will address foreign investment. All investment in this model is defined as either foreign investment strictly limited to investment through the government (I_g) or foreign investment directly into privately held properties or ventures (I_d). The key distinction between I_g and I_d is to whom the direct benefits of investment flow. In the former, the dictator receives all the benefits. In the latter, the private borrower entering into the agreement receives the net benefit, and the dictator will receive that proportion corresponding to the direct and indirect flows from taxation.

The production function for this dictator in a closed economy without foreign trade is a function of government spending and tax revenues.

Equation 2.1
$$Q = q(G, t)$$

Where: Q is national output (or GDP), G is government spending and t is the average marginal tax rate. By assumption, tax revenue (T) is proportional to Q (i.e., GDP):

Equation 2.2
$$T = tQ,$$

The dictator's cost function includes both the costs of providing public goods and services as well as the maintenance of internal security to protect his power. Total costs, therefore, can be characterized as both a function of the total government spending as well as a function of the size of the GDP, where C is a function of government spending and S is a function of GDP.

Equation 2.3
$C = c(G)$ and

Equation 2.4
$S = s(Q)$

This dictator's net income (Y) therefore equals tax revenues (T) minus the cost of governing and providing public goods and stability (C) and minus the cost of maintaining a hold on power through security forces and payments to the elites (S).

Equations 2.5 & 2.6

$$Y = T - C - S$$
$$Y = t * q(G,t) - c(G) - s(q(G,t))$$

These relationships reveal the net income-maximizing rate of taxation (t^*) and the net income-maximizing level of government spending on infrastructure and services (G^*). Taking the first order condition of equation 2.6 with respect to t and G reveals the following:

Equations 2.7 & 2.8

$$\frac{\partial Y}{\partial t} = q(G,t) + t\frac{\partial q}{\partial t} - \frac{\partial s}{\partial q}\frac{\partial q}{\partial t} = 0 \text{ at max, } t^* = t(G)$$

$$\frac{\partial Y}{\partial G} = t\frac{\partial q}{\partial G} - \frac{\partial c}{\partial G} - \frac{\partial s}{\partial q}\frac{\partial q}{\partial G} = 0 \text{ at max, } G^* = g(t)$$

With the standard assumption of concavity, the second order conditions are negative, and the first order condition will characterize the income-maximizing level of taxation and government services.[14]

Basic Comparative Dynamics

Equations 2.5 through 2.8 provide the initial dynamics. Assume an initial marginal tax rate near zero when the dictator imposes a small marginal tax. His net income would be expected to increase. Looking at equation 2.5, if T increases while C and S are held constant, then Y indeed does increase. If the dictator increases the marginal tax rate, however, to a rate near 100 percent from some lower marginal rate, his net income will likely decrease. The economy's producers, who no longer have the opportunity to keep a portion of what they make, will have no monetary incentive to work. Between these two extremes, therefore, some point must exist where average marginal tax rate maximizes the dictator's net income. This rate is indicated by t^*.

Similarly, if the government completely stopped spending money on government services and infrastructure such as roads, telephones, public health, fire and police forces, sewage, and electricity, the government's net income could be expected to decline as the productive capability of the economy suffered from deteriorating infrastructure.

At the other extreme, if the government spends all of its gross revenues on government services and infrastructure, the net income of the dictator goes to zero. The income-maximizing level of government spending, then, is indicated by G^*.

Increasing these initial control variables, tax rate (t) and public spending (G), from zero will have a positive effect on income (Y) up to a point and then each will diminish income.

By assumption, all investment in this model is either I_g or I_d. It may be argued that I_d provides greater wealth-creating potential for the economy. Intuitively it makes sense that an economy with only public investments will likely be less efficient than a government with both private and public investments. The government, for example, may be less likely to invest resources in a more profitable yet less politically desirable investment than would a nongovernment market participant. Research on market efficiency and resource allocation tends to support this argument. More important, however, I_d provides a direct source of wealth to the subjects of the dictatorship—a source of wealth that does not originate with the dictator. It therefore strengthens the independence and freedom of the people relative to the government, thus diffusing power from the center to the whole of society. It promotes the development of a middle class and civil society.

This critical point deserves elaboration. The dictator being modeled here does not enjoy political legitimacy. He does not hold a mandate to rule from the ruled. He does not hold economic legitimacy because the population lives in general poverty. And he suppresses nongovernmentally sanctioned manifestations of civil society. Lacking these basic legitimate ties to power, he sees his government in a basic power struggle against civil, economic, and political forces outside of the government. He holds power through coercion, as well as through engendering loyalty among elites by providing benefits.

It is the monopoly power over the sources of wealth, therefore, that figures prominently into the dictator's calculus of maintaining power. Through taxation, he can fund security forces that stifle opposition and he can pay for the loyalty of the elites. He maintains a relative wealth gap. If he loses this advantage, people will organize, alternative leaders will emerge, and competing sources of wealth will create new power sources and weaken existing loyalties to the dictator. So long as the dictator maintains his monopoly power over the sources of wealth, he maintains his advantage.

Economic prosperity within his domain is not, in and of itself, good or bad for the dictator. The critical element remains who controls the sources of wealth. Monopoly power over the sources benefits the dictator. Diffusion of the sources of wealth away from the dictator, in this specific case, weakens the dictator's grasp on power. Any shift of power from the center increases the risk to the dictator of losing control and thereby increases the costs of security. S, therefore, is an increasing function of both Q and I_d.

Limited Investment

Assume I_g imposes no direct costs on and poses no risks to this dictator. Further assume that this dictator can successfully insulate the domestic economy from foreign investment that goes directly into privately held properties or ventures (I_d). In other words, foreign investors must partner with the government. For simplicity, assume that they are legally prohibited both from foreign ownership of domestic enterprises and from finding private sector partners for joint ventures. The dictator then pays the local workers—the foreign investor does not get to control the wages or working conditions. The wages earned by local workers at a joint venture, for example, will be commensurate with the wage rate in the domestic economy. The impact, therefore, of I_g investment on tax revenue (T) is very small and here assumed to be zero. In the specific case of the dictator defined in this model, all of the direct benefits to foreign investment accrue to the government.

This is not the case, however, with I_d. FDI invested directly in the productive factors of the economy and not through the government will likely increase GDP. It will, by equation 2.4, therefore increase security costs (S). In this model, the diffusion of power increases the likelihood of an overthrow of the regime. If the dictator, therefore, can limit investment to I_g and he takes a percentage of this investment,

kI_g such that $0 < k < 1$, where k is the effective tax rate on I_g, as net profits from the investment, then the revised net income equation can be characterized as follows:

Equation 2.9

$$\Upsilon = T + kI_g - C - S$$
$$\Upsilon = tQ + kI_g - C - S$$
$$\Upsilon = t^*q(G,t) + kI_g - c(G) - s(q(G,t))$$

Recall that the dictator incurs no cost from I_g, and that the dictator's ability to segregate the economy is so complete that the control variables t and G remain unchanged by I_g. This implies that the income-maximizing level of I_g is unlimited. As shown in equation 2.10, taking the derivative of Υ with respect to kI_g yields a positive constant.

Equation 2.10

$$\frac{d\Upsilon}{dI_g} = k$$

Since the marginal increase in GDP arising from an incremental change in kI_g equals a constant, which is greater than zero, there is no point of diminishing returns. The slope of the relationship is linear and positive; therefore I_g can go to infinity. There is no limit to the amount of direct investment through the government for this dictator given the assumptions of the model. The dictator's net income increases in direct proportion to any increase in foreign direct investment through the government by a factor of k.

An example illustrates why this is so. Suppose a foreign investor provides $100 to the dictator in exchange for a partial interest in a coal mine, and the dictator's effective tax rate on the investment is 75 percent. The dictator's immediate net gain in income equals $75. The remaining $25 covers the costs, including labor costs at a wage determined by the dictator and not the investor. The dictator and investor would then share any stream of revenues generated by the investment. His incentive, therefore, is to encourage as much government-controlled direct investment as possible while preventing investment with the general public.

Open Investment

The final variable added to the model is foreign direct investment that is not controlled by the autocratic government: I_d. Since the economic impact directly benefits the economy, it cannot be segregated from Q, the output of the entire economy, and the dictator's benefit from this investment derives from the marginal tax rate on the production of the economy. He does not derive any direct flow of income, as is the case with investment that comes in via the government (I_g).

Equation 2.11

$$\Upsilon = t * q(G,t,I_d) + kI_g - c(G) - s(q(G,t,I_d))$$

Foreign direct investment (I_d) benefits the dictator, but not without additional cost. By providing a source of income to the economy, control of which is not monopolized by the dictator, FDI diffuses power from the center and toward those engaged in the factors of production benefiting from the direct investment.

A dictator may be tempted, however, to at least partially open his economy to direct foreign investment (I_d). The probability that the dictator loses control (P) is equal to some function of the amount of I_d, direct foreign investment:

Equation 2.12

$$P = p(I_d).$$

The probability that he keeps control while opening the economy to direct foreign investment is one minus the probability the dictator loses control ($1 - P$). Assuming the dictator is risk-neutral and hopes to perpetuate his regime forever, his decision regarding taxes, services, and FDI can be characterized as follows:

Equations 2.13 & 2.14

$$\Upsilon^e = \frac{P(0) + (1-P)\Upsilon}{r}$$

$$\Upsilon^e = \frac{(1 - p(I_d))\left[t * q(G,t,I_d) + kI_g - c(G) - s(q(G,t,I_d))\right]}{r}$$

Expected income (Υ^e) equals the probability of being deposed (P) multiplied by the wealth he will receive if deposed (zero), plus the probably he remains in power multiplied by the wealth he receives if he remains in power (Υ). Since his time horizon is assumed to be infinite, the entire equation is divided by the interest rate (r), which for simplicity is assumed to be a constant rate.

Since the dictator earns no income through the government if deposed, the first term on the right side equals zero. And since direct foreign investment (I_d) does not go directly through the government (unlike I_g, which is totally controlled by the dictator), he receives that proportion that directly affects GDP, as determined by the marginal tax.

Since r is in all terms and can be multiplied across, the first order conditions for his choice variables are identified in equations 2.15 through 2.18. A rational, risk-neutral dictator chooses the net income maximizing tax rate t^*, net income maximizing level of government spending G^*, and as much I_g as he can attract (there is no maximum level, as discussed previously). There also exists a net income maximizing level of direct investment into the economy, I_d^*.

Equations 2.15–2.18

$$\frac{\partial \Upsilon^e}{\partial t} = (1-P)\left(Q + t\frac{\partial q}{\partial t}\right) - \frac{\partial s}{\partial q}\frac{\partial q}{\partial t} = 0 \text{ at max, } t^* = t(G, I_d)$$

$$\frac{\partial \Upsilon^e}{\partial G} = (1-P)\left(t\frac{\partial q}{\partial G}\right) - \frac{\partial s}{\partial q}\frac{\partial q}{\partial G} = 0 \text{ at max, } G^* = g(t, I_d)$$

$$\frac{d\Upsilon^e}{dI_g} = k > 0$$

$$\frac{\partial \Upsilon^e}{\partial I_d} = \left(\frac{\partial p}{\partial I_d}tQ\right) + (1-P)t\left(\frac{\partial q}{\partial I_d}\right) - \frac{\partial s}{\partial q}\frac{\partial q}{\partial I_d} = 0, \; I_d^* = i_d(G, t)$$

The second order condition for I_d^* is given by equation 2.19, which is assumed to be less than zero in order for equation 2.19 to characterize a maximum.

Equation 2.19

$$\frac{\partial^2 \Upsilon^e}{\partial I_d^2} = \left[\left(\frac{\partial^2 p}{\partial I_d^2}tQ\right) + \left(\frac{\partial p}{\partial I_d}t\frac{\partial q}{\partial I_d}\right)\right] +$$

$$\left[\left(\frac{\partial p}{\partial I_d}t\frac{\partial q}{\partial I_d}\right) + \left((1-P)t\frac{\partial^2 q}{\partial I_d^2}\right)\right] - \left[\left(\frac{\partial s}{\partial q\partial I_d}\frac{\partial q}{\partial I_d}\right) + \left(\frac{\partial s}{\partial q}\frac{\partial^2 q}{\partial I_d^2}\right)\right] < 0$$

Interpretation

Three immediate conclusions stand out from the mathematical manipulation of the relationships and assumptions outlined here. First, the risk of overthrow or insurrection does not change the dictator's choices for marginal tax rate (t), level of government spending (G), or government-controlled foreign investment. Second, there appears to be no limit to the amount of foreign investment through the government (I_g) the dictator desires. Third, the risk of overthrow changes the dictator's choice level of I_d. A rational choice level would equate the marginal cost of the last unit of I_d with the marginal benefit. Stated another way, the dictator will allow I_d to enter the economy until the marginal benefit equals the marginal cost. The marginal cost of I_d is characterized by $\left(\frac{\partial s}{\partial I_d}\right)$ and the marginal benefit characterized by $(1-P)\left(Q+t\frac{\partial q}{\partial I_d}\right)$.

At the optimum level, marginal cost equals marginal benefit. If the observed level of I_d is smaller than would otherwise be expected, it may be possible to conclude that the dictator finds the additional costs associated with increased GDP unacceptable. A decision by the previously defined dictator to forgo at least some of the expected gains from I_d means (assuming risk neutrality) that his desire to remain in power requires his avoiding the risks of revolution that accompany economic growth in an open economy.

All dictatorships are not alike. We have constructed an assumed dictator, an extreme example perhaps, for the purpose of developing a set of assumptions that are easily understood and easy to contrast. For the extreme totalitarian—a leader with total control, an infinite time horizon, and no popular support or consent to rule—this model provides powerful insight into his behavior. As argued earlier,

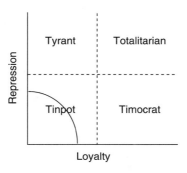

Figure 2.7

in theory, he will provide a regular system of taxation and ensure his monopolization of this power, and he will provide for public services to enhance the productive capacities of his economy. He will accept foreign direct investment to the extent that he can control it, and he will accept unlimited amounts of direct investment through the government.

We have a theory of human nature that we can apply to national security. We can build micro models with individual decision makers so we have a theory to explain the behavior of dictators. The theory and models show us that even bad people, such as tyrants, totalitarians, timocrats, and tinpots, face constraints, and we can shape behavior when we know these constraints.

CHAPTER 3

Principles for Policy Makers

Economic science grew out of an inquiry into human nature. Each individual maintains some traits common with individuals throughout the world and throughout history. Specifically, each individual desires survival and well being for self and others; the stronger the kin relationship, the stronger the shared drive for survival. Each of us is hardwired to make decisions that maximize our survival, survival for our kin, and for those in our future generations—"self-preservation, and the propagation of the species."[1] Our individual drives to maximize clash with the reality of scarcity. We have limited ability, wealth, and time, so we must make choices each day. Everyone faces scarcity of one form or another. Economics is the study of the complexity of this simple articulation of human nature; this book applies the theory and methodology to security analysis and policies.

Through the division of labor, we can attain a great deal more than we could on our own, and since we drive for maximization, we tend to "truck, barter and exchange one thing for another."[2] One person making a pin can make perhaps twenty in one day, according to Adam Smith in about 1776. Ten people each making 1/10th of a pin throughout the day can make 1/10th of 48,000 pins, or the equivalent of 4,800 pins in one day.[3] Through the division of labor, we help each other to attain more. We do not do this out of concern for our fellow man, but rather for our own self-interest.

"Give me that which I want and you shall have this which I want" describes every human interaction.[4] "It is not from the benevolence of the butcher, brewer, or baker, that we expect our dinner, but from their regard to their own interest. We address ourselves, not to their humanity but to their self-love, and never talk to them of our own necessities but of their advantages."[5]

We need each other in order to attain our goals, almost all of the time. This is true of you, me, and the best heroes and worst villains. We each face scarcity; through trade and specialization we can increase wealth, but we will rely on others for our well-being to the extent we specialize. Bin Laden needed al Zawahiri. The Taliban needs money launderers. Shorty Guzman of the Sinaloa Cartel needs bankers. Policy makers should not only understand this concept, but must apply it to their advantage. How can we appeal to the self-love of the dictator, insurgent, or terrorist in a way to advance our own self-interests?

To summarize the economics of decision making for policy makers, we propose a few rules of the economic road.[6]

1. Scarcity requires choice

You may want a new car you cannot afford; to go out to lunch with a business colleague as well as your friend who is visiting from out of town; and to run a marathon although you've not run more than 5k in five years. You can neither have nor do it all; you must make choices. The first step in applying economic analysis is to identify an individual making decisions in conditions of scarcity. Start your analysis with preferences and constraints.

- **What is this person maximizing based upon revealed preferences?**
  Sometime you will answer "money," but often observable behavior will lead you to conclude power or respect. Economists tend to speak about the notion of utility. People maximize their utility; this is theoretical because we do not know how to measure it objectively. Utility is different than money. If I can make an additional $100 today at work but would miss having dinner with my family, I may choose to go home. I opt to maximize my utility, which in my case values dinner with my family at more than $100. As a dictator, if increasing government revenues means risking overthrow and an end to my reign, I may maximize my utility by not maximizing my short-term wealth. Discerning what foreign leaders want to maximize and how they want to do it can give you the tools you need to persuade them to be on your side.
- **What constraints does this person face?**
  Include time constraints, resource constraints, and institutional constraints such as formal laws and rules, but also unwritten social norms that may be local, cultural, or religious.

2. Institutions matter

So many world events can be understood by applying the rules by which people operate—the institutions that constrain behavior.

Formal and informal, institutions tell rich and meaningful stories that capture the complexities of world events not readily apparent from the first order fact that people maximize under conditions of scarcity.

3. People seek approbation

People want respect. The need for some level of respect impacts decision making. Although we can hypothesize a leader who seeks no support, the real world's leaders seek a combination of power and support. Hitler worked hard for public support. Even Castro and Kim spend time seeking public support in Cuba and North Korea and, indeed, around the world. Leaders want to believe that they are supported, even if they are despised. So we will sometimes see instances seemingly in violation of rule 1 and 2, but these can often be explained by approbation.

4. Substitution and the next best alternative

Everything costs something, even if that something is your time. The price paid is at least as low as the next best opportunity foregone. The "free lunch" costs you at least the time you could have used to get your hair cut, for example. Nothing, therefore, is free. Terrorists hijacked airplanes when they perceived that to be their best policy tool. When countermeasures made this more difficult (i.e., costly), they changed tactic from hijackings to assassinations, the next best alternative, but a more expensive one.[7] Presidents and prime ministers consider several options at once and weigh their decisions against the next best option foregone. Formulating effective policy means influencing events and options so that the decision you want someone to make will be better than all their alternatives.

5. Incentives matter

"Incentives matter" encapsulates economic analysis, properly understood. Reward action A consistent with my preferences and make it less costly than action B, and I will choose action A. One line also tells the story: the downward-sloping demand curve shown in figure 3.1. As prices decrease, people demand more. As prices increase, people demand less. Simple, yet powerful stuff. World leaders, friendly and unfriendly, respond to incentives just like everyone else. If your security policy violates this rule, your policy will fail.

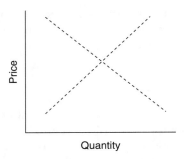

Figure 3.1

6. Decisions are made at the margin

People look at additional or marginal cost versus the additional or marginal benefit. Although I am on a diet, what is the marginal cost of eating just one potato chip versus the benefit? What is the marginal cost and benefit of getting the luxury package on the new car that I am buying? What is the marginal cost and benefit of planting one additional acre of corn this year? Leaders make policy decisions at the margins as well. What is the marginal cost and benefit of devaluing the currency by 1 percent? Of borrowing an additional amount of money from a sovereign wealth fund? Of adding another 30,000 troops to a deployment of 100,000?

7. Information is a commodity

People making trades require information in order to operate efficiently. Efficient markets assume perfect information. Empirically, we know information comes at a cost. Before buying a digital camera, we research the technologies on the market. Before investing in a foreign country's infrastructure, it's necessary to invest time to understand the associated risks. The information requires an investment of labor, capital, or both.[8] Information asymmetries exist everywhere, even in national security policy making. Be aware of it and use it to your advantage.

8. Value is subjective

People enter into trades if they think they are getting something better than they already have, and the decision is based upon individual preferences and quality of information. If I have a pineapple allergy, I will not purchase the fruit no matter how low the price.

Without the allergy, I will not purchase it if I know the fruit is rotten, regardless of the price. We buy stocks based upon expected prices of the stocks in the future. In a marketplace where preferences and constraints cause choices, and imperfect information exists, we make our choices based upon our expected utility; we seek to maximize utility, but most of the time we take our best guess at what will yield that result. If thirsty and miles from water, I will trade diamonds for water. The takeaway: trade makes everyone better off or at the very least makes everyone think that they are better off at the time of the exchange. When looking at leaders' incentives, constraints look also at level of information and try to discern relative values; the leader may prefer poverty and control to wealth and the risk of overthrow by assassination.

Evaluating Policy—Welfare Analysis

What if an economic policy takes into consideration all of these principles? Will it be successful? For example, a particular economic sanction cuts off Cuba from the U.S. marketplace. Is it successful? What if a trade policy imposes safeguards on the importation of steel into the United States, saving some U.S. jobs in one geographic area but driving up prices slightly throughout the country and preventing job growth in another area—is it a success? Suppose the converse: a particular trade policy benefits the jobs and growth of a developing country, undermining the safe harbor of terrorists, but puts a U.S. industry out of business. Have we succeeded?

Three concepts can inform our opinion of policies: Pareto efficiency, cost-benefit analysis, and individual utility maximization. A theoretical concept, a Pareto efficient policy makes at least one person better off without making anyone worse off. If, after implementation, your policy makes only one person in the world better off and makes nobody in the world worse off, then it satisfies the definition for Pareto efficiency. Policies moving an economy toward free trade surely will not qualify. Somebody will lose protection, and therefore her job. Neither will sanctions qualify, since sanctions seek to make the sanctioned dictator worse off. So this common conception of evaluation will not help.

Cost-benefit analysis, a more pragmatic approach, simply weighs the "better off" against the "worse off." If a trade policy eliminates 100 jobs and creates 200 jobs, on balance, the policy succeeds—at creating jobs. This analysis actually works and probably accurately reflects how people make decisions. The flaw, of course, is in who gets to make the analysis. Who decides that a net gain of 200 agriculture jobs in California has higher value than 100 jobs manufacturing auto parts in Michigan? Growth in a developing country may deny safe harbor to terrorists, but people in my hometown may become unemployed. If you are one of the people losing a job, your opinion will surely differ from that of the person gaining the job overseas. The politician or autocrat making the decision, likewise, will have personal passions and interests different from at least some—if not most—of those impacted by the policy.

Cost-benefit analysis can inform welfare analysis, but requires attention to the incentives of the decision maker. Consider the standard "guns versus butter" debate. Should a government spend money on defense and weapons or on welfare and food production? The answer is usually "both," but how much of each differs depending upon whom one asks.

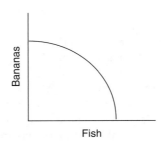

Figure 3.2

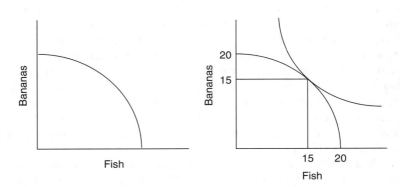

Figure 3.3

We will evaluate policies throughout this book by using a simple two-commodity model. Recall the island with one inhabitant, Robinson Crusoe; he and his island comprise an economy. He can spend his productive time fishing or climbing trees to cut down bananas. So we have an economy with one person and two commodities, bananas and fish (see figures 3.2 and 3.3).

Every decision involves a trade off—there is no free lunch. His decision is subjective, based upon his personal preferences and his expectation of the abundance of fish and bananas in the future based upon his knowledge of the market (climate, storms, infestations, etc.). Whether it's between bananas and fish, guns and butter, invasion and sanctions, trade and invasion, this choice represents a trade off.

The principle of the diagram presented in figure 3.3 works for all goods; only drawing it in two dimensions limits the current discussion to just two items. We'll revisit this graphic to reinforce the concept that economic actors must make choices amid constraints. This applies equally to Robinson Crusoe as it does to dictator X and democratically elected leader Y. We will now begin application of this first section of the book to world leaders. We begin with modeling dictators. We will study sanctions against dictators, and then move to democracies and trade policies used by and against democracies for national security reasons.

The World

In part I, we examined the immutable laws of human nature. What motivates economic man to act? Can we use our knowledge of the principles of economics to model the behavior of leaders in the real world? That is the question studied in part II of the book: how can we apply economic instruments to influence leaders to take a desired action. The opening chapter considers the longstanding U.S. embargo on Cuba. Through the use of a unique economic model, we will test the theories postulated in part 1 as they apply to policies put in place by Fidel and Raúl Castro in response to U.S. sanctions. We then turn, in the succeeding chapters, to specific economic instruments that can be utilized by policy makers to influence behavior.

CHAPTER 4

Castro's Cuba and U.S. Sanctions

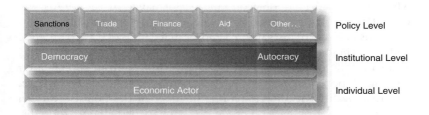

Sanctions	Trade	Finance	Aid	Other...	Policy Level
Democracy				Autocracy	Institutional Level
Economic Actor					Individual Level

Figure 4.1

The model presented in part I works in theory. But does it work in practice? If we are to make progress in advancing security in the real world, we need ideas that work. In this chapter, we will test the theoretical model in great detail. The remainder of the book consists of shorter case studies. The nontechnical reader can skip the equations and still understand the model.

Cuba lies only ninety miles from the United States. During the Cold War, Cuba fell under the Soviet Union's sphere of influence; U.S. policy treated Fidel Castro's Cuba as a significant threat. The Cuban Missile Crisis, which brought the world to the brink of nuclear war like never before or since, highlighted this threat for the world. Although Cuba's threat to America today is debatable, the Castro regime remains a sworn enemy of the United States and a target of American security policies.

Fidel Castro, who ruled Cuba from 1959 until 2008, when he handed power to his younger brother Raúl after falling ill, fits the totalitarian dictator model. He ruled Cuba with an iron fist. Although he was not the first autocrat to rule Cuba, and he was not the only totalitarian in the world, Castro's long rule of Cuba and the United States' long period of anti-Castro economic policies provide an excellent historical case study of the use of economic instruments in security policy.

First, we compare Castro in 2000 with the theoretical model. We then describe the Cuban economy with emphasis on the post-Soviet decade of the 1990s. This time period is chosen because during the first thirty-three years of Castro's regime (roughly 1959–92) Cuba received approximately $5 billion annually in Soviet subsidies, an anomaly difficult to control for when trying to extrapolate generalities that can be applied elsewhere.[1] From 1993 to 2000, however, Castro faced market pressures. After comparing Cuba's dictator with the totalitarian dictator model, we apply this model to determine to what extent Cuba's poor economic performance in the 1990s was caused by (1) external sanctions, or (2) Castro's own policies.

Let us begin with institutional and factual details of Castro's regime and how these compare to the dictator X model in chapter 3. Fidel Castro totally controlled the Cuban government from shortly after coming to power in January 1959 until 2008. While head of state, Castro's loyalist Ricardo Alarcon, a member of the Political Bureau of the Communist Party, headed the Cuban parliament (formally, the National Assembly of People's Power) and Castro's brother Raúl commanded the armed forces. Fidel Castro controlled the police and the all-powerful Committees for the Defense of the Revolution (CDR)—the neighborhood watch network that still prevents ordinary Cubans from communicating freely or organizing within their communities.[2] In any given neighborhood in Cuba, one never knows who is in the CDR. If one confides in a neighbor about a plan to organize within the community for any purpose, residents fear this information will get passed along to the security forces. A similar system existed in Saddam Hussein's Iraq, where, as Kanan Makiya describes in *Republic of Fear,* one could return home from work one day to find the government had seized your home and given it to one of Saddam Hussein's loyalists.[3]

Castro controlled the Cuban economy. He controlled the government, which set wages and standards for working conditions to supposedly ensure equality among the Cuban people. However, despite these trappings of Marxist egalitarianism, Castro's political loyalists enjoyed a quality of life superior to the masses.

Castro controlled tax rates, monetary policy, and government spending. Thus, as a totalitarian, his personal fiscal constraints were those of the government. Castro also controlled investment. Private property was and still is outlawed in Cuba, although individuals may operate self-employment businesses such as government-licensed restaurants from private homes (*palidares*). Until the mid-1990s it was illegal for anyone other than the government to own real property, including a home or a business. All foreign investors, therefore, were forced to partner with the Cuban government through joint ventures, production agreements, and joint accounts.[4] This law changed in September 1995 (Decree Law 77) with the intent to increase foreign investment. In practice, however, there has been no change in the implementation of ownership rights under Cuban law. The Cuban government still controls foreign investment, and it partners in all significant foreign investments in Cuba.[5]

Castro wanted his revolution to last forever—he had an unlimited time horizon. "I trust ideas better than people...No one has the power to change the line of the revolution because that's what people believe in."[6] It can be argued that Castro believed his rhetoric, that he was fighting a Marxist-Leninist revolution against the forces of America and Western capitalism. As such, like a monarch, he desired his rule and the reign of his ideas to continue after his departure. Once too ill to govern, he placed his brother Raúl in charge of his government and revolution. Fidel came to power as a revolutionary and never gave up that persona. He always fought the *Yanqui* enemy and the capitalistic imperialists. By observing his behavior, we conclude that he wanted more than simply money. He wanted his life to have long-lasting meaning for the world—he wanted his ideology to be continued beyond his lifetime. In this sense, Fidel Castro wanted to live forever.

Castro did not have the Cuban people's consent to rule. In effect, Fidel Castro seized power in a revolutionary coup in 1959 by ousting the dictator Fulgencio Batista. He promised reform; shortly after coming to power, however, he turned on the Cuban people by rejecting elections. On May 16, 1961, Castro declared Cuba a socialist country.[7] For now, we will take the listed assumptions at face value and argue their merits. Exceptions to any of these assumptions can be incorporated into the model and the results assessed. Having said this, all of the aforementioned assumptions, in fact, are common in the literature on Castro.[8]

It is plausible to assume that Castro wanted to maximize his power. In particular, given his lack of legitimacy, he needed to maintain his military and security forces, needed to maintain the appearance of strength and power, and needed to convince society's elites that any attempt at overthrow remained futile. To do all this he had to monopolize the nation's wealth and sources of wealth. He maximized utility by accumulating power, and power required wealth and the sources of wealth.

In the previous chapter, the dictator model assumes he

- controls government spending, taxation, and monetary policy;
- controls trade and foreign investment;
- has an infinite time horizon;
- lacks political legitimacy;
- rules by force and coercion;
- must maintain a costly system of internal security, including police and military forces, to prevent insurrection and overthrow;
- must maintain a system of rewards for the elite to engender their loyalty;
- is an income maximizer whose economic constraints are synonymous with those of the entire economy;
- rules an economy that can be characterized as in a state of general poverty.

Fidel Castro provides a superb example of the model. What are the implications for security policy?

External policies have minimal effects on the Cuban economy. The model concludes the dictator chose average marginal tax rate and government spending, limiting foreign investment to that which he can control. The possible exception to this is I_g, investment into Cuba directed by the government. Castro's income equaled tax revenues (T) plus taxes on foreign investment via the government (I_g), minus the costs of running the government (C) and the costs of security to stay in power (S).

Equation 4.1
$$\Upsilon = T + kI_g - C - S$$
$$\Upsilon = t * q(G, t, I_d) + kI_g - c(G) - s(q(G, t, I_d))$$

From this analysis, we see two important dynamics. First, investment flows must pass two checks, not just one. That is, people seeking investments in Cuba must be permitted by their government to invest, and the Cuban government either accepts or rejects these investments. Castro, in fact, prohibited the flow of private investment into Cuba. Using the terms of the model, the Cuban dictator limited investment by prohibiting I_d and by limiting I_g through rigid policies detrimental to foreign investment. Regardless of a lifting of

U.S. unilateral sanctions permitting investments from U.S. investors into Cuba, Castro faced incentives to reject some investments. These issues will be explored in the following section.

THE CUBAN ECONOMY IN THE 1990s

Cuba's economy in the 1990s went through three basic phases: collapse in the early 1990s, recovery in the mid-1990s, and contraction following 1996. The literature generally supports this taxonomy.[9] Shortly after the revolution that overthrew Batista in 1959, Castro nationalized all property and implemented a Marxist-Leninist command economy that ran production into the ground. For thirty years, Cuba survived as the Soviet Union's largest aid-receiving state.[10]

From the first Agrarian Reform Law of March 1959 and the second Agrarian Reform Law of October 1963, Cuba's ruling government actively worked to liquidate the capitalist system and eliminate market-oriented institutions that prevailed in Republican Cuba and to supplant them with institutions that supported a centrally planned economy. The full employment policies pursued by central planners meant that markets for capital and labor did not exist in Cuba. Consequently, the Cuban financial system remained severely underdeveloped, with Banco Nacional de Cuba performing both central and commercial banking roles. Credit was not allocated by the central government. There were few savings institutions, and interest rates remained too low to attract significant volumes of deposits.[11]

In the early 1990s, upon the collapse of the Soviet Union and the end of its subsidies, the Cuban economy entered a period of crisis. In the mid-1990s, the Cuban government instituted a series of reforms that turned the economy around, but only temporarily. In the late 1990s the Cuban economy again experienced weak performance.

A macroeconomic description of the Cuban economy includes these highlights. From 1990 to 1993, the country's imports and exports dropped precipitously as the Soviet subsidies ended. Cuba's fixed capital and inventories began to degrade and diminish. Merchandise imports fell by 75 percent from 1989 to 1993.[12] Prior to 1994, according to some estimates, up to 80 percent of the factories could not operate because of a lack of fuel, machinery, raw materials, and spare parts.[13] As the Cuban government maintained fixed prices and continued its priority of keeping state-run enterprises in business, the budget deficit increased from 9.4 percent of GDP in 1990 to 30.4 percent in 1993.[14] Fixed prices further exacerbated shortages and depleted inventories. In the small black market for some agricultural products, inflation increased from 2 percent in 1990 to more than 200 percent in 1993.[15]

The reforms of the mid-1990s, with associated expectations of further reforms, caused the Cuban economy to level off in 1993 and begin to grow toward the end of this period. The fiscal deficit dropped, reaching 2.5 percent in 1996. With monetary tightening, inflation returned to lower levels and national savings increased. Fidel Castro's actions improved the economy.

By 1995, however, Castro's actions and rhetoric began to raise doubts about the reforms. In fact, the government backtracked on some reforms, which likely caused the slowing of growth witnessed in the late 1990s.

The major legal changes that impacted the Cuban economy during the post-Soviet decade—what Stephen Kimmerling calls the "Special Period" of the 1990s—were:

The Constitution of 1992 (August 1, 1992)
The Law on Foreign Investment, Law No. 77 (1995)
Decree-Law No. 165: Duty-Free Zones and Industrial Parks (1996)
Decree-Law No. 173: Banks and Non-Banking Financial Institutions (1997)[16]

We note, as many observers have over the past decade, that Castro instituted these reforms to invite capitalists without the capitalism.[17] According to Kimmerling, this allowed "foreign capital inflows without compromising...government supremacy."[18] In short, as in China and many other command economies, Cuba's government wanted the benefits of liberalizing the economy without paying the cost of losing political control. When the middle class began to grow and civil society started to develop, Castro responded by retreating from the reforms and increasing repression. For example, he cracked down on Concilio Cubano in early 1996. This umbrella group, created in November 1995, consisted of 108 dissident factions. It had petitioned the government to meet in Havana from February 24 to February 27, 1996. The meeting never took place and many Concilio Cubano leaders were subsequently jailed.

In the early 1960s, private property was outlawed and the economy became closed to foreign investment. Not until 1982 did the law change to allow limited foreign investment onto the island. From 1960 until the early 1990s, Cuba received massive amounts of aid in the form of loans, and subsidies from the Soviet Union. In 1995, following the collapse of the Soviet Union, the end of the Soviet subsidy, and the implosion of the Cuban economy (noted earlier), Castro passed Law No. 77 known as the "Law on Foreign Investment."[19] In the two subsequent years he passed additional laws that sought to entice foreign investment into the still-struggling Cuban economy. Although economic performance had improved dramatically by the late 1990s, it remained significantly below its 1989 levels.[20]

In the late 1990s, foreign investment in Cuba fell. What happened during these years that would explain the decline? The quality of the Cuban workforce did not diminish. Cuban workers remained competitive among the economies against which Cuba competed for foreign investment. The Cuban economy was growing, which would have tended to boost investors' expectations that it would continue to grow. Infrastructure was not deteriorating at an appreciably greater rate. Absent some demand shock, investigated and dismissed by former IMF economist Ernesto Hernández-Catá, the problems, therefore, must have been political.

Although Cuban officials extolled the freedom with which foreign-owned enterprises were able to operate on the island, in fact there were significant restraints stemming from the government's determination to maintain control over the conduct of economic activity in the country.[21] In 1996, Jorge Pérez-López identified four manifestations of this political reluctance to embrace foreign direct investment. First, FDI into Cuba must be individually authorized by the Cuban government. Second, important sectors of the Cuban economy are off limits to foreign investors. Third, foreign investors must use the Cuban government to hire, fire, and pay workers; they cannot manage their own personnel. And fourth, the Cuban government can terminate a joint venture at will, claiming as national property any capital and assets in Cuba. The disincentive to invest in Cuba becomes apparent when foreign investors have no guarantee that the Cuban government will not seize everything. In fact, a few cases of this type of seizure actually happened.

The third manifestation—foreign investors must use the Cuban government to hire, fire, and pay workers—is an important distinction in the common public policy argument regarding dictatorships. The foreign investor's ability to improve the workers' wealth and quality of life was limited by the Cuban government's willingness to accept such improvements, in the form of increased salaries, improved benefits, and other personnel decisions. This was not the case in some other dictatorships. For example, an investment in the People's Republic of China in 2000 could have dramatically impacted the lives of workers as Western companies set wages, working and safety conditions, and even provided housing and medical care. In Cuba, however, no such power existed for the foreign investor. The government, in fact, controlled the flow of income and assets to the Cuban people.

One question remains: what political changes caused foreigners to invest in the mid-1990s but then reduce their rate of investment and even pull out of Cuba in the late 1990s? Again, the literature contains ample rational justification for this observed behavior. The slide in Cuba's economic performance leveled off in 1993. This is likely due to the policy pronouncements and laws discussed previously, and the Cuban government's concerted effort to attract foreign investment. Thus began a virtuous cycle, however brief, where investment led to economic growth, which inspired additional investment based upon expectations of additional economic growth. However beneficial to wealth creation on the island, Castro lacked political legitimacy and would lose power by giving up monopoly control over the sources of wealth. Thus, in spite of the early rhetoric, the practical value of the reforms to Castro diminished over time. In fact, the pace of structural reforms began to slow, and by 1995 fears of policies being reversed became apparent.

The unwillingness of Cuban authorities, either in Law-Decree No. 50 or in Law No. 77, to permit foreign investors to acquire title to the properties in which they invest, and statements by Cuban officials that Cuba reinforced its commitment to maintain its socialist economic and political structure, negated some of the positive climate created by the investment protection policies.[22] Sufficient research and literature exists to conclude that, during the 1990s, Cuba's internal policies were sufficient to both initially attract and then deter foreign direct investment.

The dictator model, the technical model, and the facts of the Cuban economy in the 1990s lead us to conclude that U.S. sanctions had no significant impact on the Cuban economy. Castro had the ability to control the Cuban economy. In addition, the U.S. sanctions were unilateral—the rest of the world could trade with Cuba. Castro himself limited the amount of foreign direct investment based upon his selection of internal policies in Cuba. If the United States could not stop the flow of FDI from other countries (Canada, Mexico, and Europe were the largest investors in Cuba in the 1990s), the reasons these countries reduced their rate of investment in the late 1990s must lie beyond U.S. sanctions. The U.S. passage of the Cuban Liberty and Democratic Solidarity (LIBERTAD) Act of 1996, it may be argued, discouraged FDI from other countries into Cuba, particularly as it related to sanctions imposed on those trafficking in confiscated American-owned property in Cuba. If this 1996 law, commonly known as Helms-Burton, in fact significantly impacted FDI from non–U.S. countries, it will appear in the empirical analysis that follows.

Although Castro's budget constraints corresponded to the national budget of Cuba, and his personal wealth depended upon the nation's economic performance, he did not want unlimited economic growth in Cuba. His legitimacy and his survival in office depended upon his successful management of the national budget to maximize his revenues while minimizing his security costs—which tend to rise as the middle class grows and civil society develops.

If the analysis of this study stopped with Olson's model, we would conclude that Castro sought simply to maximize his profits; that is, the Cuban government would provide the profit-maximizing marginal tax rate and level of government spending. This analysis, however, would overlook two important dynamics. First is the legitimacy of the dictator. If cattle on a ranch, to steal Olson's analogy, are not happy with the treatment they receive from the farmer, they cannot rise up and overthrow him. A dictator who fails to maintain legitimacy, however, faces threats of insurrection and overthrow. A vital element in the budget constraints of a totalitarian dictator is the cost of maintaining power.

Stability and wealth are not complementary goals for this dictator across the full spectrum of economic growth. Commentators on the Cuban economy often assume that wealth leads to stability and poverty undermines it. Therefore, sanctions are applied to undermine the regime. This was the widely held justification for U.N. sanctions on Saddam Hussein's Iraq, as well. But, in fact, wealth above a theoretical level promotes instability and below a theoretical level promotes stability. This applies to other dictatorships, but the factors facing each dictator must be looked at individually; the days of treating all dictators equally must end.

At the end of the 1990s, Cuba's low child mortality rate and moderately advanced health care system were often praised by those who defended Castro's policies. But he came to power in a country with a per capita income among the highest in Latin America and a health care system that was already quite advanced. Did Castro create or simply maintain? Today Cuba is poor. Did he destroy the economy, or did the embargo impoverish the Cuban people?

Let us quickly clarify what we are arguing. Castro's actions, some analysts may say, caused the United States to sanction Cuba; the United States seeks to impoverish the island, sowing the seeds of discontent among the population in order to bring about insurrection or overthrow. To support this argument, advocates simply point to U.S. laws that prohibited trade between the United States and Cuba in addition to the president "encouraging foreign countries to restrict trade and credit relations with Cuba," according to the Helms-Burton Act. Therefore, some conclude, although the dictator chose to persecute the Cuban people and deny basic freedoms, it is in fact the external policies—the economic sanctions of the United States, the world's largest economy—that caused Cuba's poor economic performance.

We argue the opposite. Castro's internal policies—lack of freedoms, property rights, and the rule of law; the use of repression, fear, and other totalitarian tools to maintain power domestically—accounted for Cuba's poor economic performance. The general dictator model applied to Castro's Cuba demonstrates that the incentives and behaviors of Fidel Castro have contributed to the island's impoverishment since 1959. Furthermore, it provides the basis for an argument that he is completely responsible. While some may argue that the U.S. trade embargo starves Cuban children and deprives the people of medicines, this model demonstrates that the failure to benefit from foreign direct investment resides with Fidel Castro. Therefore, to the extent that Cuba's economic performance can be attributed to the dictator's actions, it cannot be attributed to the sanctions. The next section of this chapter will test these conclusions empirically.

If correct, that unilateral sanctions did not impact Cuba's economic performance, then what was their value? Did the president of the United States have influence over Castro? If one supports unilateral sanctions as a way to harm the dictator economically so that his behavior will be modified, this model suggests that the policy will be ineffective. And if we cannot influence his behavior, then how are we advancing security? However, if one opposes unilateral sanctions on Cuba because of the resulting economic harm to innocents, the model also suggests that one need not worry. At the end of this Cuba case study, people can intelligently argue both for or against sanctions; they will not, however, be able to argue that the economic impact of unilateral sanctions is the essential element of their position.

Dictating Economic Performance

A reader of political and policy debates during the late 1990s might conclude that U.S. sanctions on Cuba either impoverished the island, and therefore caused innocent Cubans to suffer, or kept valuable resources from Castro rendering him unable to build his military and maintain his security forces and control. Both sides in the debate assume that sanctions prevented wealth from entering the Cuban economy, and thus both sides focus on who felt the brunt of the impact: the dictator or the people. But what if—as the findings of our study indicate—the sanctions actually had a negligible impact on domestic economic performance? Then, the question of "who feels the impact?" is misguided. We applied economic theory to national security policy through the modeling of the behavior of a totalitarian dictator. Using that theoretical totalitarian dictator model for Cuba, we found strong descriptive power of Fidel Castro's Cuba from 1994 to 2000. Now we collect data to test the theoretical model to real world events to determine the effectiveness of the economic analytical tool kit.

In the general dictator model and the discussion of Cuba, we argue that sanctions may not affect economic performance as intended by policy makers. In this case, policy analysts might ask two questions: what did the United States gain and lose from its sanctions, and why did the Cuban people live in poverty? The debate over "who the United States is harming, the dictator or the people" must end. It is time to address the causes of poverty and the constraints placed upon a totalitarian dictator by the circumstances of his power.

To conduct the empirical analysis, we develop a way to measure the impact of U.S. sanctions on the Cuban economy vis-à-vis the impact of Cuba's domestic policies on its economy. If the data indicate that Cuba's domestic policies—and not U.S. policies—caused the macroeconomic changes to Cuba's economy, then the data will support our theoretical model. If, however, U.S. sanctions cause significant shifts in Cuba's economy, then our theory, although logical, will not withstand empirical scrutiny from the real world.

The main difficulty in analyzing the issue empirically lies in the scarcity of reliable data. The Cuban economy has operated as an independent entity only since about 1993 with the end of the Soviet subsidy. It took several years after that for the government to implement and adopt accounting standards. The reported numbers, moreover, contain inconsistencies and inaccuracies.

To overcome the difficulties in using Cuba's internally generated data, we use the stock price of companies outside of Cuba that made investments in Cuba from 1994 to 2000. This approach provides two specific advantages. First, analyzing the micro-level data on companies that made such investments gets directly at the relevant issue—foreign direct investment in Cuba. Second, the specific data used, daily stock prices, comes from a well-functioning global capital market, specifically the NASDAQ, and therefore not subject to government manipulation.

The empirical methodology employs an event study. We compare the performance of the Cuban foreign investment portfolio to a general market portfolio over the period of foreign direct investment in Cuba during the 1990s.[23] If external policies such as sanctions have little or no impact on the Cuban economy, then changes or anticipated changes in such policies should not produce significant changes in the Cuba portfolio relative to the benchmark. In contrast, Cuban domestic policies should have an impact on the Cuban stock portfolio when compared to the general portfolio.

To assess the impact of policy events, we look for significant external and domestic policy changes that could reasonably be expected to alter Cuban economic performance and the risks associated with foreign investment in Cuba. One would expect to find that the performance of foreign companies investing in Cuba would react to significant U.S. or other external policies, but to a much smaller extent than to Cuban domestic policies. Restated in the general terms of the broader argument, we expect the dictator's policy choices will have a greater impact on the domestic economy than will the policies of the outside sanctioning economy. In this instance, Fidel Castro had the ability to increase and decrease the performance of foreign investment in Cuba irrespective of the external policies of the United States.

Recursive Regression

We use the FTSE All World Actuaries Index as the general market portfolio benchmark. This index assigns a daily value to a portfolio designed to proxy for the entire world market, a composite of stock performance throughout the world. We use the Herzfeld Caribbean Basin Fund, a mutual fund traded on the NASDAQ exchange under the ticker symbol CUBA to proxy for foreign investment in Cuba. This fund's managers seek to provide investors an opportunity to invest in Cuba indirectly by investing in companies that invest in Cuba. Therefore, investors in this fund bypass U.S. restrictions on investing in Cuba while maintaining a focus on assets invested in Cuba.

Each of these data series is nonstationary, and to correct for detected serial autocorrelation in these data, a recursive least squares technique is employed. Specifically, the dependent variable is CUBA and the independent variable is the market portfolio (World), and we estimate the equation by repeatedly adding a daily value to the set with each estimate until all observations are used. At each step the last estimate of the coefficient vector, *b*, can be used to predict the next value of the dependent variable. The one-step forecast error is defined to be the recursive residual. The recursive residual w_t is formally described in equation 4.2.

Equation 4.2

$$w_t = \frac{y_t - x'_t b_{t-1}}{\sqrt{1 + x'_t (X'_{t-1} X_{t-1})^{-1} x'_t}}$$

where:
y_t = the dependent variable CUBA
x_t = the regressor variable, World
X_{t-1} = the $t-1$ by k matrix of the World variable

The residual from the recursive model, w_t, is independent and normally distributed with mean equal to zero and variance equal to σ^2. The residuals thus reflect random shocks, or unanticipated deviations from the time series pattern. The analysis focuses on the significant variations when the World portfolio fails to predict the CUBA portfolio to within two standard deviations.

This recursive residual is measured on the vertical axis in figure 4.2. In addition, we plot lines representing two standard errors from the residual. Points falling outside of two standard errors indicate a time of instability when the World portfolio failed to predict the

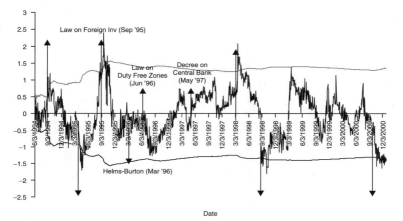

Figure 4.2

CUBA portfolio. Moving forward in time, the outlying values will be incorporated into the model for the next least squares prediction, so the mean would again be expected to be zero. For those time spans during which the residual falls outside of two standard errors, we examine the historical record to determine whether a policy change or other event specifically affected the CUBA portfolio, externally or internally. The most significant events inside of Cuba as well as in U.S.–Cuba relations are indicated along the timeline to illustrate the impact of these internal and external events on the regression.

The regression graph plots 1,537 daily observations on portfolio prices between June 3, 1994 and December 29, 2000. By using Flexible Least Squares, any nonstationarity is directly visible because of the simple fact that by reducing the weight on measurement error and increasing the weight on parameter error, the unit root disappears. In other words, some econometricians who use FLS claim that unit root/ nonstationarity problems are a figment of the assumption that regression parameters are constant.[24] Once you relax that assumption, nonstationarity should disappear.

In the six-and-one-half years of data, it appears that only during six time periods did the market portfolio fail to predict the CUBA foreign investment portfolio, using the two-standard-error criterion.[25] Had the number of time periods been much greater, other independent (control) variables would have been added to look at further restrictions on the model. We examine these six periods to determine what might have caused the instabilities in the model.

Of immediate importance are the Law on Foreign Investment of September 1995, arguably the most important piece of domestic legislation passed in Cuba during the 1990s,[26] and the Helms-Burton Act of March 1996, the most significant U.S. legislation specifically directed at Cuba during the sample period. In the months prior to September 1995, Castro instituted changes in policy, law, and even rhetoric to address severe economic conditions in Cuba. This was the time in Cuba's special period of transformation when the government was likely compelled to experiment with market openings in order to generate some economic recovery.[27] In fact, the international press covered this event to a great extent. The largest variation from the world portfolio occurs about the time of this change in Cuban policy.

The Helms-Burton legislation was considered a landmark U.S. law. This act codified the previous laws and executive orders currently in effect toward Cuba; that is, the president lost the authority to rescind the executive orders that comprised many of the sanctions on Cuba and only Congress would be able to lift these sanctions in the future. Since Congress was considered to be more "hard line" toward Cuba, this was clearly considered by all to be a significant tightening of existing sanctions.

In addition, Helms-Burton sought to place new and significant disincentives to foreign investment in Cuba. This law contained two provisions that received heavy criticism in Europe and Canada as being extraterritorial. Under these provisions, the law provides for recourse in U.S. courts for any American who has property in Cuba that is being trafficked in by foreign investors. For example, if a mining company in Canada purchases from the Cuban government a parcel of land for a mining joint venture, and if that land in Cuba had been confiscated by the Cuban government (which was common shortly after the Castro revolution and the nationalization of the economy) from someone who is now an American citizen, that American can sue the Canadian company in U.S. federal courts for trafficking in stolen property.

The graph in figure 4.2 highlights these two events with arrows. The Helms-Burton Act, the single largest U.S. policy change during the observed period, did not significantly impact the Cuban foreign investment market when compared to the magnitude of the change from the Cuban Law on Foreign Investment. This seems to indicate that Helms-Burton did not counteract some often-claimed great desire to invest in Cuba by the non–U.S. companies of the world.

We conducted a search of fifty-two major newspapers using LexisNexis to determine what events occurred during the six periods of instability when the World portfolio failed to predict the Cuban foreign investment portfolio.[28] Significant events based upon a general literature review of U.S.–Cuban relations are listed. Figure 4.2 reveals six periods from mid-1994 to the end of 2000 (roughly the period in which the Soviet subsidy ended and the Cuban government could have been expected to seek foreign investment to supplant the lost income) of Cuba-specific economic shock. These peaks and valleys indicate times when the World portfolio fails to predict the Cuban foreign investment portfolio, using the FLS method. By identifying the dates that correspond to these failures of the FLS model to predict CUBA, we move to the events study.

The theoretical model led us to the hypothesis that the dictator's domestic policies, and not those of the United States, drove domestic economic performance, including that of FDI. The peaks and valleys, therefore, should correspond to domestic events, and the significant U.S. policy events should not register as significant in figure 4.2

(see appendix). The six significant time periods and corresponding events are as follows.

1. September 1994

In 1994 Cuba permitted farmers' markets—farmers were allowed to sell their surplus crops directly to Cuban citizens willing to pay, and for any price they could obtain. It is interesting to note that these types of market reforms instituted in the People's Republic of China in the 1980s led to significant increases in productivity and improvement in the economy. Perhaps, in the autumn of 1994, investors expected Cuba to follow China's model, and that in time the market would be opened to the same extent as China's market. Whatever the case, this period of marked improvement shows no sign of having been caused by external policy changes.

2. Spring 1995

On May 28, 1995, the Cuban government showed its first signs of retreating from its newly implemented, relatively open investment policies when, in violation of what should have been legally binding contracts, it expelled the Spanish managers of four joint-ventured Cuban hotels. In a country such as Cuba, where the government is subject to little or no oversight—no checks and balances exist on government action—what matters to foreign investors may be how investors are actually treated rather than any protections afforded under the law.[29] Although the world seemed to react with enthusiasm to the domestic posturing of Cuban officials designed to attract foreign investment, this first public act of abrogating an otherwise enforceable agreement probably sent shivers down the spines of existing and would-be investors. During this period, the CUBA portfolio underperformed the World portfolio and no external events can be assigned the blame.

3. Summer and autumn 1995

The Cuban foreign investment portfolio outperformed the World portfolio during this period. A review of international press reveals no significant external policy changes during this period. Internally to Cuba, the Law on Foreign Investment was passed and signed, as discussed earlier.

4. February 23, 1998 to June 11, 1998

The United States and the European Union reached an agreement on the implementation of the Helms-Burton Act. Specifically, the

United States agreed not to take retaliatory action against foreign firms operating in Cuba; in exchange, European governments agreed to prohibit aid to companies doing business in Cuba. During this time period, this external event likely influenced the investment market in Cuba; it represented an agreement on behalf of those who were investing in Cuba, represented by their governments, and the sanctioning U.S. government. No significant internal policy changes took place in Cuba during this period.

The performance of the Cuban investment portfolio during this time period, therefore, could be the exception to our expected finding: only domestic policies matter. In fact the external event—the U.S.–EU agreement on investment in Cuba—may have had enough impact on the foreign investment market in Cuba to cause the CUBA portfolio to significantly outperform that predicted by the model. This makes sense intuitively; the multilateral agreement of this time period directly impacts a significant number of those investing in Cuba. It is not the impact of the U.S. law, however. Recall that the passage of Helms-Burton did not upset the model to a significant level. The European Union's agreement to impose its own policies governing European companies investing in Cuba, in response to the U.S. law, seems an obvious and significant factor on these foreign investments in Cuba.

5. August 31, 1998 to December 11, 1998

No relevant events external to Cuba appeared in the international press during this period. No relevant events internal to Cuba appear in *El Nuevo Herald* either. This deviation from the predicted values for the CUBA portfolio cannot be explained by the methods employed in this events study.

6. October 12, 2000 to December 29, 2000

No relevant events external to Cuba appeared in the international press during this period. However, the Cuban government actively pursued policies of domestic repression.

It is only during the fourth time period that an external event—the U.S.–EU agreement—appears to coincide with a significant variation in the Cuban market from the world market. This result is interesting in that it reflects a multilateral agreement that created disincentives to invest in Cuba. Furthermore, perhaps the unique attribute of the Helms-Burton legislation was not the codification of U.S. sanctions, but the ability of this law to impel action by the European Union.

Without exhausting this point in this study, it appears worthwhile to investigate in another venue the relative impact of unilateral versus multilateral sanctions on the economy of a totalitarian dictator as generalized in this study. One possible conclusion from further investigation is that a dictator may be willing to accept more risks, or accept great compromise, in order to avoid multilateral sanctions. As the data shows, multilateral sanctions likely impacted the flows of foreign direct investments to Cuba. Castro received some benefits from foreign direct investment. Therefore, multilateral sanctions impacted Castro's ability to maximize these benefits given the constraints. Consequently, multilateral sanctions may be able to impel a change in the dictator's behavior.

For the purposes of this study, however, in the six years following the end of the Soviet subsidy and subsequent pressures on Castro to open his economy to foreign investment, it appears that the policies of the Cuban government, and not those of the United States or other external powers, bear the blame for Cuba's economic successes or failures. It appears that Castro himself was responsible for the poor economic performance of his economy, given his choices as laid out previously. Without the U.S. embargo, would Castro let the Cuban economy flourish? With the expectations of the model now shown to be supported by the data, we can be reasonably sure that he would not. He had the entire world to trade with, except the United States. He had the opportunity in the 1990s to open the economy to a much higher level of foreign investment but made policy decisions that limited further investment.

Lessons from the U.S.–Cuba Case Study

Sanctions against Cuba advanced U.S. security policy, according to advocates of the policy. Depending on one's perspective, this may be true. That sanctions did so by limiting the wealth of the Cuban dictator, however, appears untrue. If U.S. sanctions altered Castro's behavior, the policy did so for reasons other than economic impact. Likewise, those who opposed U.S. sanctions on Cuba often did so while crying foul over the economic impact upon the poor and starving Cuban people. This claim also appears baseless. Was the policy effective at advancing U.S. security? If it was, the direct economic impact has nothing to do with the success.

Using Castro's Cuba as a case study, we evaluated unilateral U.S. sanctions as a legitimate tool of security policy against a totalitarian dictator. The literature on this topic has been sparse. This study finds that the Cuban economy from 1994 through 2000 reacted both positively and negatively to events inside of Cuba. Contrary to popular belief, however, external events, including the landmark U.S. Helms-Burton Act codifying U.S. sanctions against Cuba, did not significantly impact Cuba's foreign investment.

Recalling the complete relationship of the elements of the general dictator model, the dictator's net wealth increases in direct proportion to that part of FDI that he controls (I_g); he must limit FDI outside of his control (I_d), however, because his net wealth decreases when I_d exceeds a critical value.

Equation 4.3

$$\Upsilon = t * q(G, t, I_d) + kI_g - c(G) - s(q(G, t, I_d))$$

Essential to arriving at this dynamic, the costs associated with maintaining power—the costs that accompany illegitimately holding total control—are included in the model (supported in the theories of Wintrobe and others). The dictator, therefore, will have a net income-maximizing level of FDI. And since he has total control over the economy, he can impose limits. We conclude from this dynamic that, even though additional benefits from trade may occur between the economy of the dictator and the world, and investors may be willing to provide FDI to the economy, investment will not exceed the optimum level for the dictator. Stated another way, even though investment capital may actively seek entry into the economy, the dictator will choose to limit that investment to his own optimum level. From this dynamic we see that the internal policies—the limits placed by the dictator in spite of a willing foreign investment community—limit FDI.

The surveyed literature shows conclusively the positive relationship between FDI and economic growth and, therefore, we are able to conclude that the dictator's decisions, given his constraints, can impair economic growth. When applied to Cuba, these arguments are supported by the general literature on Cuban economic performance, as well as the empirical study using a measure of FDI in Cuba. The policies of the Cuban government between 1994 and 2000 had the most dramatic impact on the performance of FDI in Cuba, and significant U.S. sanction laws toward Cuba did not significantly impact the economy.

The model, however, contains several assumptions that might be challenged. Therefore, specific opportunities for follow-up study are identified. First, if the dictator did not maintain monopoly control over the sources of wealth and could not control the flow of FDI into the economy, then FDI may bring about political change. It is often assumed that opening the floodgates of investment to closed economies will bring down the dictatorship. If investment cannot be totally controlled centrally, I_d cannot be stopped. Foreign investment into the economy can benefit the economy directly, diminishing the wealth gap and undermining the totalitarian dictator's abilities to employ repression and loyalty to maintain power.

Second, critical to the dynamic model, is the assumption of an unlimited time horizon. Contrary to the previous model, should the dictator believe that he will remain in power for a short amount of time, the tools of power become less important. The marginal benefit from any public spending (G), for example, must exceed the marginal cost. If building a road from a river to a town will take the dictator ten years to amortize, and he anticipates being in office only five years, the road will not be built. In fact without this time horizon assumption, the dictator becomes Olson's roving bandit, with net income a function of his ability to plunder.

Third, legitimacy would greatly decrease the costs associated with maintaining power. The model assumes the dictator resides in power without legitimacy. With associated decreased costs (S) from changing this assumption, the dictator could afford a greater amount of FDI without increasing his risk of overthrow.

In addition to these assumptions, the research revealed two additional points for further study. First, to what extent do multilateral external policies affect the target economy more than unilateral policies? For example, the data shows that the Helms-Burton Act did not significantly impact foreign investment performance in the CUBA portfolio until the European Union agreed on implementation measures with the United States. This effect, however significant at the time, appears to be fleeting. The general thesis of this model was that a dictator with total control, an infinite time horizon, and a lack of legitimacy will choose to control the level of economic performance. So it can be acknowledged that multilateral forces may be able to limit market access to a dictatorship, and that even with unlimited access to the world market, the dictator will eventually be the actor limiting economic performance.

It may be useful to develop measures of total control, expected time horizon, and legitimacy, and conduct comparative analyses of various governments. Having identified these critical attributes of a totalitarian, modeling can begin to differentiate dictators. Even cursory analysis reveals stark differences between the Cuban and the Chinese Communist regimes. Understanding the Iraqi regime under Saddam Hussein or Haiti under Aristide, for example, using the dynamic model may better inform policy makers on the efficacy and efficiency of sanctions and other external policies. In the end, one may conclude that sanctions amount to symbolism—a condemnation by one country of another. U.S. presidents and the Congress may choose these policies anyway. But the debates regarding these policies should be based upon a realistic understanding of the extent to which sanctions actually matter.

Sanctions: Truth in Advertising

Such sanctions serve important purposes. Politically, they assert America's world leadership role in working to expand the realm of peace and freedom. Morally, they refuse U.S. economic participation in egregious evils. Militarily, they can isolate dangerous regimes and weaken their threat to regional and global security. More cynically, according to sanctions expert Douglas Paal, "Sanctions always accomplish their principal objective, which is to make those who impose them feel good."[30]

What U.S. economic sanctions alone do not do, however, is what they explicitly aim to do: make an authoritarian regime change its behavior.

Superficially, economic sanctions offer a target government a choice: comply with the requirements of sanctions or suffer the consequences. In the case of Saddam Hussein's Iraq, for example: verify disarmament or suffer growing economic deprivation. For Cuba: institute democratic reforms and receive the benefits of trade and investment from the United States. To many observers, a government that does not eventually comply seems irrational, even mad. This might be true, if maximizing national wealth were its leader's primary aim. For totalitarian regimes, economic analysis and experience suggest a more sophisticated story.

Viewed as an economic actor, a dictator seeks a level of growth that balances maximum regime revenue and minimum security costs. His economy has a two-fold job: fund the regime's extensive security needs and also control society. Control mechanisms include tools like taxation, monetary policy, state ownership, and rules governing trade and foreign investment. A totalitarian regime cannot afford unbridled economic growth, which would promote the emergence of a middle class with growing expectations and independence. This only raises the cost of control, and often does so quite sharply.

Power is an economic good that a dictator purchases at a price. He might not choose, but does not necessarily fear, actions that impoverish the public. A dictator can and will pass the costs of economic sanctions to society at large while he works to maintain the core sources of regime stability: a security apparatus capable of suppressing rivals and a political system that rewards loyalty among the elite. Sanctions become a waiting game between the dictator, a hardened power-seeker, and the sanctioning powers, compassionate observers of the worsening public situation.

Moreover, the nature of the sanctions program may not harm the dictator and may actually tend to solidify his power. When sanctions are unilateral and a dictator can turn to other partners for trade and foreign investment—as in the case of Cuba—empirical study shows that sanctions effectively have no impact. Cuban economic performance tracks Castro's economic choices, not U.S. sanctions policies. In the case of multilateral sanctions, such as those imposed by the United Nations, loopholes can paradoxically give the dictator advantages that enable him to sustain and prolong his control.

Saddam's Iraq is a case in point. Economic sanctions were imposed by the U.N. Security Council in 1990, and remained in place after the first Gulf War in order to pressure Saddam to disarm as he agreed. As economic analysis might have predicted, Saddam not only failed to comply with U.N. mandates; he actively molded Iraq's sanctioned economy to bolster his regime. State resources flowed to the military and elite, especially those involved in sanctions-busting smuggling, while public welfare declined. The regime launched a propaganda campaign to blame the sanctioning powers, especially the United States, for Iraqi deprivation. It was asserted that sanctions starved the population, destroyed public services, and caused the deaths of 500,000 Iraqi children.

The full story of how Saddam manipulated the sanctions is just now emerging from a freed Iraq. It's also clear that by the mid-1990s the sanctions myth was in full bloom, and a conscience-stricken West responded with the Oil-for-Food Program (OFP) that allowed Saddam to sell oil to buy food and other permissible imports. Ironically, the program played directly into Saddam's hands. Both sides of the OFP equation—the national oil industry and the state-run food rationing system—were under Saddam's authority. The regime issued contracts (and reportedly demanded that oil buyers deposit surcharges to private accounts, evading U.N. scrutiny), favored supporters, and took credit for the food that reached the population. Eventually, an estimated 60 percent of Iraqis were dependent on the oil-for-food ration and, therefore, directly upon the dictator.

While OFP funds kept the population at subsistence levels, Saddam continued to drain the nation's resources to support his palaces, security forces, and government's survival. Indeed, Saddam's levers of power were increased by this program: he had the ability to line the pockets of his elite supporters while blamelessly keeping the masses powerless and poor. As long as he was willing to hold his people hostage, the OFP became a means to prolong his rule—an issue we will revisit later.

Did sanctions have no economic impact on the regime? Arms embargoes and other limitations likely debilitated the Iraqi military so that when war came, the regime quickly crumbled under the U.S. assault. Yet years after the U.S.-led invasion of March 2003, Iraq remained in crisis. Throughout the Arab world and elsewhere, the sanctioning powers—especially the United States—are held responsible for what were Saddam's actions.

Clear economic analysis helps answer questions about sanctions policy before this kind of crisis occurs. In today's globalized economy, sanctions can remain a credible policy alternative, but policy makers must be aware of what they are purchasing. Unilateral sanctions can provide meaningful and necessary symbolism and political favor at home. Multilateral sanctions can influence the prices paid by target countries, but the costs of compliance with sanctions must be less than the costs of noncompliance before behavior is altered.

The evidence shows that dictators like Saddam are supreme calculators of economic costs. Only when Western policy makers also make these calculations, and correctly measure the outcomes of economic action, can they hope to prevail.

Is there a cost at which a tyrant or dictatorship like Castro, Kim, Sassou-Nguesso, or the Burmese military junta would meet conditions associated with sanctions, and can sanctions impose this cost? If not, then do not look for proximate regime change. Can sanctions affect other meaningful impacts? If so, sanctions may be a part, if only a part, of a strategy designed to genuinely transform behavior.

To complete this discussion we need to finish nailing down the moving parts. The actor is defined. The institution—totalitarian dictatorship—is described in detail. The democrat—the actor imposing the unilateral sanctions in this chapter's example—will be thoroughly addressed in the next chapter. The building blocks of this book are the actor, the institution, and finally the policy. To complete this first case study, we need to look at the policy and ask, "What is a sanction?"

Academic literature explains the topic of sanctions thoroughly and, therefore, it will not be repeated here. We will, however, examine the different ways in which people can describe sanctions. In critically evaluating a policy, getting the terms right must be a prerequisite to debate. Serious disagreements exist and must be considered; in fact, these debates provide the most interesting frontier of the current debate on sanctions.

Country A can end all trading with country B. This is a sanction. Country A can stop some trade with country B. Country A can end all or some of its financial flows with country B, perhaps by denying country B access to country A's currency. Development assistance or other unilateral aid can be stopped. Support at international financial institutions can be cut off for financing or aid. Are all of these sanctions?

A team of scholars at the Institute for International Economics seems to think so. They have published a series of works on sanctions.[31] Hufbauer and Oegg define sanctions as, "deliberate, government-inspired withdrawal, or threat of withdrawal, of customary trade and financial relations with a target country in an effort to change that country's policies." They emphasize two aspects of the definition. First, the importance of the threat of withdrawal, pointing out that the threat itself often carries as much significance as actually withdrawing the customary trade and financial relations. Second, they point out the importance of the customary relations, meaning that existing financial relationships allow for the opportunity to influence policies through the threat of ending those relations.[32] Hufbauer and Oegg employ perhaps the broadest definition of sanctions when conducting their empirical research. Well beyond trade and finance, they include aid. They also go so far as to include relations such as sporting events, intercountry civil aviation, and telecommunication between countries.

Based on this definition, they conduct empirical studies into the effectiveness of sanctions to determine if they achieved their intended foreign policy goals. They conclude:

1. The success of U.S. sanctions has dropped since World War II (although sanctions are more successful in achieving modest

policy goals and seldom work as a substitute for military force in achieving major goals).

2. There has been a decrease in unilateral U.S. initiatives since World War II.
3. Globalization is the proximate cause of both prior conclusions, which has made it nearly impossible for a sender country to deny access to resources when acting alone.

Hufbauer and Oegg identify the evolution of sanctions, from broad policies designed as substitutes to military force to focused policies that can go beyond traditional confrontation to include promoting democracy and human rights, stopping the production or transshipment of illicit drugs and fighting terrorism.

Elliott and Oegg continue the inclusive definition, including any actions or threat of any action between countries.[33] Interestingly, as they point out, the nature of sanctions has changed since the early twentieth century from entire trade embargoes to more limited measures such as arms embargoes or embargoes on other strategic measures, travel restrictions, and even freezing of assets.

In contrast, Senator Jesse Helms, then-chairman of the U.S. Senate Foreign Relations Committee, offered a completely different definitional view of sanctions in the January/February 1999 issue of *Foreign Affairs*.[34] For Senator Helms, sanctions include bans on bilateral trade and finances; they do not, however, include denial of aid. What right does an aid recipient have to that aid? The U.S. taxpayers, he argues, provide aid voluntarily and can stop at any time they find it within their interest to do so. Therefore, the denial of aid cannot be seen as a sanction.

At the time of Helms' article, a massive lobbying effort was being undertaken by a coalition of U.S. businesses—led by the U.S. Chamber of Commerce. The business coalition titled their lobbying group USA*ENGAGE. The baseline rhetoric for this initiative was based upon data issued by the National Association of Manufacturers (NAM). Before explaining the data and Helm's response, it's instructive to consider the interests of NAM. Surely we can assume that NAM's membership, comprised of American citizens, support the strongest employment of tools in defense of U.S. interests. They are also leaders charged with increasing profits—corporate executives answerable to shareholders and boards of directors. So what happens when these two demands compete for the individual's loyalty? If the United States were to employ sanctions, it is possible that present or future sales would be negatively impacted. Perhaps immediately, a U.S. manufacturer would need to shut down some operations because of the loss of a market. Or maybe even the threat of U.S. unilateral sanctions would provoke foreign customers to purchase their manufactured goods from a non–U.S. competitor. For all of these reasons, one could argue that the leadership of a U.S. manufacturer would oppose sanctions, especially U.S. unilateral sanctions. This apparent tension between commercial and national security goals will be explored throughout the remaining chapters.

NAM published data that indicated that between 1993 and 1996 the United States imposed more than sixty new unilateral sanctions against thirty-five countries and 42 percent of the world's population. USA*ENGAGE members walked the corridors of the U.S. Capitol and adjacent offices. They threw their hands up in exasperation, both figuratively and literally, and exclaimed that the United States must end this "sanctions epidemic." Specifically, they proposed Congressional constraints over the president's ability to impose sanctions under existing legal authorities such as the Trading with the Enemy Act and the International Economic Emergency Powers Act. More significantly, USA*ENGAGE proposed limiting the U.S. Congress's ability to impose sanctions.

Amidst this battle, Senator Helms questions, "What sanctions epidemic?" He states that 75 percent of the so-called NAM sanctions are conditions, limitations, or restrictions on U.S. foreign aid. Of the forty-four presidential or executive branch unilateral sanctions, five are not unilateral but rather U.N. sanctions, seven were counted twice, two cases were never put in place, eight placed limits on foreign aid, five banned military exports, and thirteen were limited to a specific person or company. Therefore, in spite of the NAM numbers and the so-called epidemic, from 1993 to 1996 Congress passed five new sanctions laws and the president imposed four—far less than the number claimed by NAM.

Any listing of important work on sanctions must include Dan Drezner's *Sanctions Paradox*. He uses the Hufbauer et al., statistics that may be more similar to NAM than Senator Helms in terms of definitional boundaries. His approach on effectiveness, however, provides for interesting insights. He argues that leaders usually put sanctions in place without regard to the prospects for success of the policy choice—a thesis consistent with and supportive of that argued in this book. Between 1914 and 1990 Drezner counts

116 sanctions. Drezner finds that one-third of the sanctions failed; one-third succeeded; and one-third showed partial success. Perhaps counterintuitively, he demonstrates that sanctions are most successful when imposed against allies as compared to against adversaries and that there is no correlation between international cooperation and success.

CHAPTER 5

Democracies and the
Politics of Trade

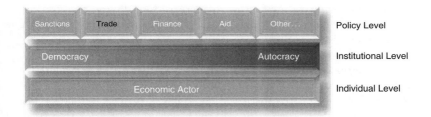

Figure 5.1

If trade makes everyone better off, shouldn't democratic governments embrace unqualified free trade? Empirically, they do not—for reasons that differ from those at play in dictatorships. In this chapter we'll explore the factors bearing on trade decisions in a democracy, opening with a prosaic reference and then moving to political reality. When we understand the theory and practice of trade in a democracy, we will apply our understanding to national security.

At the time of a trade, each party receives something of greater subjective value than that which it gives up. If I have a dollar but am thirsty, I will exchange that dollar for a bottle of water. If I valued the dollar more than the water, I would not part with my dollar. If the merchant valued the water at more than $1, his vending machine would not be programmed to give me the water in exchange for my dollar, but would perhaps require $2. I am better off with the water than with the dollar, and therefore engage in the trade. The vendor is better off with the dollar than with the water, and therefore engages in the trade. Both the vendor and I, from our own points of view, are better off because of the trade. We are richer.

Nobody had to create anything in the transaction; trade itself creates value. Because of the trade, both parties increased wealth. The act of the trade itself created wealth for the vendor and me. This principle holds when extended to international trade. The world buys U.S. management expertise and the United States sells it; both parties are better for the trade. The United States imports oil and textiles. Americans would not spend dollars on gasoline and clothing unless the expense made each better off.

One might expect all democracies—and elected officials—to support free trade. If I am a member of a legislature or a head of state, my reelection chances tend to improve if the economy, jobs, and consumer confidence increase.

In the same vein, one often encounters assertions that dictators' chances of longevity increase with increased GDP, and they should also embrace trade. In the earlier discussion of autocracy, however, we demonstrated why a dictator will not favor unlimited free trade, and therefore can be expected to impose limits.

In a democracy the decision-making dynamics differ, but again we do not see unequivocal embrace of free trade by democratic governments. One cause is the institutional constraints in a democracy. For example, popularly elected politicians must take positions that serve some constituencies more than others; they must make choices. A look at recent U.S. presidential conduct is instructive.

INSTITUTIONAL CONSTRAINTS

President Bush initiated a new global round of trade negotiations in 2001, the "Doha Round." Throughout his presidency, moreover, the United States signed ten bilateral trade agreements—the most under any president—as well as the multilateral Dominican Republic–Central America Free Trade Agreement (CAFTA-DR). Yet the Bush administration also imposed safeguards on steel imports into the United States—a decidedly anti–free trade move, but a decision made in the interest of protecting the workers and owners of the American steel industry. In the election campaign to choose President Bush's successor, leading Democrat candidates, then-Senators Barack Obama and Hillary Clinton, advocated a review to determine whether the United States should remain a party to its free trade agreements, including longstanding agreements such as the North American Free Trade Agreement (NAFTA). Presumably, this position was intended to appeal to the national labor unions, which have considerable influence in the Democratic primary process. Once in office, however, President Obama abandoned this position.

Constraints from Electoral Politics

Elected officials tend to utilize antitrade rhetoric and policies to address the anxiety felt by those struggling to compete in a challenging global economic environment. In spite of the antiglobalization rhetoric published daily, the world economy is actually much less globalized than it was 100 years ago. Prior to 1914 and the outbreak of World War I, trade, people, and currency moved freely across borders—more freely than today. World Wars I and II and regional conflicts severely curtailed free movements throughout the twentieth century. The globalization of the early twenty-first century represents only the beginning of a return to the levels of free trade achieved 100 years ago.[1]

For the developed world—the major trading nations—the return to free trade has been hindered by powerful domestic political interests. Although economists almost universally agree that trade makes all people better off, the time horizon of most politicians and workers is too short to appreciate the nuances of this theoretical argument. Workers want a paycheck to meet this month's rent. Politicians want to give workers what workers think they need from their governments in exchange for votes and campaign dollars.

Debates on free trade persist in spite of the candidates' shared knowledge about the benefits of free trade. Democratically elected politicians argue for constituents—for targeted voters. Free trade may be better for some constituents and not beneficial, at least in the short run, for others.

Returning to our Cuba example from the previous chapter, we can look at the dictator, Castro, and ask why a U.S. president would support unilateral sanctions against Cuba—a policy position that was particularly popular during the 1990s. There is the "good government" case raised earlier: the symbolic importance of the United States refusing to support the Castro regime in any way, even though this position has no real impact on Cuba's economy. Digging deeper, however, uncovers the role of institutions.

U.S. presidents do not gain office directly by a nationwide popular vote, but instead via votes in the electoral college. Each state is allotted a number of electoral college votes in proportion to the population of the state. More accurately, it has the same number of votes as the state has in its delegation to the U.S. Senate and House of Representatives.

When political strategists run a campaign, they look at states with close votes and weigh these states by their size. Florida has a few attributes that make it a pivotal state for a U.S. president. First, it is a closely divided state; that is, in recent elections, the vote has been closely split between candidates. Second, it is a large state and thus delivers significant electoral college votes to the winner. Finally, Cuban Americans comprise a large ethnic minority and voting bloc in Florida. Although Cuba is not the only issue Cuban Americans care about, and they are not a majority or even a plurality of the population of the state, U.S. policies toward Cuba remained a front-burner political issue in Florida, particularly throughout the 1990s.

Members of the U.S. House and Senate from South Florida and New Jersey embody a powerful voting bloc in Congress. They also represent the largest Cuban American populations of any states in the country. Together with the president, politicians from these states have successfully ensured that the United States remains staunchly anti-Castro.

Electoral politics also helps to explain the steel safeguards imposed by the Bush administration. During the 2000 campaign, Republican vice presidential candidate Dick Cheney promised the steelworkers of West Virginia that a Bush presidency would mean swift action to insulate the U.S. steel industry from injurious imports. The people of West Virginia voted for President Bush in one of the closest elections in U.S. history and the steel safeguards were put in place soon after President Bush took office.

Readers may react with support or anger at this explanation. As is the case with dictators, however, democracies place constraints on decision makers. Politicians derive their power and legitimacy by standing for election. This means that they must represent the interests of their constituents. True, the good politicians both lead and listen, and will not support a "bad" policy. On the other hand, if the elected politicians do not represent the interests of their constituents, then the system fails. This often produces "bad" policies in a normative sense. The role of democratic institutions differs from autocracies, but similarly constrains behavior. How do economic theories appear in democracies?

This is where Adam Smith, the framers of the Constitution, and current politics converge. Recall the discussion in chapter 1 on Adam Smith's conception of human nature as a constant and independent variable; providing insights into leaders, both democratic and autocratic. Man, like other animals, seeks survival and continuance. And for man, this appetite for self-preservation is best attained through cooperation. A related drive is the need for approbation, according to Smith, which functions in direct proportion to proximity. The thread of man's fundamental nature unites seemingly disjointed ideas in describing theories of government.

James Madison, an author of the U.S. Constitution, believed in government designed in consideration of man's nature. His theory of constitutionalism relies on a theory of man consistent with Adam Smith's. Madison's conception of constitutional government understands that different people express different views. These differences, according to Madison, are not appropriately decided by "enlightened statesmen" but are best balanced by competing interests.

> The latent causes of faction are thus sown in the nature of man.... It is in vain to say that enlightened statesmen will be able to adjust these clashing interests, and render them all subservient to the public good.[2]

Madison offers the best explanation of the link between human nature and politics in *Federalist No. 51:* "The Structure of the Government Must Furnish the Proper Checks and Balances Between the Different Departments."

Thinking about this in the context of national security, we will review the decision-making process in a democracy by looking at the U.S. government, as we looked at Cuba to understand dictatorship. All leaders maximize utility and face constraints. Illegitimate totalitarians need power obtained from maintaining a wealth differential with the population. Democratic leaders, in contrast, must obtain popular support from critical—not all—constituencies in order to maintain power. National security decisions take place in this context.

The causes of differences "sown in the nature of man" are immutable. People seek survival and the maximization of their conditions. They fight for their own interests, strive to prosper, and want those in their closest circles to thrive comfortably as well.

Government, therefore, according to Madison, should aim to remedy the possible negative effects of a society of people motivated by self-interest. Democratic society gets sculpted not by preventing expression, but by relying on competition from opposing interest groups and the fundamental need for approbation. People remain free to pursue their passions while the legitimate institutions of government balance interests and control conflict.

The decades-long passionate support of some members of the U.S. Congress for unilateral sanctions against Castro's Cuba is one example. They argue sanctions can bring about economic and political change over the long term. They might simply believe in the potency of American symbolism, or they may adhere to the principle that the U.S. government should not allow U.S. economic actors to take part in supporting a repressive regime through trade. Each of these arguments may appear right or wrong to the reader. Surely at least part of the U.S. farm lobby disagrees with the justification for sanctions on Cuba. USA*ENGAGE, the affiliation of companies opposed to sanctions that we introduced earlier, lobbies Congress against what the industry group considers excessive use of U.S. sanctions. While the Cuba policy of the United States has been shaped for years by political pressures on elected leaders, it is clear that lobbying efforts for free trade are assuming an enhanced role that counterbalances the pressure of voting blocs.

Perhaps the most robust interests in the United States focus on trade. The stakes are high. Data gathered by the research group Center for Responsive Politics from the Senate Office of Public Records indicate the Washington, D.C., lobbying industry spent nearly $3.5 billion in 2009. The largest amount by far ($144 million) was spent by the U.S. Chamber of Commerce and other business interests. Madison's factions are hard at work on the trade front.

Constraints from Constituent Concerns

The economic debate over trade is finished; trade is a good and it makes people better off. There is one caveat: international free trade often hurts workers close to retirement in locations that have a high cost of production. In the United States, textile workers and steelworkers are particularly vulnerable. While Congress has attempted to alleviate the burden on these workers through Trade Adjustment Assistance and other social benefits, laid-off workers may not have enough time in their working careers to seek training for new vocations, and their local economies may not recover during their lifetimes.

Other than this kind of exception, trade makes all people better off. Still, empirically, we do not see global free trade. We see countless barriers to free trade around the world—in democracies as well as autocracies. If trade is so good, why do sane, rational, and self-interested people restrict free trade?

We have already noted the role of the electoral college in U.S. elections and the competing interests of factions within American civil society. The diffusion of decision making in democracies is also a significant factor. The U.S. model, which involves government and interest groups, provides insight. To provide checks and balances on power, Madison designed the three branches of the U.S. government: the executive branch, the legislative branch, and the judicial branch. Regarding the daily operations of the democracy, however, influence in Washington is a function of the president, Congress, and the countless constituencies that reflect the many passions of people across America.

Let us deconstruct the executive branch for a moment. The executive branch includes the president, his staff, and members of his cabinet. The secretary of commerce, a cabinet member, shoulders the mission of promoting the growth of the entire U.S. economy. His core constituency, however, is only part of that economy: U.S. business.

For the U.S. secretary of the treasury, who represents the entire country's financial interests, U.S. financial institutions are a primary constituency. The State Department often represents the interests of foreign governments to the U.S. government, in addition to representing U.S. interests around the world. And so goes the rest of the cabinet: each has a boss—the president—and a core constituency. When we consider the competition of interests and the missions of each leader in terms of constituencies, we have a better understanding of the clash of interests in the democratic system of governing.

The legislative branch, which consists of the House of Representatives and the Senate, experiences similar conflict. In Congress, in addition to the geographic constituencies of each member, there also exists a committee structure and leadership structure. Within these institutions, members advocate for their respective interests and constituencies: farmers, textile workers, ethnic groups, etc.

Each of these government institutions possesses the authority to influence U.S. trade policy. Though the president—the head of the executive branch—is often viewed as the primary actor in how the United States engages economically with the rest of the world, trade authority is granted by the Congress, whose power to regulate foreign commerce derives from Article I of the U.S. Constitution. This shared power arrangement provides multiple entry points for constituencies seeking to influence government policy making.

K Street, in Washington, D.C., houses the offices of many of the over 20,000 active lobbyists in the United States. Colloquially,

Washington insiders refer to the influence industry as "K Street."[3] The U.S. Constitution protects the rights of individuals, groups, or corporations to lobby the government, and organized participants include trade associations, law firms, boutique lobbying firms, public relations firms, and advocacy groups such as AARP, the powerful lobby for seniors formerly known as the American Association of Retired Persons.

By looking at the important constituencies and power brokers in the U.S. government, we see how decision making appears more diffuse in a democracy than in a dictatorship. For the Commerce Department—a nontraditional actor in national security policy making with the exception of a role in enforcing export controls—trade primarily serves as a policy to create jobs and grow the economy. Trade promotes economic growth, and less trade diminishes it. For members of Congress, trade is either good or bad for jobs back home. And in every instance of its use, all of the aforementioned groups try to weigh in on how, when, and for whom decisions are made.

By seeking to understand decision making by democratic leaders, in addition to the earlier discussion of autocrats, we can better craft policies to advance national security. Any country with an economy of significance regards trade policies as tools of national security. Trade is a power tool for wielders of authority and welders of policy. At home, within the confines of their governments and institutions, they can assert themselves through trade policies in order to grow the GDP, create or protect jobs, represent constituents, and perpetuate positions within the government or institution.

Beyond borders, trade policies can promote, limit, or prohibit trade to alter the behavior of foreign leaders with proverbial carrots and sticks. What if we cannot directly influence a specific leader—a sponsor of terrorism, for instance? Theory and experience prove it is also possible to affect him through our trade practices with the nations that surround him—"surround and conquer." This approach throws into stark relief the U.S. decision-making process, the value created by trade, and a backdrop for the phenomenon that while free trade makes people better off, it is not always the strategy of choice.

Let us build on our theories in this chapter, spotlighting the two categories from the trade tool kit, analyzing them as tools-in-action, and evaluating them for relative effectiveness. First, we look at the broad class of bilateral and multilateral free trade agreements—and the threat of revoking trade agreements. Second, we discuss a myriad of more surgical policies that fall under the broad category of limits on trade. Specifically, we explore export controls and import restrictions as tools to change behaviors of leaders, and therefore states, with the goal of advancing national security.

Free Trade Agreements

Promoting trade agreements, exports, and imports also promotes access to marketplaces. A policy that limits trade also limits market access. Decisions to open the U.S. economy to the world, then, must be guided by an understanding that the decision benefits both the United States and the country receiving the access. Policy makers can, therefore, use free trade agreements as tools of security policy.

Historically, the promotion of trade may have been considered a means to enhance GDP. But it is so much more. The United States has the largest and most successful economy in the world, and access to this marketplace benefits the world. The more access provided by the United States, the greater a target economy benefits. This "good"— access to the U.S. marketplace—therefore presents the U.S. president with a powerful tool. When you have a good, you have a tool.

These tools of statecraft can advance national security; think about how they are used and not just who they are used with and against. The prioritized trade agenda of the United States over the past few years, in fact, confirms the use of trade agreements and access as a tool of security policy. The case of a U.S. Free Trade Agreement with Jordan demonstrates the point. Why was a free trade agreement with Jordan a top priority for the United States? Clearly, this small economy was not going to provide jobs to American workers or increase take-home pay across the U.S. economy. By trading with Jordan, however, the United States can gain influence with Jordanian leaders, and Jordan with U.S. leaders. Given the relative sizes of expected economic benefit, however, the greater leverage may flow to the United States. The president of the United States can make requests of the Jordanian leadership to the extent that Jordan values the trading relationship with the United States to a degree greater than any cost of the policy concession on Jordanian leadership. And U.S. leadership can revoke market access to Jordan only to the extent that the cost of such revocation does not exceed the benefit. If the United States never had the preferential trading agreement with Jordan, then the corresponding leverage would not exist.

How might this be used? The choices made by Jordan's leaders pose tremendous potential benefits and threats to U.S. national security. With Jordan's role as a critical actor in the Middle East, the United States seeks to improve relations with the Arab state.

By viewing trade promotion as a tool, and ensuring that policies are crafted to optimize the employment of trade as a lever of influence, the United States increases its arsenal of nonmilitary instruments of national security. As we review the list of other U.S. bilateral free trade agreements (FTAs), think of national security implications of trade with these countries/regions. The Caribbean Basin Initiative (CBI), Andean Trade Preference Act FTA, Chile FTA, Dominican Republic—Central America–FTA, and Panama FTA help to develop this important region in the United States' hemisphere; it also impacts source and transit zones for illegal drugs being smuggled into the United States. The U.S.–Bahrain FTA, like the FTA's with Jordan, Morocco, and Israel, help the U.S. reward friends in an important and turbulent region and maintain and increase influence for the future.

Think of a simplified world, such as the one pictured in figure 5.2. Countries A, B, C, D, E, F, and G are all participants in the global economy to some extent. Think of the relative sizes of the boxes as a representation of the relative sizes of their domestic economies. Leaders in countries A and F, however, consider each other's national policies as hostile, and therefore have strained bilateral relations or none at all. A and F do not trade with each other. Working from the gross to specific, leader A can offer targeted trade promotion policies to seek to get leader F to change policies. If, however, this change would likely get leader F's head chopped off, literally, he is unlikely to make the change, even if trade will expand. Leader A can then seek to engage other world leaders who may be better positioned to influence leader F, such as leaders in E and G. Leader A can also look past leader F and simply seek to increase the wealth of the general population in F as a method to advance national security. We will continue to

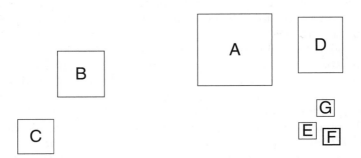

Figure 5.2

explore the incentives facing the leaders, and we will begin this discussion with the wealth effect. The link between poverty and security will be explored in depth in chapter 6.

The Wealth Effect

Trade is leverage: the steward of the tool can leverage the behavior of a target country's leader with incentives that can alter behavior. In addition to influencing the leadership of the target country, the flip side of the trade-as-a-tool coin is that it offers incentives to the populace of the target country. It creates wealth. Trade can help to build a middle class. If there is a link between poverty and national security, then trade is one "cure" to poverty and therefore a tool of national security.

Trade impacts the behavior of a target country through the "wealth effect." Recall, for example, the constraints facing a totalitarian dictator. Trade with the general economy increases the costs (S) of maintaining power. Therefore, if an autocrat allows—or perhaps more likely, is unable to prevent—trade-generated wealth in the general economy, then trading with a country ruled by some sort of autocracy can in fact reduce the leader's control; it can undermine his authority and weaken his rule. Trade can undermine the relative power of an illegitimate government over its people. It can weaken the grip of a dictator. Trade, therefore, impacts the incentives facing the citizens of a country. It impacts their behavior.

This is exactly why Castro limits free trade. He understands the power of trade to weaken his grip. Trade with the Cuban people that benefits the people significantly more than it benefits Castro can, on balance, hurt Castro. Similarly, free trade in some African kleptocracies might promote the development of a middle class motivated to challenge a tyrant. In the People's Republic of China, we have witnessed trade's impact and learned lessons regarding theories of trade as a tool.

CASE STUDY: THE PRC AND MOST FAVORED NATION STATUS

Trade between the United States and the People's Republic of China (PRC) may be justified on the basis of mutually beneficial market sizes. However, in light of human rights concerns, the United States chose to limit trade with China and engaged in an active debate over the proper role of trade. The debate came to a head in 2000 with the

U.S. Senate eventually granting permanent Most Favored Nation/ Normal Trading Relations status to the PRC. (As a biographical note, while serving on the staff of the U.S. Senate, the authors had occasion to work on issues related to trade and sanctions policies directed at influencing the behavior of the leadership of the People's Republic of China.)

U.S. industry and business lobbied hard for granting China permanent most favored nation (MFN) trading status. The United States has on the books a law that requires nonmarket economies to be certified by the president of the United States as being in compliance with certain human rights standards. The law, known as the Jackson-Vanik Amendment, conditioned Soviet trade concessions on the free emigration of Soviet Jews out of the Soviet Union when the law was passed in 1974.

From the early 1990s, however, the law began to be used as an annual opportunity for some lawmakers to make an issue of human rights conditions within the PRC. According to China scholar Bob Manning in 1997:

> Under the Jackson-Vanik Amendment to the 1974 Trade Act, in order for non-market economies to receive MFN status, the President must determine that the country meets emigration criteria or waive the ban on MFN annually by June 3. Jackson-Vanik is an outmoded piece of Cold War legislation, originally intended to aid the emigration of Soviet Jews, by holding out MFN to Moscow (with whom the United States had little trade). But it is a convenient legislative vehicle for Congress to express post-Tiananmen outrage. As Senator Connie Mack (R-FL) said recently, "The reason we annually consider China's trade, human rights, and national security behavior during the MFN renewal debate is because we do not have an acceptable alternative."[4]

Under the Jackson-Vanik Amendment, as Manning notes, nonmarket economies could receive MFN status on an annual basis only if the president determines that the country meets the Act's emigration criteria or the president waives the ban on MFN status. A presidential determination to waive the ban takes effect unless Congress passes a joint resolution denying the waiver.

Each year, including the year following the 1989 Tiananmen Square massacre, the presidential waiver was upheld by Congress. Therefore, the president of the United States, the leaders of the PRC, and those active on China, trade, or human rights issues in the U.S. Congress would engage in an annual debate, which continued annually until permanent MFN status was granted in October 2000.

Though grossly oversimplified, a summary of the positions of each of the three players—the PRC, human rights advocates, and business groups—provides a dramatic backstory. The PRC seemed annoyed with the process and usually took actions, such as freeing a prominent dissident, in exchange for some support within the U.S. government—in both the executive and legislative branches. The president and Congress were caught between two points of view: the human rights caucus and the business lobby. Of note is that the House of Representatives had previously named a "Human Rights Caucus." The Senate did not have an official caucus, but the senators most involved in activist human rights issues, regardless of political party affiliation, worked together quite effectively. The human rights caucus argued that the PRC's widely recognized and reportedly gross violations of basic international human rights standards should not be tolerated. Trading with the PRC, at a minimum, turned a blind eye to the atrocities and, at worst, provided a reward to the PRC leaders who should instead be held criminally responsible for their actions. PRC human rights violations include: forced abortions and sterilization in support of the PRC's one-child policy; operation of the Laogai slave labor camps where political prisoners were shown "education through labor" as a way to give up on political reform; abuses of the Tibetan people including cultural genocide, kidnapping the child Panchen Lama, and failing to hold talks with the Dalai Lama; and many more.

Of course the PRC leadership would either deny these accusations or deny that they were any concern of the United States. The leadership would, however, usually make some concession to the United States around the time of year that the debate occurred. For example, Wei Jingsheng and Wang Dan, prominent pro-democracy advocates in the PRC, were each arrested, imprisoned, and subsequently released in what most U.S. human rights observers view as political gestures in 1993.[5]

The other viewpoint within the United States was not a defense of the PRC or a dispute of the charges. However, the U.S. business lobby was eager to gain friends and influence people within the PRC so that a hoped-for market share of the billion-person economy would soon follow. The lobby would maintain that engagement would mitigate the PRC's human rights evils. The business logic trail was that by trading with the PRC, U.S. businesses would be exporting American values and standards to China. Only through this engagement could the United States ever hope to see real political change in China. IBM and Motorola, for example, would hire workers, pay good salaries, ensure good living quarters and working conditions, protect the environment, and train a cadre of Chinese managers who would appreciate free market dynamics and the power of empowering individual workers. The employees of these American corporations would become America's human rights ambassadors. While making products in China, they would also bring democracy and respect for human dignity to the PRC, it was argued.

The opposing camps fought over how best to bring democratic reform to China in order to mitigate the possible threats to the United States, as well as advance global standards of human dignity. Business fought the battle in Congress against the human rights caucuses over how to advance these interests. In 1998, the Senate Committee on Finance changed the name of most favored nation (MFN), the status that the U.S. business community sought for the PRC in order to avoid the annual waiver and debate. The MFN name morphed into "normal trade relations" (NTR) status. In effect, the absence of Jackson-Vanik was "normal" trade treatment. This change, along with the retirement of some of the strongest advocates for the annual PRC debate, allowed the U.S. business lobby to carry the day. As of now, the PRC holds permanent NTR status under the Jackson-Vanik Amendment, as modified. There is no annual certification, but a commission was created to specifically assess and report on human rights in China every year. Without the threat of removal of MFN, the report attracts a fraction of the attention that the human rights agenda used to magnetize.

Who was right? The jury is still out and time will tell. U.S. business continues to invest and build infrastructure in China. American companies continue to employ Chinese workers. But the Communist Party of China still rules the national political institutions of the country and sets national policies that impact human rights conditions. According to U.S. State Department annual reports, human rights conditions remain abysmal.

Essentially the United States traded the use of one tool—the annual MFN debate—for another: trade. Maybe trade—specifically, proactive bilateral trade—will ultimately prove to be a tool of change in the PRC. By removing post–Tiananmen trade restrictions on the PRC, the United States is seeking to promote economic and political freedom. And, the theory goes, with wealth and an emerging middle class, political power devolves to the people, decreasing the relative power of the autocratic center. This shift in power brings about a decreasing security threat. If successful, we will know that this tool works.

Providing Economic Opportunity

The wealth produced by commercial engagement through free trade can not only be a tool to create change in an autocratic regime, it may provide an incentive for groups of individuals to cease engaging in destabilizing behavior within a country or region. The activities of Islamic radicals in Afghanistan and Pakistan jeopardize the civil society in those countries and provide a base for terrorists seeking to do harm to Western interests in the region and abroad. The terrorists thrive in these countries due to weak, complicit, or corrupt central governments. The lack of economic opportunity provides a fertile ground for new recruits.

Both the Bush and Obama administrations have proposed the establishment of Reconstruction Opportunity Zones (ROZ) as a means of enhancing economic opportunity in Afghanistan and Pakistan. A business located in the ROZ would enjoy duty-free access to the U.S. market for its products. If successful, the economic activity generated by a ROZ would have several positive effects. A middle class could begin to develop that would demand enhanced security to conduct its economic activity, perhaps helping to fund a strong central government that would marginalize extremist elements. In turn, U.S. security is enhanced by reducing terrorist havens in the region. By choosing to engage in free trade, the United States creates wealth abroad and enhances security at home.

FTA Carrots and Sticks

Trade agreements are a carrot, or incentive, for a leader whose behavior we want to change. When a leader recognizes the benefits of access, we can tell him, "If you do the following, we will give you a trade agreement that benefits the population." The stick is the threat of removal. Once he gets a trade agreement, he wants to keep it.

The serviceability of the threat of removal is more than theory; it is a proven practice of statecraft. In the preceding section we explored the annual debate in the United States over human rights in the People's Republic of China. The debate did impact behavior among the Beijing elite, but the threat of removal of trade status from the U.S. market is what really mattered. Only countries with access to a market can be threatened with a loss of that access. A country with a healthy economy can apply two facets of the bilateral trade agreement as tools. Trading with another country benefits both countries' economic growth, and the growth can encourage political change—if you accept the arguments of U.S. businesses. Also, the bilateral trade relationship will bind the two countries together and nurture relationships.

CASE STUDY: PISTACHIOS, RUGS, AND RELATIONSHIP BUILDING

Recall the U.S. decision to allow the importation of some products from Iran in early 2000. Iran–U.S. relations have been abysmal since the Iranian revolution and U.S. Embassy hostage-taking in 1979. Pistachios and rugs were not going to cause the mullahs to abandon any nuclear weapons ambitions. Neither would they push a GDP upswing in either country. The action was symbolic—a taste of carrot, a taste from the menu of opportunity if they became friends with the United States. President Clinton, as positive reinforcement for some desired and witnessed behavior in Iran, changed U.S. regulations under the Iran and Libya Sanctions Act (ILSA) to allow Iran to export to U.S. consumers certain nonoil items such as carpets, caviar, pistachios, and dried fruit.

Would granting this limited access to the U.S. market increase jobs in the United States? No. It might help the Iranian economy to a limited extent, but the trade allowed was so narrow that the impact across the country would be small. The stated purpose of the policy goal was linked to symbolism. The message: if you continue to take actions consistent with our interests, we will open up even more of our economy to you. It was a teaser, perhaps. Get them in the door and maybe they will want to sell more.

The problem with this policy, of course, is that the benefit to the Iranian leadership was so small, and the price for maintaining power in Iran so high, that no rational domestic Iranian policy would warrant serious concessions to the United States by the religious leadership of the state. Concessions would run counter to their own interest in keeping power. The decision-making scale would weigh their personal benefit in gaining more market access to the United States with their personal cost. Recall the security costs (S) from the dictator model; they apply in Iran as well.

$$(\Upsilon = R - C - S)$$

The religious hierarchy in Iran controls about 80 percent of the power in that country. Those who favor reform and opening to the West, although prominent and in the news, hold very little power.

When those in power fail to hold popular legitimacy, they must spend capital on the tools to stay in power. It is only when a policy effectively changes the 80:20 split in power in Iran by empowering those who seek reform that the simple and symbolic policies of the United States toward Iran can have an impact. It is unlikely that a policy can be crafted that would advance U.S. interests in Iran as well as benefit the theocratic leaders more than it costs them.

Driving Up the Cost of War with Trade

Some argue that trade agreements are an especially viable tool of national security because countries that trade with each other do not go to war with each other. The assumption is that the benefits of trade are great, so the costs of war are higher between countries with healthy trading relationships. When the potential cost of war exceeds the potential benefit, then war becomes a less likely choice. Therefore, the promotion of trade is a tool that makes the cost of military conflict greater than the absence of trade.

Application of this cost-benefit analysis requires great care. To think that Castro desires to maximize wealth above all else is too simple, and would be inaccurate. A declared war with the United States, according to Castro, keeps him strong and in power. Opening up to free trade with the United States may be perceived as a loss of control and may damage the image of his invincibility; he would lose power shortly afterward.

The Cuba case reminds us again of the role of the individual decision maker—on both ends of the policy. In each foreign policy scenario, U.S. policy makers, keeping in mind domestic political constraints, must also think about the target country's individual actors and then analyze their incentives, institutions, and constituencies, if any. At first blush it may seem that wealth-maximizing individuals will choose trade promotion over the absence, and will choose trade over conflict or war; this can often be wrong. Nationalism and theocratic dogma, for example, given the constituencies, can present a leader with scenarios in which war is the rational maximizing choice. This is true for the dictator; given his personal preferences, war might be the rational answer. For example, if his choices are to face immediate and near certain insurrection via armed rebellion or go to war against a third party and remain in power longer, albeit of a poorer country, the choice for a tyrant may be clear.

Bilateral Stakeholders

While the tyrant's choice of war may be rational in some cases, trade creates constituencies on each side of a bilateral trade relationship that often serve as a check on a leader's actions. Bilateral economic engagement creates new companies and high-paying jobs related to manufacturing, exporting, and importing. Cross-border service providers benefit from an expanded customer base abroad. Investors direct capital across borders to take advantage of an expanded labor force, new technologies, and new markets for their products. Consumers in each country begin to demand the products of the other as they gain exposure to new and different goods and services. Take a look at the products on the shelves of your local grocery store to appreciate how Americans have developed a taste for products such as French wine, Italian pasta, and Belgian chocolate.

These stakeholders—those who make a living from serving the foreign market—have a strong interest in the maintenance of good relations between their native county and its trading partner. These stakeholders operate much like constituents in the domestic politics of trade. But as these constituencies pursue their own self-interests, namely access to the foreign market, they influence individual leaders to adopt policies that enhance stability and security between nations. As the trade relationship grows, the number of stakeholders increases and the more likely it is that the leaders of the respective trading partners will pursue policies friendly to each other.

Trade Incentives, Creative Thinking, and the Republic of Congo

How about when a leader seems intractable? The Republic of Congo is an interesting study. The United States has not yet been able to use trade to get the dictator to change his behavior. He is reportedly building houses on the French Riviera while presiding over one of the poorest populations in the world. Is there an opportunity for us to use trade as an incentive for Sassou-Nguesso, the president of the Republic of Congo, to promote freedom, democracy, and economic growth in his country, regionally, and throughout Africa? Can we structure trade with the Congo so that benefits accrue to the people for economic growth and political development?

Sassou-Nguesso likely makes a tremendous amount of personal money ruling his oil-rich (and yet financially poor) country. The World Bank estimated that revenue from its oil sector accounted for approximately 65 percent of Congo's $10.7 billion GDP in 2008. The country, however, lacks transparency over government books, and the president is in power thanks to a military coup and subsequent elections that were later determined to be unfair. In spite of the rich oil production, the annual per capita income of the country ranks among the lowest in the world.

Where does the money from oil revenues go? If we assume that the autocrat personally profits from millions of dollars per year, and personally spends millions per year to keep the forces of repression and loyalty in place to keep him in power, then we can better assess policies aimed at this country. How will Sassou-Nguesso react to demands of compliance to international rules of trade such as transparency and compliance with the rule of law? If he can skim millions of dollars under the status quo but avoid additional foreign direct investment, diversification of the economy, and spreading of wealth among the population, he may choose to keep things as they are. A dictator with a short-term time horizon may choose to enrich himself as long as it lasts, not risking the threat of overthrow in exchange for any possible long-term benefits of a healthy and diversified economy. And besides, the likelihood of personal enrichment in an internationally friendly, legal, and transparent economy probably seem small to him.

Is President Sassou-Nguesso a threat to the United States? Perhaps not specifically to the United States; however, as we look at tools to impact the world—the nature of interactions between world leaders—the Republic of Congo presents an interesting case study. If we adopt the broad view, to be addressed later in this book, that the alleviation of poverty supports efforts to combat terrorism, then the Sassou-Nguesso example matters. First, by fighting poverty, we impact in some way the terrorist leaders' abilities to act. And second, by developing tools that actually work on influencing the behaviors of world leaders or the people of autocratic regimes, such as Sassou-Nguesso and the people of the Republic of Congo, we have developed a nonmilitary arsenal for the next kleptocrat posing a real threat to national security. While trade, the focus of this discussion, has yet to be an effective tool for influencing the behavior of Sassou-Nguesso, in January 2010 the International Monetary Fund and World Bank agreed to support $1.9 billion in debt relief for the Republic of Congo, following reported progress made by Congolese authorities to improve transparency. We will return to this case study and the tool of debt relief in our study on lending and borrowing in chapter 8.

"Surround and Conquer"

Jordan's ruling monarchy, while less oppressive toward its own people than leaders of other countries in the region, faces serious legitimacy concerns.[6] Free trade with Jordan makes sense for both the U.S.'s decision makers and for Jordan's. For the United States, Jordan is a strategic country on the border with Iraq, Syria, Saudi Arabia, and Israel. Good ties and the potential ability to influence the actions of this country's leaders can improve the United States' ability to exercise power in this part of the world. Consider the countries surrounding a "bad" country. If the United States cannot influence the "bad" country directly, an alternative is to develop influence with all of the countries around the target country. Ties with Jordan, therefore, are of profound interest to the United States. The Jordanian monarchy, likewise, has good reason to trade with the United States. The monarch relies on a great deal of loyalty; to the extent he can provide for the economic growth of the country, it is likely that he perceives his chances of staying in power as increased.

Limits on Trade

As discussed previously, once the tool of trade is employed and economic engagement established, the withdrawal of trade itself can be used as a means to influence a leader's behavior. The most comprehensive use of this tool is typically referred to as a sanction, or a trade embargo. In the previous chapter, we discussed U.S. sanctions in the context of the trade embargo on Cuba. Sanctions are the deliberate withdrawal of trade or financial relations with a nation in order to influence a leader's behavior. Sanctions generally are characterized by a refusal to engage in virtually all trade with the sanctioned country, except for food, medicine, and other humanitarian items. The prohibition on U.S. companies doing business with countries such as Iran and North Korea are examples of trade sanctions. In addition to direct sanctions, the United States has also attempted to impose penalties on foreign companies for doing business with a sanctioned country. These secondary, or extraterritorial, sanctions have proven to be ineffective in stopping trade with the sanctioned country and their use has declined in recent years. Laws such as Helms-Burton and the Iran-Libya Sanctions Act are examples of secondary sanctions.

The reasons countries employ sanctions can vary widely, but all involve influencing the behavior of the foreign leader. Sanctions can be aimed at containing the aggression of another country, keeping it from obtaining critical technologies, or even encouraging regime change. Sanctions often fail to meet their objective because they are ill-designed to accomplish their intended purpose. In *Shrewd Sanctions*, for example, Meghan L. O'Sullivan argues that much of the ineffectiveness of U.S. sanctions against Iran is due to ill design.

> The United States relied on sanctions both as a means of containing the Islamic republic and in an effort to sway the regime to stop its support for terrorism, opposition to Israel, and pursuit of weapons of mass destruction. In pursuing these goals, the Unites States put in place one of the most rigid sanctions regimes possible but failed to get multilateral support for most elements. As a result, the sanctions regime was neither suited to the containment of Iran (given that is was unilateral), nor flexible enough to serve as a basis for a more gradual approach between the two countries.[7]

A 2007 Government Accountability Office review of U.S. sanctions targeting Iran stated similar findings: "For the past 20 years, U.S. sanctions against Iran have been an important element of U.S. policy to deter Iran from weapons proliferation and support for terrorism...However, the overall impact of sanctions, and the extent to which these sanctions further U.S. objectives, is unclear."[8]

As discussed in detail in chapter 4, sanctions merely provide the leader with a choice of whether to comply with the sanction or continue their offensive behavior and bear the cost of the sanction. As we've seen, the leader will tend to comply with the sanction—or change his behavior—if the cost of doing so is less than not changing his behavior.

Short of a comprehensive sanction, more precise tools involving the withdrawal of trade benefits can be employed to influence behavior. On one hand, certain exports of U.S. goods and technology can be withheld from trading partners or, alternatively, our market can be closed to certain imports from trading partners.

Export Controls

Export controls protect American technological advantages, maintain security, and further U.S. foreign policy objectives. Toward this end, policy makers use export controls to regulate, and in some cases prevent, the sale of technology and goods to certain countries. They are a security policy justification to limit free trade. Export controls are implemented and enforced by a number of agencies within the U.S. government. For instance, munitions are controlled by the Department of State. Items known as "dual use," which can serve the civilian sector as well as have military applications, fall under the oversight of the Department of Commerce. Overall general trade embargoes are enforced and regulated by the Treasury Department and now the Department of Homeland Security where the Customs Service—now U.S. Customs and Border Protection—resides. Federal agents enforce these laws. A system of licensing transactions provides for the sale of munitions list items, dual use items, and exceptions to trade with embargoed economies.

The United States has been controlling exports in a meaningful way since the development of the anti-communist export control network in 1942. For the United States, the Cold War against the Soviet Union marked the heyday for export controls—a tool to keep weapons, parts, and technologies from the Soviet Union. Our allies of the Coordinating Committee for Multilateral Export Controls (CoCom) provided a multilateral mechanism to prevent the transfer of military-related technology from the West to the Soviet Union and Eastern Europe.

The CoCom multilateral system of export controls worked. The member nations united against a common threat—the communists. The critical technologies were primarily owned by the governments; research and development dollars during the 1960s through 1980s overwhelmingly resided within governments.

Within the United States, this tool of security—denying U.S. exports of controlled items, munitions and otherwise—arises from specific legal authorities. In the U.S. system, it is important to remember that all authorities not given to the executive or judicial branches in the U.S. Constitution are authorities owned by the Congress. Only through enactment of legislation—through a law—can the executive have a power not articulated in the Constitution. The U.S. president's authority to regulate exports began with the 1979 Export Administration Act, which allows the president to implement and enforce the export control laws.

In the early twenty-first century, however, the export-control world faces three existential challenges. First, no consensus exists regarding the threat to unify allies as existed during the CoCom era. The United States maintains an arms embargo on China while our close allies in Europe and Israel freely sell weapons systems to the Chinese. Our trading partners supply Iran with its nuclear technologies as the United States calls for tighter sanctions.

Second, the private sector now owns most of the technology. The 1990s technology boom helped to create massive pools of venture funding, fueling remarkable technologies not controlled by government. Even the U.S. Department of Defense buys critical technology from the private sector, some of which is globally available. Globalization has dramatically changed the way companies design and produce key technologies. A multinational corporation often brings together scientists and engineers from several countries to design a single product, blurring the definition of what is "U.S. technology" and, thus, subject to control.

Finally, the Export Administration Act has not been rewritten since 1979, before the end of the bipolar world and the powerful effects of globalization. The EAA has even been allowed to lapse several times by an inattentive Congress, calling into question the political legitimacy of U.S. export controls.

For export controls to continue as a valid tool, Congress must update the law to reflect new global realities. This means addressing the twin concerns of effectiveness and efficiency. The end of the bipolar world and increased globalization coincided with a rise from new threats: adaptive nonstate and substate actors. While the leaders of certain states continue to seek technologies for government-led weapons of mass destruction programs, it is nonstate groups that have attacked the U.S. homeland and our military personnel in several countries abroad. Effective export controls must address these new risks.

First, to be effective, enforcement efforts should be focused on denying technologies to groups and individuals, in addition to countries, and to the front companies often created to serve them. It may mean expanding controls to classes of goods that serve terrorists on a battlefield, such as night vision technology, that were previously uncontrolled. Furthermore, it means imposing meaningful penalties on U.S. companies who violate export controls. At times, during lapses in the EAA, the paltry penalties for violating U.S. export controls failed to act as a deterrent to those wanting to place profit over compliance. A new export control regime has to recognize that the expected cost of an action (the penalty) must exceed the expected gain (the profit) if a policy maker seeks to deter the illicit behavior. Finally, effectiveness is enhanced when a policy is implemented multilaterally versus unilaterally. Policy makers can multiply the economic impact of a policy by getting other countries to go along. Every effort should be made to convince other leaders to implement export controls in a similar fashion. The consequences of the failure to achieve multilateral consensus among leaders is explored next.

Second, to be efficient, an optimal export control regime must place a high value on economic efficiency that strengthens combat effectiveness. America's military advantage, in large part, is based on the ability of U.S. companies to innovate faster than the rest of the world. U.S. companies provide the most cutting-edge technologies to our war fighters, giving us a tremendous technological advantage on the battlefield. In the post–Cold War adaptive adversary environment, the battlespace, not just the weapons, evolve with the technology. To the extent that U.S. companies, or global companies with a U.S. footprint, create the leading-edge technologies, U.S. government policy makers can employ tools to control access for the rest of the world. These technologies can be kept solely for U.S. military use or shared with only the closest allies, if desired. This model—often referred to as "running faster" than our potential adversaries—is contingent on the ability of U.S. businesses to continually innovate. Domestic innovation in a globalized economy relies on the proper incentives so that private sector investors are motivated to invest in new technologies through research and development. Efficient export controls will incentivize domestic innovation in technologies relevant to both economic growth as well as national security.

Efficient policies also protect "choke point" technologies. Since a given technology can represent a breakthrough innovation while many others do not, the restrictions on exports should focus on high payoff innovations, and especially during the time in which these technologies can drive other innovations. Think of a device helpful in weaponizing a nuclear device. If this device represents an innovation not previously known anywhere in the world, then the control of this technology through export control regimes will produce a high payoff in terms of security. If, however, the technology can be obtained throughout the world, via the internet, for example, then U.S. controls of this item may seem futile. Simply put, efficient export controls focus on critical technologies, produced primarily by U.S. firms. An exception to this would be if all major supplier countries multilaterally agree to control the export of an item, which is often the case with key nuclear technology.

In order to achieve efficient and effective export controls, the policy makers should consider the following questions.

1. If a technology or product is available from other foreign vendors, is it likely that others will sell the technology to the target country even if the United States refuses to do so? An answer of "yes" does not necessitate that the United States sell the product, but rather that we assess the response in crafting an efficient policy. In other words, should we deprive a U.S.

company revenue from a sale that could be used for additional research and development when the alternative is the end user will simply obtain the good from another source?

2. Does a product exist in the mass market? The United States may be the only country in the world to purchase a technology, but it may be so ubiquitous in the United States that controlling the product may be nearly impossible. An example is a product readily available at a common electronics store in the United States and sold in millions of units per year, even though it is only produced in the United States. Resources spent on attempting to control this item could be better utilized elsewhere.

3. Are we using the best sources of strategic intelligence to prevent unauthorized export of the technology? Should resources be targeted more toward interdiction of illicit trade rather than an overly broad licensing structure?

4. Who is the end user, and beyond controlling items, can we match lists of items with specific users? Stated another way, can we be more precise and surgical in the application of export controls so that, instead of blanketing an entire country with a label, we can distinguish between illegitimate end users and trusted customers that would, in fact, be eligible to purchase otherwise restricted items?

5. And finally, efficiency demands the application of discretion. An effective and efficient export control system would ensure that the focus on *transactional* risks do not cause *systemic* risks. In the past, U.S. leaders designed the export control system simply to address the risk of particular transactions: adversaries obtaining key technologies that could jeopardize our national security. Continuing to devote finite resources to control all but the highest-performing computers and semiconductors is a misguided use of resources when cell phones can now perform the functions of the supercomputer of the last decade. Today, an overly broad and prescriptive export control system would also result in a systemic risk: the degradation of our own industrial base, U.S. tech companies, which provide us with the most capable military in the world.

As with the other instruments explored thus far, various domestic constituencies affect the nature and implementation of U.S. export controls. In this case, the private sector is in the unique position of seeking revenue from exports of U.S. technology and, at the same time, being in the best position of furthering U.S. national security goals by preventing the release of its technology to end users of concern. Domestic institutions and regulations must be in place in any country in order to provide proper incentives for the private sector to comply with these national security policy goals.

CASE STUDY: INDIA AND COMMERCE

Let's look at a case study of meaningful export policies with a passage through India, while picking up a thread from earlier in the book: the U.S. Department of Commerce as a nontraditional contributor to national security. The U.S. Department of Commerce, while not a national security agency, can contribute to national security objectives. The secretary of commerce fosters American business at home and abroad, promotes U.S. exports, enforces international trade agreements, and regulates the export of sensitive goods and technologies, among other things.[9]

India and Pakistan detonated nuclear devices in 1998, becoming nuclear states outside of the Nuclear Non-Proliferation Treaty (NPT). India's nascent but growing trading relationship with the United States came to a screeching halt. At the time, one of the authors worked in the Senate on a bipartisan "Sanctions Task Force" called for by Senate leadership. The so-called Glenn Amendment to the Arms Export Control Act prohibited U.S. foreign assistance to any nonnuclear weapon state as defined by the NPT that, among other things, detonates a nuclear device. India has never signed the NPT and refuses to do so as a nonnuclear weapons state. President Clinton invoked the Glenn Amendment against India on May 13, 1998. In addition, he immediately tightened export controls. As a nuclear state in contravention to the NPT, U.S. laws basically halted American businesses' ability to trade with India. Even after the Glenn Amendment restrictions were lifted, the ban on sales to certain prohibited entities in India remained.

The Department of Commerce created a list of entities that were in some way involved in India's nuclear program, and these entities were put on a prohibited list. Think about this. U.S. firms—by order of the secretary of commerce—were prohibited from trading in nuclear-related goods with the listed Indian firms. The Indian leadership was paying a price for its decision to detonate a nuclear device and declaring India a nuclear power.

Then, in 2002, things changed. From 1998 to 2002, Indians lobbied U.S. congressional leaders and the president to reinstate trade in the prohibited classes of technology. In 2002, India's leaders reached out to their U.S. counterparts asking what actions would be required to facilitate trade in the prohibited areas. The Department of Commerce identified International Atomic Energy Agency (IAEA) safeguards and proliferation issues as the behavior to be modified. The U.S. officials backed up their assertions with proof of inadequate nuclear safeguards, as well as proof of India's proliferation of weapons or related technology.

The president wanted safety and proliferation behaviors changed; he had instituted prohibitive export controls following the 1998 nuclear detonation. Four years later, the Indian leadership wanted to make a deal. They had responded to an incentive to change—a meaningful incentive.

Within the next year, sufficient progress on proliferation and safeguards had been made, and the U.S. export controls began to relax in 2003. In 2008, moreover, President Bush signed legislation that agreed to civil nuclear energy cooperation with India, though at the time of this book's publication the agreement has not yet entered into force.[10]

Cooperation between the United States and India on technology in the private sector has been increasing, as both Indian public and private sector entities now have access to U.S. technologies. In return, the United States receives from Indian leaders specific actions on nuclear safeguards. The policies of the U.S. secretary of commerce certainly played an important national security role, and the case study is a reminder that trade is a good, and therefore can be used as a tool.

CASE STUDY: THE PRC, PUBLIC DISCLOSURE, AND VERIFIED END USERS

A second case study of how export controls can be used in an effective and efficient manner to create incentives for change is the use of the "unverified list." A U.S. publication of Chinese companies that received U.S. technology but did not allow the use of the technology to be verified by U.S. officials, the unverified list was created by the Commerce Department in response to the People's Republic of China preventing the United States from conducting end-use verifications at Chinese companies that received U.S. technology subject to an export license.

The publication of the list caused embarrassment to most of the PRC-housed companies and jeopardized their businesses by depriving them of desired U.S. goods. The implication was that they were employing the technologies for illegitimate purposes under the cover and protection of the PRC government. U.S. companies, list in hand, were less likely to export to these companies for fear of the same embarrassment and public derision. Instead, U.S. technologies began to flow to PRC-based companies that were not on the list. Many of the Chinese companies, once they understood the United States was serious in not allowing exports to unverified firms, willingly invited U.S. officials to conduct end-use visits, contradicting their own government's policy.

The PRC government was not pleased. But the business constituencies in China would not be deterred; they desired the U.S. technology. The Chinese companies lobbied their own government to change its policy. As discussed previously, stakeholders in the bilateral relationship can check the actions of their leaders. As a result of this public disclosure method, and after only about eighteen months from implementation of this policy, the PRC government began to make concessions on end-use verification inspections and acknowledged the legitimacy of the U.S. government making these inspections on Chinese territory. The United States and the PRC continue to have differences and conflicts on export controls. However, the publication of the end-use verification list proved to be a tool with heft: effective and efficient.

Moreover, the success of publishing the names of end users in order to facilitate checks on exports raised a more hopeful question among leaders. What if regulators could verify the bona fides of certain end users in advance, and allow expedited exports of certain technologies to these trusted end users? The mutually beneficial nature of the economies of the United States and China has been discussed in other publications and need not be repeated here. But as certain industries rise in prominence in China, they have a voracious appetite for U.S. goods and technologies. As strong, predictable commercial relations develop between certain American and Chinese companies, trade volumes increase and a heightened level of confidence emerges. For these special commercial relationships, the Commerce Department recently developed a Certified End User list, a specific list of companies in China to which American companies can export controlled goods on an expedited basis. This type of system allows American companies to reap the benefits of selling into this burgeoning market with confidence that the technology will not be diverted for nefarious use. It also creates a strong economic incentive for Chinese companies to put in place the export control safeguards and measures necessary to be included on the list.

The India and PRC cases emphasize that despite the merits of free trade, security policy can justify restricting trade. Leaders make decisions that, on the surface, seem to contradict tenets about human nature, choosing to forego the short-term benefits of trade and opting to use it as a tool for reaching larger security interests. In these cases, trade was interrupted. But once the national security concerns were addressed, trade began again. These tools worked.

Export controls are one means to limit trade. Import restrictions are another tool affecting the complex networks of movement of goods around the world, and are the subject of the next section.

Import Restrictions

Restrictions on imports can protect American businesses from certain unfair advantages of imported foreign goods. Otherwise known as trade remedies, import restrictions include policies such as antidumping, countervailing duties, safeguards, and what is known in the United States as Section 337 of the 1974 Trade Act.

Leaders design and implement trade remedies for three basic reasons. First, people argue that they level the playing field. In other words, some market failure exists and some sort of government intervention will make trade "fair." Second, these policies can limit other actors' access to the U.S. domestic market for a particular trade benefit. Finally, remedies can be used to influence the behavior of an international economic actor.

Antidumping

Antidumping laws have been in place in the United States since 1916. Initially consisting of a private right of action, as of the 1979 Trade Act responsibility for administering the laws moved to the U.S. Department of Commerce. Antidumping actions, in essence, penalize the actions of private persons who trade "unfairly." A manufacturer, for example, "dumps" goods in foreign markets by selling at a price below their cost of production or for the price they sell in their closed, home market, thereby causing harm to the domestic industry. This predatory pricing behavior could allow the foreign producer to come in at a later time and recoup the leading losses incurred, and eventually profit at a much greater level than if the U.S. industry had remained unharmed and intact. The Department of Commerce will levy a duty on the dumped imports in these circumstances in order to offset the price advantage enjoyed by the foreign competitor.

Antidumping actions are aimed, then, at private company behavior. What leverage does this give the policy maker with the foreign leader? Dumping traditionally occurred in situations where the foreign exporter enjoyed a protected market at home. Unburdened by competition, the firm charged high prices to its domestic consumer and used the profits to sell at a level below cost of production in foreign markets. In that way, the firm captures market share abroad, adding to its global revenues. Closed markets, such as Japan in the 1970s and Korea in the 1990s, were subject to a multitude of trade remedy cases on their exports. The antidumping laws, and their application against the major companies in these markets, led to trade negotiations between government leaders and, gradually, opening of these markets.

The antidumping laws also offer a powerful tool to influence systemic changes in certain economies, designated as nonmarket-oriented economies.

CASE STUDY: THE PRC AND NONMARKET ECONOMIES

Two kinds of economies exist in the world, as classified under U.S. trade law: market economies and nonmarket economies (NMEs). The PRC is a nonmarket economy, although Communist party leaders argue to the contrary with U.S. leaders. The implications of this designation are severe. Because of the way the antidumping laws are implemented, a nonmarket economy faces many more antidumping actions than a market economy and the duties put in place by the Department of Commerce are very steep. The PRC leaders have an incentive to be designated a market economy. This provides leverage to the U.S. policy maker.

In order to attain a market economy designation, the PRC—or any economy—must attain six criteria. First, they must have a fully convertible currency. The press well documents the claims that the PRC leadership pegs its currency at an artificially low exchange rate with the United States. It is not freely convertible. Second, domestic wage rates must be set by the market; in the PRC, wages remain highly managed. These first two items alone give the PRC significant trading advantages in the short term over market economies that must compete to keep currencies sound and workers competitively paid. Third, government ownership in the private economy must be limited. Fourth, the government must not engage in the allocation of resources to industry. Fifth, the government must freely allow foreign investment.

The sixth category, "other," gives U.S. policy makers a catch-all category. Some may consider this a political option: a chance to withhold market economy status when the justification does not fit neatly into categories one through five. What it provides, in fact, is subjectivity—an opportunity for the secretary of commerce to apply subjective reasoning. For example, think of Russia and the Ukraine. Russia was granted market economy status in 2005 and Ukraine followed in 2006. Are these countries more market oriented than China? The line can be difficult to draw without the ability to apply subjective criteria. Here is perhaps the most interesting point when we consider the role of institutions in this question. The assistant secretary of commerce for import administration sets these import restrictions. Of all the decisions this person makes, only this one—nonmarket economy status—is not subject to judicial review. All other decisions before this government official can be challenged in court and overturned by a judge if the decision is not based on facts and law. The NME decision, however, in addition to having this subjective caveat, can be neither appealed by any stakeholder nor overturned by a court.

The nonmarket economy status of the PRC gives the United States tremendous leverage to demand changes in the Chinese economy. Until Chinese currency and trading practices become more market oriented—and thus more "fair" from the perspective of their foreign trading partners—Chinese exporters will continue to be penalized by antidumping cases. This seemingly intractable situation has resulted in the creation of a high-level working group between officials of the two countries that is outlining the specific steps China must implement in order to become market oriented. These changes will, ultimately, lead to a more balanced commercial relationship between the United States and China.

Countervailing Duties

Countervailing duties (CVDs), another import-restricting policy, seek to undermine a foreign government's subsidies. A foreign manufacturer that receives a financial benefit from its government for the production or export of a good can sell its product at prices lower than its competitors. If the foreign subsidy results in harm to a U.S. industry, the Commerce Department will implement import duties to offset the value of the subsidy, thereby leveling the playing field for U.S. producers.

Access to the largest market in the world, the United States, is a good sought by foreign companies. A countervailing duty deprives the foreign company of this good and has the effect of reducing the value of the company's subsidy. What is the point of a subsidy if the company loses its ability to access the most important market in the world? The use of the countervailing duty laws has been an important tool in forcing foreign leaders to reevaluate the use of subsidies as a means of promoting their exports. The WTO Agreement on Subsidies, which prohibits export subsidies, is a recognition by the member countries that subsidies are trade distorting and economically unproductive. It is unlikely that the WTO Agreement would exist without the leverage of the countervailing duty laws, and export subsidies would continue to be used by governments seeking a commercial advantage in world markets.

An example of the success of CVDs in curbing export subsidies can be found in the longstanding dispute between the United States and Canada on softwood lumber. Since 1981, the U.S. lumber industry has argued that imports of subsidized Canadian lumber were hurting U.S. producers because the Canadian lumber industry operates under rules characterized by most in the U.S. government as mercantilist, or at least not free. Under this system, Canadian producers received government subsidies that drove less than fair market prices for Canadian lumber sold in the United States.

In order to avoid years of fighting with our largest trade partner over lumber, in 2004, the Department of Commerce issued a blueprint for a market-oriented Canadian lumber system, free of subsidies and, thus, immune from future CVD costs. This plan provided Canadian lawmakers an incentive to change its system and resume normal trade relations with the United States. Many Canadian leaders and officials understand the benefits that free trade will bring to Canada should the artificial pricing system end and have been able to push for free market reforms. For example, the United States and Canada reached a seven-year Softwood Lumber Agreement in 2006, which seeks to balance Canadian export and U.S. lumber prices. This progress toward normalizing trade would not have been possible without the application of the CVD laws.

In another example, many members of Congress recently called for the United States to expand its use of countervailing measures against Chinese products. These critics of Chinese trade policies contend that the Chinese government provides significant subsidies to many of its industries through preferential bank loans, debt forgiveness, and tax breaks. Until 2006, the U.S. Commerce Department argued that countervailing laws could not be applied to a nonmarket economy, such as China, because the government determines most of the production and prices and it would, therefore, be too difficult to calculate the duty to counterbalance the government subsidy. This decision was reconsidered in 2007, and the Commerce Department has since issued rulings to impose CVDs against certain Chinese paper products, off-road tires, and steel pipes. Some U.S. lawmakers are hopeful that the use of countervailing duties will force Chinese leaders to reevaluate the use of subsidies as a means of promoting their exports.

Safeguards

The U.S. government implements safeguards to address a sudden surge of imports that injures a U.S. industry. Steel safeguards during the first term of President George W. Bush, for example, resulted from a finding that the domestic steel industry in the United States was being damaged by the low price of foreign steel coming into the United States. Safeguards go beyond placing a duty on an import. Safeguards block the importation of the product altogether. When the government imposes a safeguard, however, there does not need to be any finding of an unfair trade practice on behalf of the foreign government or exporter. For this reason, safeguards are assumed to be more political in nature than other trade remedies and their use is often controversial.

By imposing safeguards on steel produced in Europe, Asia, and South America, the United States provoked a heated debate among the participants in the global trading system. The Bush administration argued that the safeguards were necessary to offset the huge oversupply of steel being dumped into world markets fueled by government steel subsidies. In the end, the United States removed the steel safeguards, but not before using the leverage of closing the world's largest market to launch historic negotiations. A dialogue under the auspices of the Organization for Economic Co-operation and Development (OECD) was begun to lower steel subsidies globally. All participants, OECD members plus India and China, agreed that global steel subsidies had led to overcapacity and a decrease in world steel prices, harming steel producers in all countries. The downturn in steel demand beginning in 2008 has reduced the sense of urgency for global subsidy reductions, but the OECD participants continue to closely monitor global steel production and the use of subsidies.

Can the use of trade remedies—such as antidumping actions and safeguards—actually lead to more trade and greater engagement between nations? President Obama often cites his administration's trade enforcement agenda (the use of trade remedies) as a primary means to gain public interest group support for an expanded free trade agenda. The argument is that certain, powerful groups, such as labor unions, have opposed new free trade agreements because of the government's failure to invoke trade remedies to protect workers in times of increased imports into the United States. If the administration shows a propensity to use enforcement tools more regularly, it is thought by some, new trade agreements can be adopted and the tool of free trade can be employed with additional trading partners.

Upon taking office, the Obama administration acted quickly to impose trade remedies on China, including invoking a special safeguard to impose steep tariffs on Chinese tire imports. These actions were highly praised by labor unions and other constituencies concerned with imports but, to date, these groups have not embraced a more open trade agenda.

Patent Protection

An emerging trade remedy tool is the use of safeguards to block imports of goods manufactured abroad that have been found to infringe upon U.S. intellectual property. Section 337 of the Trade Act of 1974 provides a remedy for U.S. companies whose intellectual property has been pirated. Under Section 337, if the International Trade Commission finds that a patent has been infringed abroad, that product may not be exported to the United States. The 337 process is becoming the most widely used trade remedy, reflecting increased piracy of U.S. technology in key export markets such as China. Of course, a nation's ability to innovate is reflected in its patents. As national security depends on innovation for the economic prosperity that fuels defense spending and the development of new technologies to maintain our military competitive edge, innovation depends on the protection of intellectual property. The increased use of 337 safeguards could provide leverage to U.S. officials to strengthen the international rules and enforcement of intellectual property protection, much like past application of trade remedy laws was used to open foreign markets.

Trade as a Tool: Roundup

Trade policy as a tool of security policy operates on many levels and has demonstrated capability of changing behavior. The opportunity

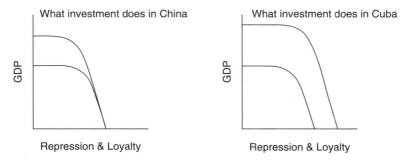

Figure 5.3

to open markets to domestic producers and consumers may reap benefits for a leader, democratic or autocratic. Providing for the needs of the people of a country can confer legitimacy. Therefore, the provision of trade can be easily viewed as a "carrot," or positive incentive for a leader to change a behavior; likewise, the removal of trading access can negatively reinforce a foreign leader's behavior.

Trade also promotes wealth within an economy, and wealth creates or grows a middle class; therefore, this growth can lead to political reform and openness. Similarly, the wealth effect guides a population's attention to policies that might jeopardize a trade benefit. The threat of loss of market access to or from a specific country can incentivize a population to change a behavior.

Beyond the legitimacy attributed to a leader, and the wealth impact on the general population, specific and surgical policies can be employed. Export controls of specific materials and to specific purchasers can effectively promote national security. And finally, targeted import restrictions can be an impetus for leaders to alter their behavior in order to maximize utility.

While constituencies, geographic or industry-specific, work within a democracy to limit free trade, the totalitarian dictator discussed previously may limit free trade to maintain a wealth differential, and so limits trade.

For the dictator, trade can be a "bad," something he wants to reduce. If trade makes an unpopular dictator more susceptible to insurrections and overthrows, then clearly a dictator will limit free trade. As argued previously and shown in figure 5.3, there may exist a level above which the dictator begins to spend more on security (repression and loyalty) than he gains in revenues. This point, which may be no trade or may include a great deal of trade, defines the profit-maximizing level of trade for the dictator. We will not see free trade with dictators facing such constraints.

CHAPTER 6

Money and Finance as Security Tools

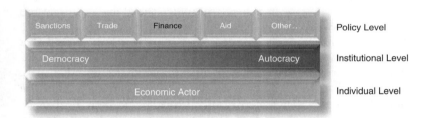

Figure 6.1

The movement of money—how it's bought, sold, borrowed, loaned, and invested—creates opportunities to leverage world leaders and, therefore, world events. We will explore the fundamentals of international finance, but with particular interest in finding tools for national security. Like the free trade agreements, export controls, import restrictions, and sanctions covered in the preceding chapters, international finance influences national security as well as the decision makers whose choices make a difference in the global struggle for peace and security. The next few chapters will explain money and finances. We will cover topics one could address in several volumes; we will cover the brief knowledge necessary for the policy maker and analyst, however, and not the academic. This will be the international finance fundamentals followed by real-world scenarios. As usual, throughout this book, the concepts will be covered so that the list of policy tools derivable is limited only by the creativity of the reader.

MONEY

Money can be traded, and people want more of it, not less. It is traded just like a banana or a fish. One fish can equal $1, and $1 can equal three bananas. We carry money in our pockets because it is much easier than carrying fish or bananas. It is portable. It is divisible. It is widely recognized and difficult to forge. This makes it good money, and good money gets traded as a commodity.

This is quite remarkable. A U.S. dollar, coveted around the world, is not a commodity currency. Hold up any U.S. currency note. The intrinsic value of that bill is almost nothing, regardless of the markings denoting 1, 10, or 100. *Commodity money,* a term of art in economics, refers to currencies such as gold and silver, which have value regardless of the images stamped on them. Gold coins retain their value even if melted down; currency minted from gold thus trades as commodity money. The U.S. dollar, and most currency around the world, however, is what we call a *fiat currency.* When ripped into pieces, we destroy its value. Amazingly, the global economy and financial system largely trade currencies with no intrinsic value. In fact, a 2003 study for the International Monetary Fund found that only twenty-two currencies are backed by a commodity or some combination of commodities. Even within the countries found to have commodity-backed currencies, which include commodity-exporting industrial countries such as Australia, Canada, and New Zealand as well as commodity-dependent developing countries in sub-Saharan Africa, most use paper-and-coin fiat money.[1] How does this reliance on fiat currency work? Faith.

The dollars in my pocket have value because they are backed by the good faith of the U.S. government. To be more precise, because I trust the U.S. government will accept dollars in payment of taxes, I believe the U.S. government backs the U.S. dollar. And because of that backing, I can offer my dollar to a merchant in exchange for some good. The merchant takes the dollar based upon the confidence that tomorrow he can use that same dollar to purchase something else, and that another person will accept it from her in an exchange. That's it. The merchant could be in a Wal-Mart in Peoria or at a souk in Istanbul; they take the dollar today because they trust it will hold value in the future—faith based upon trust that the U.S. central bank will preserve the value of the dollar in the future. We all—each of us in this marketplace—function based upon faith we have in the leaders of our country and central bank to preserve the value of the currencies in our pockets. And if we lose that faith, we treat the currency accordingly.

What are the implications for a nation's security? The value of a fiat currency, which most countries use, depends upon the good faith of the government leader not to destroy the value of the currency. It makes sense, then, that the world buys "good" money for savings and investments—money that people expect will hold value. The glimmer of international finance as a tool of security policy radiates from an understanding of currency, why it has value, and its exchange as a good.

INFLATION

Inflation is a general increase in prices. We can explain inflation in several ways: the exchange ratio of money to goods decreases; more money is required to purchase a product; the value of money decreases. Inflation can be caused by an increase in demand for a product, a decrease in supply, or a change in technology. Inflation becomes problematic, however, when governments abuse authority over the money supply and print money for short-term political, rather than economic reasons. Politicians break the faith of the users of the fiat currency, therefore devaluing the currency relative to other currencies and goods in the marketplace. Problematic inflation is almost always a function of an increase in the supply of the domestic currency—a choice of a political leader.

At the local grocery store, bananas cost more in some years than others. First, think in terms of supply and demand. If we assume that there is a new banana diet fad causing a global surge in demand for bananas, then we know the price of bananas (relative to dollars) will increase. If, however, some unusual weather pattern has caused a massive overabundance of bananas this year, without an increase in demand, then we expect the price of bananas will drop.

Return to our hypothetical small island economy mentioned at the beginning of this book with Robinson Crusoe. Let's assume a group of people survive the sinking of a boat or a plane crash and are stranded on an island. On the island we have a fixed number of dollars—these survived the boat wreck and landed on the island with the people. And we have two items in our economy: bananas and fish. On the first day, one dollar buys one fish and four bananas. If the supply of bananas doubles, then one dollar will buy one fish and eight bananas. To understand abusive inflation, picture a box floating ashore with another 100 one-dollar bills inside. Holding bananas and fish and all things constant, the prices of both will double; it will take twice as many dollars to buy the same product. Two dollars will now buy one fish.

Governments almost always control the monetary base—the number of units of currency actually in circulation. Although not literally accurate, think of the president of a developing country with his hand on the on/off switch of the printing presses for the local currency. Just as when the second box of dollars washed ashore and the ratio of bananas to dollars decreases, when a government prints new money, the ratio of bananas to dollars decreases. It now takes two dollars to buy one banana where before it only took one. This represents inflation—inflation that harms an economy.

This, in its simplest form, describes what happens in the world when a country experiences severe inflation, which is called hyperinflation. Russia experienced inflation over 1,000 percent per year in the early 1990s, as did Argentina (1989–90), Bolivia (1984–85), Brazil (1989–90, 1993–94), Bulgaria (1997), Congo (1991–94), Peru (1989–90), and Nicaragua (1988–91). More recently, Zimbabwe became the first country to hyperinflate in the twenty-first century with inflation over 100 trillion percent in 2008, though this astronomical rate has since subsided, ending in 2009. In each case, excessive printing of domestic currency provided the proximate cause of the inflation. The subsequent loss of confidence in the currency causes it to lose further value. People begin to anticipate that the government will print more money, which means currency values will decrease again and people will need to exchange even more money for goods. This creates a vicious cycle, where the leader will try to print money faster than the market participants anticipate devaluation.

We apply this understanding of money and inflation to security policies. Just as we can trade different products in the global economy, we can trade different currencies. The value of a fiat currency requires faith in the monetary authority, and many countries have terrible histories of abuse of that monetary authority. Money is a good, but people do not hold all currencies in equal esteem. Economists may say that good money is a better good than bad money. People throughout the world desire currency that they can rely upon: money that will hold its value and not be devalued through sovereign leaders printing currency notes whenever it is politically expedient. Understanding money, and further understanding the differing qualities of sovereign currencies, allows us to consider crafting policies that influence foreign leaders. If foreign leaders want money, and especially if they want good money, policy makers have levers of influence by controlling access to money.

Case Study: Swiss Dinars
and Saddam Dinars

Pre- and post-war Iraq presents an interesting case study in currency, foreign exchange, and the quality of a currency. Prior to the Gulf War of 1991, the Iraqi dinar, the national currency, was printed by a Swiss company. The last printing of the currency occurred in 1989. Following the Gulf War, however, and the creation of a no-fly zone over Northern Iraq, an autonomous zone for the Kurds of Northern Iraq was created. So now there were two regions within Iraq: the North controlled by Kurdish Iraqis and the rest of Iraq controlled by Saddam Hussein. The 1990s, especially prior to the Oil-for-Food Program sponsored by the United Nations, proved economically difficult for Iraq. Saddam, short of cash and running a budget deficit, resorted to printing dinars. As Mervyn King, governor of the Bank of England, wrote:

> Unable to import notes printed abroad because of sanctions, the regime printed low-quality notes in Iraq that bore Saddam's image. In May 1993, the Central Bank of Iraq announced that the 25 dinar note, then the highest denomination note in circulation, would be withdrawn and replaced by a new locally printed note.[2]

So Saddam instituted a mandatory money exchange, forcing all people of Iraq to turn in their Swiss-made dinars in exchange for the new "Saddam" dinars.[3]

Since the Iraqis in the North, however, did not trade with the South, they did not need to turn in their Swiss dinars and continued to use them as their currency. So by the late 1990s, Iraq was one country with two currencies. One currency was a remnant of the previous national currency, and the other, the Saddam dinar, was the new national currency of Iraq. One was a fiat currency not backed by anyone; the other was backed by the good faith of the Iraqi ruler.

The interesting thing is, the Saddam dinar was considered the worthless currency, and the Swiss dinar held its value. Both currencies were traded internationally, so it is possible to compare values of the currencies. Contrary to what one might expect, the currency backed by nobody and nothing held its value. The currency backed by the government—in this case the government of Iraq—failed to hold its value.

After the 2003 Iraq War, the United States combined both currencies into one by destroying both the Saddam and the Swiss dinar to end the monetary separation between the regions, and produced a new, third dinar.

Money, as a good, is traded: bought, sold, and loaned; and people want more of it. We're familiar with interpersonal financial flows; most of us manage personal bank accounts. World leaders also deal in money denominated in particular currencies. They need it and want it. Often leaders require it to stay in power. But beyond quantity of a currency, people also care about the quality: Saddam dinars versus Swiss dinars exemplify the distinction. Leaders, like you and me, prefer good money.

The process of buying and selling goods, services, and currencies in the international market and the domestic monetary and fiscal policies of a government sets the price of a given currency in terms of another currency. A given despot or even a president may be able to control the monetary authority of his country, and therefore control the quantity of domestic currency. Some things are easily done, like diminishing the value of a currency through excessive printing. Increasing its value, however, is less easily controlled and often cannot be done. Actions taken by others—states or even large financial actors—can impact the relative price of a domestic currency. Economic actors want money and prefer good money to bad. Both the quantity and quality of money available to a leader is subject to not only domestic policies, but also outside manipulation. Understand these levers, and you've found tools to influence behavior—economic tools of security.

CASE STUDY: INTERNET MARKETPLACE

So how is money traded? The relative qualities of currencies do not matter unless there is a marketplace for money. In the presence of a market, people will seek good money over less good, and avoid bad. We measure this like we do any other commodity—by the price, or the exchange rate. The marketplace allows for the valuation of currencies in terms of other currencies. First, we will explore a marketplace and its powers, followed by a discussion of exchange rates and the marketplace for currencies. This will lead to exchange rates as a tool of security.

The price of money is set by markets. Efficient markets, with a large number of participants with access to information and low transaction costs, set accurate prices. An accurate price is a powerful thing. In fact, only markets can efficiently set prices. With the global proliferation of access to the internet, online markets have made proving this assertion easier.

Recent academic literature highlights the predictive power of markets.[4] A favorite recent example is the Iowa Electronic Markets (IEM), an online marketplace affiliated with the University of Iowa, the alma mater of one of the authors. According to its Web site, http://www.biz.uiowa.edu/iem/, "The Iowa Electronic Markets are real-money futures markets in which contract payoffs depend on economic and political events such as elections."

How does it work? IEM participants enter the market by opening accounts with real money. Once in the market, futures contracts are bought and sold in an online marketplace. The electoral marketplace produced impressive results during the 2008 U.S. presidential election. Contracts in the winner-take-all contest between President Obama and Senator McCain paid $1 if the designated candidate won the U.S. popular vote, and paid nothing if the candidate lost. At midnight on November 3, 2008, a $1 futures contract on President Obama was selling for 53.55 cents, and a $1 contract on Senator McCain was selling for 46.45 cents. The popular vote on November 4, in fact, reported 52.9 percent for President Obama and 45.7 percent for Senator McCain.[5]

As shown in figure 6.2, most pundits and political experts failed to accurately predict the election results that individuals, voting with their real dollars and facing real incentives, aggregated by an efficient

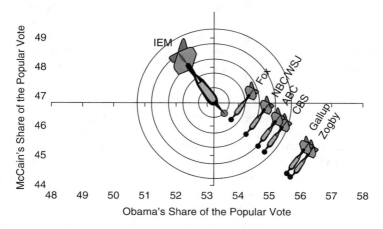

Figure 6.2

marketplace predicted. The market coordinated the opinions and, in fact, set an accurate price on the contract as of midnight the night before the election.

Multiple components merge to make these markets powerful. First, they employ real incentives—people must use their own money. Second, a large number of incentivized people participate in the market. Their purchases are weighted by their respective confidences in the outcome. Those best informed may be more confident, and therefore more likely to invest more in the futures contracts. Less informed people will invest less. And, of course, those with no sense of the outcome will not participate if the price of losing exceeds the benefit of participating in the process.

The results of an online marketplace can be startling, and can sometimes have unintended consequences. When the Defense Advanced Research Projects Agency tried to create an online political action market to better inform policy makers, they chose to begin the project with futures contracts on terrorist incidents in the Middle East.[6] Politicians in the United States found the action untenable and cut funding in 2003. Opponents argued that terrorists may be able to purchase contracts on an event, and then carry out the event, thereby profiting from the government-sponsored online marketplace. This could be a legitimate risk, but the policy makers monitoring the market would also see a spike in the price of a terrorist event and have cued intelligence that the threat of attack is high, and have the opportunity to take action.

The same principles that characterize these market examples apply to the market for currency. The U.S. dollar bill in my pocket has value for only one reason—it is backed by the good faith of the U.S. government. The value, in short, derives from faith that the U.S. government will not devalue the dollar by printing to excess. Based on this faith alone, people buy and sell the U.S. dollar as the currency of choice for savings, investments, and international transactions.

Policy makers can use this desire for good money as an economic tool to advance security objectives. Specifically, by granting or denying access to currency, policy makers can influence the behavior of foreign leaders. For example, policy makers can incentivize a dictator they want to reform by cutting off access—or threatening to cut off access—to good money, thereby limiting the dictator's ability to conduct international transactions that could increase his wealth. Alternatively, policy makers can reward leaders that reform by granting access to the currency. In fact, both of these scenarios unfolded as the United States sought reform in Ukraine.

CASE STUDY: MONEY LAUNDERING IN UKRAINE

In December 2002, Bush administration officials announced plans to take punitive steps against Ukraine, which had been found to be doing too little to prevent terrorists from using its banking system for money laundering purposes, making it one of the first countries to be singled out for financial countermeasures under the USA Patriot Act that President Bush signed in the wake of the terrorists attacks on September 11, 2001. While we will describe in more detail the mechanics of the antiterrorist finance legislation in chapter 10, broadly speaking, the legislation gave the Bush administration the authority to identify financial activity that threatened U.S. national security and the power to take action against it.

In the case of Ukraine, U.S. banks faced additional reporting requirements for doing business there, which impeded access to savings, investments, and international transactions in U.S. currency. Discussing the decision to use the financial countermeasure, one administration official said, "This is perhaps the most muscular financial tool in the Patriot Act toolbox . . . This will send the message to the international financial community that they need to get their act together."[7]

Denying access to U.S. currency proved to be a power financial tool. Consistent with United States and international standards, the Ukrainian parliament passed anti–money laundering legislation. In return, the U.S. Treasury Department rescinded Ukraine's designation as a primary money laundering concern.

In effect, the White House denied access to U.S. currency to influence the behavior of Ukrainian policy makers. When Ukraine mitigated the threats posed to U.S. national security with legislation aimed to prevent money laundering, potentially by terrorist organizations, American policy makers granted Ukrainian investors increased access to U.S. currency.

The economic tool to grant and deny access to U.S. currency is powerful because of the value of the American dollar, which, as previously stated, derives from faith that the U.S. government will not devalue the dollar by printing to excess. By contrast, some currencies seem to drop in price regularly, in spite of promises by the leader of the country and head of the monetary authority to strictly limit policies that may devalue the domestic currency. The market, which weighs many factors, including the statements of a head of state, determines the price of a currency through international exchange.

The choice of exchange rate regime and central bank structure impacts the well-being of an economy; money, at least in the short term, matters. This is why we see world leaders manipulating domestic monetary issues and exchange rates, and many democracies trying to protect monetary and exchange policies from political leaders. Can this powerful lever over an economy be exploited by foreigners? Do global financial flows provide opportunities for offensive policies, and could they therefore be considered a tool of security policy short of military action? In the next chapter, we apply the basics of international finance to our understanding of national security.

CHAPTER 7

Exchange Rate Choices and National Security

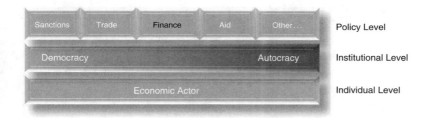

Figure 7.1

A country can be more or less susceptible to external monetary actions based upon the way in which its currency gets traded internationally. Think of a domestic currency in three ways: as the domestic money produced by a state, as a medium of exchange that allows for international trade in goods and services, and as a good itself, traded in international financial markets. We will explore these three sides of the concept with the goal of considering specific policies—ways to use international finance to influence foreign leaders.

Think of our island economy being open to the world, and the world includes one other economy but only one currency. If we think of gold as the one currency, we have the example of a model that all economists learned at one point: David Hume's specie-flow model.

In this explanation, keep in mind the laws of scarcity, supply, and demand. The known and available gold is limited and mostly stays the same year to year. Thus, assume for this model that the supply of gold in the global economy does not change. Trade in goods causes gold to flow between countries as goods flow, as shown in figure 7.2. If someone in country A buys a sweater knit in country B, the sweater goes from B to A and gold flows from A to B.

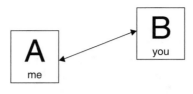

Figure 7.2

Figure 7.3

After the transaction, A has less gold but more sweaters, and B has more gold but fewer sweaters. In A, with less gold, the price of gold to all other commodities increases; gold is scarcer and therefore more expensive. It now takes less gold in A to buy the same product than required prior to the transaction.

After just one sweater changes hands, and assuming no other transactions, perhaps the magnitude of the change in the relative price of gold in A may not be significant. But if a large trade imbalance persists such that A sends a lot of gold to B in exchange for a lot of goods, at some point, the price of goods in A will decrease significantly (as the price of gold increases). Also, in B, the price of goods will increase significantly (as the price of gold drops).

Taking stock, goods are now more expensive in B and cheaper in A, as shown in figure 7.3. This should swing the flow of trade. People in A will slow their purchases of goods from B, which are now more expensive, and people in B will purchase more goods from A, which are now less expensive. Gold will flow from B to A as goods flow from A to B.

A couple of noteworthy conclusions emanate from this model. First, trade deficits will not persist, all things being held constant. The flow of trade will naturally shift, as will the flow of finance. If

A can purchase goods from B while also technologically advancing faster than B, then the trade deficit can persist; otherwise trade will balance. A looming question for the early twenty-first century: can the U.S. economy continue to grow fast enough to keep up with the American trade deficit? Second, assuming market efficiency and therefore equilibration between the two countries, the price of a sweater manufactured in B will sell for the same price, regardless where it may be in the world.

To explain this, let's make the model more complex. Instead of two countries using gold as the same commodity currency, we will assume each country has a separate and independent fiat currency. Currency A and currency B trade freely and are both freely convertible to gold. Sweaters are also freely traded; no duties or tariffs protect a domestic wool, yarn, or knitting industry in either country. The law of one price says that the product manufactured in B and sold there for the equivalent of one-quarter ounce of gold will be sold in A for the same price, plus the transaction costs, such as the cost of shipping it from B to A.

An exchange rate is the price of one currency in terms of another— the price of one Mexican peso in terms of U.S. dollars, for example. Where P is the domestic currency and P^* denotes equivalent value of the foreign currency (in the example, P is the U.S. dollar and P^* is the Mexican peso), the exchange rate "e" can be expressed as:

$$e = P^*/P$$

The price of a product in U.S. dollars (P) equals the price in Mexican pesos (P^*) divided by the exchange rate and, conversely, the price of a product in Mexican pesos (P^*) equals the price in U.S. dollars (P) multiplied by the exchange rate:

$$P = P^*/e \quad P^* = eP$$

The foreign exchange market determines e. The respective presidents do not. And market forces react to information and actions taken by monetary authorities. The Swiss dinar held value against the U.S. dollar and other hard currencies while the Saddam dinar lost value: e dropped. It required more Saddam dollars to purchase a U.S. dollar over time, while the exchange rate of Swiss dinars to dollars proved less volatile.

Earlier we demonstrated how leaders can both promote and restrict trade. The complex topic of international finance hinges on appreciating that a currency represents a commodity like gold—and also like a sweater. International finance describes how money moves around the world. We will discuss money and its movement in three ways: a domestic currency's relationship with the domestic government, with goods in the international market, and with other currencies from countries around the world. Now we can begin to think of specific policies—ways to use international finance to influence foreign leaders. In the next section we will look at exchange rate regimes as a policy choice.

Choosing an Exchange Rate

We know that individuals seek to maximize. Some leaders will seek political longevity, personal wealth, and power; each leader to a different degree. How can the international flow of money provide a mechanism for that leader to maximize? How can the international flow of money allow for us to craft policies aimed at influencing the decisions made by the leader of a foreign country?

A country can be more or less susceptible to external monetary actions based upon its choice of exchange rate regime. Think of a domestic currency in three ways: as the domestic money produced by a state, as a medium of exchange that allows for international trade in goods and services, and as a good itself, traded in international financial markets.

From the background provided, the intuition should begin to solidify. We will walk through specific choices, particularly related to exchange rate policy, to further understand this complex issue. A leader can choose between three basic types of currency regimes: a floating currency, a fixed currency, or an intermediate currency between the two such as some pegged regimes. In a floating regime, the monetary supply is not manipulated to maintain an exchange rate with another currency. The monetary authority allows the rate to float up and down without buying or selling domestic or foreign currency. The market sets the exchange rate, not the sovereign or central bank. In a pegged system, both the exchange rate and monetary base (amount of currency in circulation) are managed in order to keep the exchange rate pegged to a certain value as measured against another currency. Maximum opportunity for political interference exists in a pegged regime. A fixed regime sets a fixed exchange rate but does not manage the monetary base. Gold and silver formerly were used to fix a monetary regime. Today, countries can use hard currencies such as the U.S. dollar, euro, yen, or a combination of the three as a base, or the leadership can dollarize, using only U.S. dollars as their domestic currency, as a way to "fix" an exchange rate.

Floating Regime

Under a floating currency system, the U.S. dollar floats, as do the yen, euro, British pound, and many of the world's major hard currencies. Their values fluctuate daily and are arbitraged almost constantly on the global currency markets. Monetary policies are chosen according to guidelines handed down from the political leadership to the monetary authority.

For example, the U.S. Federal Reserve, America's central bank, has a somewhat ambiguous mission, but it can be summarized as taking some responsibility for dampening the impact of unemployment and inflation on the domestic U.S. economy. With an eye on unemployment and inflation, the Federal Reserve meets eight times per year to set monetary policies. More specifically, the Federal Open Market Committee of the Federal Reserve Board meets to set policy. As its Web site explains:

> The Federal Open Market Committee (FOMC) is the monetary policymaking body of the Federal Reserve System. It is responsible for formulation of a monetary policy designed to promote economic growth, full employment, stable prices, and a sustainable pattern of international trade and payments. The FOMC sets monetary policy by specifying the short-term objective for open market operations—purchases and sales of U.S. government and federal agency securities. Open market operations, the principal tool of monetary policy, affect the provision of reserves to depository institutions and, in turn, the cost and availability of money and credit in the U.S. economy. Currently, the objective is a target level for the federal funds rate (the rate that depository institutions charge on overnight sales of immediately available funds among themselves). The FOMC also directs Federal Reserve operations in foreign currencies; such operations are coordinated with the U.S. Treasury, which has responsibility for formulating U.S. policies regarding the exchange value of the dollar.[1]

The U.S. system created a politically independent central bank, striving to prevent the president and other political leaders from setting monetary policy. There is a good reason for this political insulation of the central bank—the bank leadership can remain beyond the reach of the political leadership. Without subjecting the monetary authority of the United States to political influence, the participants in the global marketplace for currency can find greater confidence in the long-term value of the currency. Stated more directly, the more insulated a monetary authority from political influence, the more likely the currency will not be devalued for political expediency.

Pegged Regime

Under a pegged currency system a government's leader often directs monetary policy. This allows for opportunities to extract personal benefits (rent seeking) from public policy—for both dictators and democrats—through manipulation of the currency. When the system works, a government pledges to peg the value of the domestic currency to another currency or basket of currencies. Recall that the value of a fiat currency depends on faith in the government. Most countries that descend into inflationary and hyperinflationary trouble have pegged systems with a history of government devaluations caused by printing money so that the supply of currency grows. If the money supply in the United States doubled overnight, and everyone knew it, the value of the dollar in my pocket would be cut in half when exchanged the next morning.

As long as the interests and constraints on a government's leader are appropriately aligned, then the peg will hold. Sometimes a monetary regime will designate a range of values within which the currency can float. However, when the alignment of incentives changes, the pegged system usually does not sufficiently constrain decision making, which runs counter to the overall long-term economic growth of an economy in favor of short-term benefit to the leader.

For example, picture a leader—democrat or autocrat—running a country in which his choices have led to a budget deficit. Foreign debt payments are due. Domestic spending is up. In the worst kleptocracies, the dictator simply prints money without telling anyone, using the newly minted money to pay debts and purchase government goods and services, as well as pay for loyalty and repression. Even in a democracy, however, the central banker can succumb to political pressures and loosen monetary policy. Facing a need for short-term money and insufficient constraints on the treasury, often the peg gets broken. In these regimes, the printing presses that produce the currency, in effect, fall under the decision-making authority of the political leader or dictator.

Printing presses cannot print value. They can only print a currency, like dollars, yen, and pesos. They print paper. When the number of pesos in the world increases, holding all other currencies equal, then the value of each peso has decreased.

Revisiting the island example, if the economy has bananas and fish, and the survivors of a shipwreck have 100 U.S. one-dollar bills, then a price, an "exchange rate" of dollar bills to bananas, can be established—this is the price of bananas in terms of dollars, or dollars in terms of bananas. If a bag of currency from the ship floats ashore so that there are now 200 U.S. one-dollar bills on the island, with the same number of people and rate of production of bananas and fish, then the price of bananas and fish will double. If one fish was traded for one dollar prior to the doubling of the money supply, then the arrival of the second bag of money (provided that everyone on the island knows about the arrival of the money and the doubling of the money supply) will double the number of dollars required to exchange for one fish. It will take two dollars to buy one fish.

The caveat in that last example—that everyone on the island knows about the arrival of the money and the doubling of the money supply—explains how leaders can exploit the system for personal benefit. In debating the relevance and irrelevance of monetary policy on GDP, inflation, and unemployment, economists often cite Robert Lucas and his famous "surprise" supply function. For the policy maker and analyst, the Lucas critique offers another lesson. In the function, it is understood that only unanticipated changes in money supply— inflation—alter the levels of GDP output and unemployment in an economy. If the marketplace knows the central bank will alter the money supply in a known direction, then the policy will not work. The lesson for economists is that monetary policy may be irrelevant over the long term.

Policy makers, however, take heed. In the short term, monetary policy matters.[2] Consider the following equation:

$$Y - Yn = k(P - Pe)$$

Y is output—GDP—of a certain economy at a given time, and Yn is the natural long-term output of the same economy. Deviations from long-term output are a function of (k is a constant) deviations of actual price level (P) from expected price levels (Pe). Back to the island, if the incidence of 100 dollar bills washing up on the island is widely known, then producers in the economy will expect prices to double and will know that increased demand for production arises from the currency and not a change in demand. Nobody on the island is richer—they just hold twice as much currency worth half as much. The production on the island will not change—it will not deviate from Yn, the natural long-term output.

If, however, the money is found by only one person, and she does not tell anyone, she will begin to spend more money. The increase in spending will lead to others on the island earning more money and then themselves purchasing more goods and services. The producers cannot be sure of the cause of the increase in demand. Fish and banana merchants will notice an increase in demand and raise prices above expected price levels. Unaware of the increased amount of cash on the island, they will interpret an increase in demand for their products and increase production. In a large economy, unexpected changes in the quantity of money will, in the short term, increase output and reduce unemployment.

What autocrat or democrat would not want this seeming increase in demand? And without constraints on the leader's control over the mint, the printing presses would run while no one is watching— especially before elections. Give a politician an opportunity to increase incomes and decrease unemployment and, without constraints, you will see monetary authority abuses. Historical evidence demonstrates that a pegged system proves most advantageous for kleptocratic leaders, since it allows them to choose personal optimal outcomes without sufficient constraints to avoid harming the domestic economy over the medium to long term. For example, the currencies of Colombia, Argentina, Brazil, and Costa Rica lost about two-thirds of their value from 1994–2004. Ecuador's lost 90 percent of its value. Chile, the Dominican Republic, Guatemala, Honduras, Jamaica, and Peru are among the other big losers of currency value during this decade.[3]

Fixed Regime

The third general category of monetary regime is known as a fixed regime. Like a peg, this exchange regime is tied to another currency or basket of currencies but, significantly, political leaders need not be trusted to maintain the peg. The monetary authority, under a fixed regime, exercises independence and must abide by rules that lack discretion on anyone's part. For example, a currency board, a type of fixed-rate regime, allows a monetary authority to print domestic currency only in direct correlation to hard currency held in the reserves of the central bank. Thus, a currency board with a mandate of a fixed exchange rate of 1:1 with the U.S. dollar can provide as much domestic currency in circulation as it has U.S. dollars in reserves. A central bank with $100 million in reserves can have 100 million units of domestic currency in circulation, maintaining the exchange rate of 1:1. Clearly this type of regime provides the most predictable exchange rate.

Case Study: Dollarization

Dollarization is a fixed exchange rate in which the country simply eschews a domestic currency and uses U.S. dollars or another hard currency as its own. The United States often encourages dollarization of foreign countries because many U.S. policy makers believe that it's better for the U.S. economy to have stable economies in other countries and stable trade flow between these countries. Ecuador and Panama use the U.S. dollar as their domestic currency.

Why is this important to a policy maker? Whether a country dollarizes or not, the U.S. dollar serves as the international currency of choice. People choose to conduct international transactions in U.S. dollars. As Jim Saxton, the former chairman of the Joint Economic Committee of the U.S. Congress, notes:

> There is a growing recognition of the fact that financial capital is increasingly mobile, and financial markets are evermore globally integrated. At the same time, varying degrees of dollarization have occurred in several emerging market economies and the dollar remains the world's principal international currency despite evolving developments in exchange rate arrangements.[4]

The decisions of the U.S. Federal Open Market Committee, therefore, reverberate around the world. In the world today, a leader of an open economy can choose to set domestic monetary policy or set an exchange rate. He cannot, however, set both. And depending upon the size of the economy and the soundness of the domestic currency, if the decision is made to set an exchange rate, then monetary policy will be largely influenced, if not set, by the FOMC. For a dollarized country, this will absolutely be the case. If, however, the leader actively sets monetary policy to target domestic interest rates and unemployment, for example, then he cannot, in practice, fix the exchange rate.

Thirty-three territories use a foreign currency as their domestic monetary base.[5] Think about it: thirty-three countries' domestic interest rates can be dramatically influenced by another country's monetary authority—for better or worse.

CASE STUDY: THE PRC CURRENCY POLICY

The Chinese economy has grown at a stunning rate in recent years, lifting tens of millions of people out of poverty. Some policy makers in the United States, however, believe China's economic miracle has come at the expense of American jobs because of currency manipulation.[6]

From 1994 to 2005, China pegged its currency to American currency. As China's trade surplus with the United States rose over time, China intervened in the global exchange markets, purchasing dollars in order to maintain the peg. As a result, the exchange rate between the two nations was not allowed to adjust through market forces and bring the bilateral trade account into balance. Although the yuan's value rose modestly against the dollar after China began to peg the yuan to a basket of currencies (including the dollar) in 2005, some commentators in the United States argue the yuan remains devalued by 40 percent vis-à-vis the dollar. If true, the price of Chinese imports into the United States are artificially low and the price of U.S. exports to China are artificially high, contributing to the yawning trade imbalance. This competitive imbalance, based on the Chinese government's intervention in the exchange markets, has resulted in significant job losses, according to those in the U.S. manufacturing sector. A 2008 report by the Economic Policy Institute that was well received by U.S. manufacturing and union organizations ties the nearly 2.3 million lost or displaced American jobs between 2001 and 2007 to the growth of U.S. trade with China. A major cause of the U.S. trade deficit with China, the report argues, is Chinese currency manipulation.[7]

Do Chinese currency practices actually pose a risk to the U.S. economy? The size and diversity of the U.S. economy would make it very difficult for another nation to maintain a currency intervention strategy that is sufficient to do lasting damage. Members of Congress have responded, however, by introducing legislation imposing steep duties on Chinese imports in order to offset the advantage gained by the currency practices. As of this writing, no such bills have been signed into law, and China has not been officially deemed a manipulator of its currency under the Treasury Department's semiannual review process pursuant to the 1988 Omnibus Trade and Competitiveness Act. Instead, U.S. officials continue to urge China to allow its currency to float instead of maintaining a peg to other currencies. Could the security of a nation be threatened by being subject to this or other types of currency practices from a major trading partner? This question is discussed in the following section.

CHOOSING POWER OVER GROWTH, AGAIN

Now let us look at these exchange rate regimes as choices in the national security context. We can review a large body of academic literature on how to choose a regime—all measuring economic benefits. That is not our purpose. We will explore exchange rate choices to

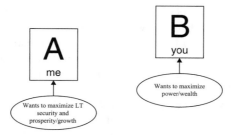

Figure 7.4

the extent that they make the world a safer place—safer from attack, whether it be interstate warfare or terrorism.

First, if you accept the proposition, defended earlier in this book, that economic growth for both countries A and B promotes each country's national security, then by all means a leader must choose the best exchange rate regime for economic growth. This is where the analysis usually ends, but it cannot—because people make decisions, not states. And the leader may choose to maximize his own personal wealth, longevity in office, or some other factor other than long-term economic growth and stability of the country he leads, as shown in figure 7.4.

If the utility maximization function of the leader of country B, for example, causes him to sacrifice long-term growth for short-term political and/or economic gain, then a suboptimal security policy choice will be made. Policy makers note: first ask yourself what the leader seeks to maximize. For example, moving from a pegged to a fixed exchange rate regime may be the best long-run policy for economic growth in country B. In the short term, however, moving to a fixed regime might cause an increase in unemployment and short-term economic disruption. The leader, whether elected or not, may not choose a stable currency and instead choose a weak peg. In the real world, this is often the case in developing countries and nondemocracies.

Referring again to the two-country world diagram, let us assume country A adopts a floating or fixed-rate regime. In a floating regime, the monetary authority allows the domestic currency to compete without manipulation against the other currencies of the world. In a fixed regime, the monetary authority fixes the currency to a foreign currency or bundle, leaving no room for manipulation for political or personal gain. In a "float," the market makes this manipulation difficult to hide. In a pegged regime, the monetary authority retains the right to manipulate the value of a currency and often does so. Sometimes he does so for reasons many economists would consider valid. Sometimes his reasons would be considered suspect. The point being, the currency in a pegged system gets manipulated much more than in a fixed regime.

Country A will develop a stable and therefore "good" currency, desired by consumers. Demand for country A's currency promotes trade and development. The kleptocracy in country B, however, will devalue country B's currency, harming chances for long-term prosperity. Notice also, the world marketplace will prefer A notes to B notes—good money to bad. Not only might A become richer than B over time, but the policy choice creates a virtuous cycle whereby A will have more leverage in global trade by virtue of having a sought-after currency compared to B.

Beyond what we would call the passive impact of choosing an exchange rate—economic growth and the benefits, which promote national security—the choice of exchange rate provides an opportunity for active offense and defense. One need only think of the so-called currency crises of the past two decades. In short, it goes like this:

- Country B pegs its currency (B notes) at an exchange rate to country A's currency (A notes).
- Because of poor economic performance and/or excessive government spending, leader B's government is short on B notes. He borrows B notes, driving up interest rates and making B notes expensive.
- With the economy stagnating, a shortage of money for government programs, and a shortage of money for private investment, leader B chooses to relax the peg. He announces a floating peg and promises to keep the B-note: A-note ratio close to the previously promised exchange rate. He then prints more money.
- A few months later, he slides the peg again, printing more money.
- Now the people in the domestic and international economy begin to expect future devaluations of B notes, and the value of the B note further declines.
- Now country B finds itself in an inflationary spiral.

This scenario happens in the real world.

The policy implications are fascinating. If we know B has weak monetary policy, we know several things. Long-term stability and growth will require significant effort to improve confidence in the B notes. The need for the leader to choose further devaluations of the currency will be strong. The ability of country A to out-compete country B in a global economy will grow. These last points are part of the vicious cycle. And finally, country A can take advantage of this weakness in country B. By buying and selling B notes on the international exchange market, leader A can literally strike at the government and people of country B, further exacerbating the weakness of the poor monetary policies of country B.

One further variation on this point: leader A need not be a sovereign leader. A nonstate actor—political, religious, commercial, or even a leader of a terrorist organization—can engage in this foreign-exchange attack. What is the prerequisite? Anyone able to control significant amounts of money relative to the cash reserves of country B can attack the monetary base of country B.[8] Consider the case of George Soros, the Hungarian-born billionaire speculator and philanthropist who was once called "The Man Who Broke the Bank of England." The Bank of England had recently joined the European Exchange Rate Mechanism (ERM; a predecessor to the Euro). At the time the UK currency, the pound sterling, was a relatively strong currency vis-à-vis its European partners, even though the UK economy was entering a recession. The Bank of England resisted allowing its currency to float, however, and intervened in the currency market to maintain parity with other members of the ERM. The situation was deemed untenable by many investors. In 1992, Soros "shorted" almost $10 billion worth of the pound sterling, betting that eventually the Bank of England would have to devalue its currency. Finally, the Bank of England buckled under the pressure of Soros and other investors, pulled out of the ERM, and saw the value of the pound sterling plunge. On a single day, Soros made an estimated $1.1 billion while the Bank of England estimated the loss to the UK Treasury at 3.4 billion pounds.

Private speculators also played a role in a significant financial crisis later in the decade, the East Asian Financial Crisis. Though the high levels of debt accumulated by Southeast Asian nations created the environment for the crisis to occur, currency speculation ultimately was the match that lit the fuse. Beginning in Thailand in 1997, high debt levels enticed foreign, private investors to speculate that the nations of Southeast Asia would be forced to undertake significant currency devaluation. Bowing to the pressures of speculators, the government of Thailand allowed its currency, the Thai baht, to float, removing its peg to the U.S. dollar. Its value plunged, rewarding the speculators but driving the region into economic crisis. As a result, the currencies of neighbors such as Indonesia, Malaysia, Korea, and the Philippines would face speculation and devaluation as well. The crisis, caused in no small part by exchange rate policy, led to the overthrow of governments in countries like Indonesia, a massive loss of wealth in the effected countries, and a sustained period of unemployment and economic recession. In the following chapter, we examine the role of international financial institutions in the East Asian financial crisis.

The relative advantage matters slightly. A poor country can be attacked by a slightly less poor leader. And can the people of the United States, the United Kingdom, or other so-called first-world nations find themselves susceptible to currency manipulation? Absolutely. Look at the United States for an example. The benefit of the stable U.S. dollar described earlier demonstrates its demand. People around the world, including foreign governments, buy the U.S. dollar. They denominate their debt in dollars. And they buy U.S. government debt—among the safest places in the world to put money. So actors in the rest of the world can collectively hurt the U.S. economy, and therefore the American people and leaders, by selling off U.S. debt. The severe economic downturn that began in 2008 and the massive amount of deficit spending by the United States to attempt to counteract the recession raised the prospect of this occurring for the first time in generations. It still remains an unlikely scenario for several reasons. However, let's look a little closer; this scenario deserves some careful consideration, even if academic for now.

Assume country A has a strong economy and strong currency, the A note. The rest of the world includes hostile country B. Over time, and for the purpose of financial stability, leaders in country B have purchased A bonds—country A's sovereign debts. The rest of country A's bonds are in circulation in country A and some are held by people in country B, also seeking safer money than B notes. If the leader of country B needs leverage over counterparts in country A, he can threaten to sell his entire share of country A's bonds. If acted upon, leader B will flood the market with country A's bonds, dramatically increasing the supply. Country A will experience higher interest rates. If the size of B's investment in A bonds equals a significant amount when compared to economy A, then leader B could do some real damage to economy A. Depending upon the institutional constraints facing leader A, this could jeopardize his legitimacy to continue leading the country. Leader B has just caused significant financial damage to economy A. This will absolutely impact the people of A, and depending upon the political situation at the time, could mark the end of the political control of leader A.

In a pegged regime, where the currency may have stability problems from years of devaluations—occasional or regular—the potential for damage from this or other types of currency manipulations is greatest. Sovereign A would need to expend a large amount of domestic currency in order to purchase these bonds to prevent interest rates from skyrocketing. This will cause a spike in the value of the A notes at home, as A notes go to country B to purchase the A bonds.

In a fixed regime, speculators will be less inclined to bet against A notes; they may be more willing to jump in and buy the A bonds being sold by B at fire-sale prices, betting that the value will hold over time and that they are getting a bargain.

In a floating exchange rate regime, if the size of country A's economy sufficiently exceeds country B's such that no long-term threat to the economy exists, then leader A will need to suffer through some short-term economic volatility, but the market will expect country A to continue to be strong over time and not bet against the A note. If, however, the amount of A notes held by country B can significantly drain the reserves of country A and threaten a long-term spike in interest rates, then the scenario will play out like in the pegged economy described earlier. Leader B will have caused serious and long-term damage to country A.

Currency, like goods and services, is traded around the world. Good money has more value than weak money. Exchange rate regimes create institutions that bind the political leadership of a country in ways that can help defend against speculative or aggressive attacks. The choice of exchange rate regime matters for national security. The lesson to be learned from this is that small countries may be better off with fixed (rather than floating or pegged) exchange rates when it comes to protection from currency attacks.

CHAPTER 8

Maximizing over Time through Lending and Borrowing

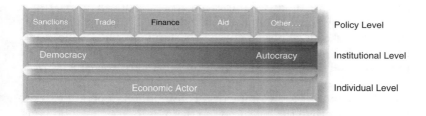

Figure 8.1

Borrowing and lending—the ability to participate in the credit market—makes people better off. Credit is a good and people want it. As a policy maker, if you can provide, deny, or manipulate another's access, you have an economic tool of security policy.

Beyond using money to facilitate the trading of goods and services in international markets, people trade money itself, intertemporally, in the lending and borrowing markets. In addition to exchanging dollars for foreign currencies, traders exchange today's money for tomorrow's money in the market for debt. We call these trades *intertemporal transactions*—exchanges in time.

Since money you have in hand today can be used, and money you do not get until later cannot, we place a premium on money we have in hand today. This premium is the interest rate, and can be thought of as the price differential between the values of money today versus tomorrow. It is the price of spending tomorrow's money today, or the price of today's consumption put off until tomorrow. By lending or borrowing money, consumption can be moved up or back in time. By investing $100 today, I forgo consuming with that money today, but I do so in exchange for something I expect to be greater than $100 in the future. Like all trades discussed in this book, intertemporal trades occur only when all participants view themselves as better off for having made the trade. Therefore, the ability to borrow and lend money makes people better off. We go back to the beginning: people maximize. By entering into voluntary trades, people create wealth. Money, like goods, gets traded in foreign exchange markets. Now we introduce the debt market as a potential tool of national security.

In today's terms, we account for today's use as consumption and tomorrow's use as savings or investment. Recalling figure 1.3, we have a production possibility frontier and a choice between two alternatives. Earlier we discussed our island economy of bananas or fish as production possibilities. Now, we shift the same diagram and explain the debt market as a choice between consumption and savings. Refer to figure 8.2 with savings—that is, tomorrow's consumption—on the y-axis and today's consumption on the x-axis. By reducing your consumption in time period one, you increase your savings in period one. Based upon the rate of interest, consumption in period two can thus be higher than the consumption that was forgone in period one; this is the reward for deferring consumption.

Intertemporal saving, investing, lending, and borrowing, like trading in goods and services, produce wealth; they are transactions that people enter into because all parties view themselves becoming better off. These actions, therefore, bestow benefits; they are good in that people want more ability to engage in these trades. Therefore, access

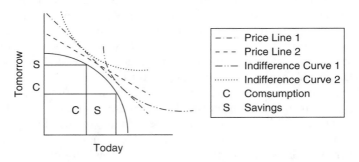

Figure 8.2

to the credit/debt market can be used as yet another tool to advance national security.

INTERNATIONAL FINANCE

Access to the international market for debt provides value to a leader. If a leader chooses to forgo current consumption and invest in a foreign country, he can reap benefits otherwise unavailable. For example, the differences between country A and country B may allow an investor in country A to receive a higher return by loaning money in country B. These country differences include many factors, such as the preferences of each country's citizens, risk associated with the debt investments, efficiencies gained from specific country advantages, availability of capital and labor, level of technology, regulations, property rights, the state of the rule of law, rules about contract sanctity, and government's stated and real monetary policies.

Diversification, which comes from access to the debt market, also provides value to a leader. Return on investment is the reward for taking risk. Think about personal investors purchasing mutual funds instead of individual stocks. Or consider the U.S. dollar—traditionally a very safe, stable currency as a result of America's stable political climate and monetary policy. This means that there are huge investment flows into the United States, but the return on those flows is not very high. U.S. Treasury bills illustrate the point: they provide a low return rate, but also very low risk. On the other hand, most developing countries have volatile political and economic climates, but if you make the right investment you can get a higher rate of return.

Return on investment should be correlated with the risk associated with that investment. Whereas many wealthy individuals from developing countries seek the stability available in the United States, many U.S. investors are willing to endure high risks associated with investments in the developing world. These riskier investments offer the promise of higher returns. We know what a market is and how it operates efficiently. We know about trade in goods, services, and money.

The international financial market, when unhindered by government interventions, efficiently channels savings and investments to the highest return at the lowest risk and optimizes international financial flows on a continuous basis. We observe government intervention, however, so leaders must see some benefit in these actions.

Government and Institutional Backing

Government leaders intervene in the market process; they must be doing so for a reason. Why do leaders intervene? Why do we have a World Bank? To be more accurate, we call the institutions known as the International Bank for Reconstruction and Development (IBRD) and the International Development Association (IDA) the "World Bank." Why do we need the International Monetary Fund (IMF)? Do regional development banks, backed by local governments, play a necessary role? Do they play a useful role? Given that these institutions exist, do they provide an opportunity for policy makers to use them to otherwise advance national security concerns?

The short answer to why governments intervene is the perception of market failure. Specifically, it is a result of the belief that political and national security imperatives may supersede economic realities. After World War II, there was a consensus about the need for a lender of last resort. People believed that given political instabilities, economic constraints, and social or public good benefits, there needed to be some sort of nonmarket intervention. People believed that private lenders either would not or could not provide loans in certain circumstances in which they would be needed.

Market failure describes the condition when the efficient market, described throughout this book, does not provide the "right" or "best" solution in a normative sense—that is, what "should" occur. So the consensus view in the late 1940s was that the global financial marketplace needed help from sovereign leaders—political intervention was necessary. This is an interesting thought to consider today. If a private institution will not loan money to a sovereign, should the money be loaned? If Citibank or Bank of America or any other banking institution that regularly loans money to sovereign governments turns down a country, this must mean that the risk exceeds the potential reward for the loan. It means the loan is not commercially viable, by definition. So the government-backed international institutions step in.

If someone knows that they are getting a loan even though they are not paying enough given their level of risk, they feel great. In reality, I may be happier and better off fixing my credit even though in the future it means paying full price for borrowed money after I lose my subsidy. The advantages of overall good standing in the credit marketplace must be significant to encourage that behavior. They must exceed the benefits of aid and assistance I can get from a subsidy for those with bad credit.

For example, if I wish to buy a used car for $5,000, but I pose a considerable credit risk, I will need to pay a high-interest loan. Assume my principal and interest will exceed $10,000 over the term of the loan. But through a government subsidy for people with bad credit who need cars, I can actually get the car for $5,000. What could possibly justify public monies covering that $5,000 gap? What could possibly justify IMF funds going to a country when Citibank refuses to loan money? The answer must be that there is some perceived public good that exceeds the cost of the subsidy. Reverting to the car example, the $5,000 subsidy to me has to be exceeded by the good the public gains from me getting the car.

Beyond the recipients—the obvious beneficiaries—the donors must also benefit. The individual participating governments of the international institutions must get some benefit out of the existence of the institution that exceeds the cost of participation. From a broad public-good perspective (assuming you trust me to have your "good" in mind), the benefit of participating in unprofitable loans to a country must exceed the cost associated with making unprofitable loans. Since not financially profitable, some other profit, either in international politics or national security, must be made by someone.

Many believe that World Bank financing for building infrastructure justifies the existence of the World Bank. The argument goes that the market would make some loans to a certain sovereign, but not for public goods such as roads, clean drinking water, and the like. Therefore, government intervention is needed to loan money to targeted projects.

Some institutions exist not to lend the money (like the IMF does), but to address the additional costs associated with risks in the developing world that prevent private lenders from making the loan. These include the Overseas Private Investment Corporation, or OPIC, which is a U.S. government organization that provides investment assistance and political risk insurance for investments in developing countries; the Multilateral Investment Guarantee Agency (MIGA), which is an international organization and member of the World Bank Group that provides investment assistance and political risk insurance to investors from all member countries of the World Bank; private political risk insurance companies, including Lloyd's of London and the American International Group (AIG), as well as brokers such as Chartis Insurance, Zurich, Sovereign Risk Insurance Ltd., and Chubb,[1] a large number of nonprofit organizations that facilitate trade and investment in specific countries.

CASE STUDY: INTERNATIONAL FINANCIAL INSTITUTIONS AND THE EAST ASIAN FINANCIAL CRISIS

Acknowledging that these nonmarket international financial institutions have power and an ability to make a positive difference opens the possibility that they can also do harm. This is often argued in the instance of the so-called East Asian financial crisis of the late 1990s, discussed in chapter 7. The argument goes that the IMF provided money for badly needed liquidity—the economies were solvent but had loan payments due and no access to affordable credit to make those payments—but extracted reforms that exacerbated the liquidity problems. Through the contagion effect, bad IMF advice in one country spread the crisis throughout Asia, to South America and even eventually to Russia.

Agree or not with these specific arguments, the role of international financial institutions continues to be a topic of some controversy. Their existence continues to provide tools of influence; their proper role continues to be debated. Originally created to provide liquidity to otherwise solvent sovereigns, many see the IMF's role as having evolved and grown since its creation. Beyond the economic missions, think about the recurring theme of this book. Access to assistance from international financial institutions represents a good—something leaders would want more of. If leader A can influence country B's access to World Bank assistance, then leader A has influence over leader B. Access to World Bank programs could either be a carrot to get a leader to change behavior, or a method to empower people in a struggle against a dictator. In a national security context, the World Bank, therefore, presents yet another policy tool for policy makers.

Critics of the international financial institutions often suggest that this policy tool is available primarily for the benefit of the United States. Because of the way the voting rights at the IMF and World Bank are allocated, the United States essentially enjoys veto power over major policy changes at the institutions. This, combined with the fact that the United States is the largest donor of capital to these institutions, certainly provides leverage for the United States to influence the policies advocated by the institutions. Consequently, critics have named the purported free market ideology of the international financial institutions the "Washington Consensus." The Washington Consensus typically refers to the institutions' advocating policies of fiscal austerity, privatization, and liberation of trade and capital market flows to donee countries. In other words, critics charge, the United States uses the leverage of the international financial institutions to push its own global economic agenda on developing countries.

If this is the case—that the United States works through international institutions to promote its own agenda—why would the United States do this? We have already discussed the leverage available to the United States because of the global demand to access its vast consumer market. Couldn't the United States simply achieve the same objectives working with individual countries on a bilateral basis? The use of a multilateral institution as a tool could have many benefits to a country like the United States. Politically, the leader of the country being asked to accept the policies of the IMF or World Bank may be able to do so much easier if the policies are seen to have the multilateral support and legitimacy of an international institution. This is usually preferred to being seen as giving in to the demands of the United States. The United States can also leverage the capital and intellectual resources of the institution to pursue its agenda without consuming all of its own resources to do so. Finally, if the policies fail it is the institution that typically receives the blame—as it has in the East Asian financial crisis—and not the United States. The United States can hide behind the institution itself. International financial institutions provide a good that is demanded by other leaders. This provides the institution—and primarily its most influential members—a tool to influence these leaders.

CASE STUDY: TIBET VERSUS THE WORLD BANK AT QINGHAI

In summer 1999, one of the authors participated in a debate over $160 million in World Bank loans to the People's Republic of China. The Bank claimed a great success in supporting development in rural China by repatriating people from one part of the country to another. Human rights groups and nongovernmental organizations (NGOs), however, opposed a proposed loan to move 60,000 non-Tibetans into a historically Tibetan region. Of paramount concern, the Tibetan community in exile claimed that this large-scale 60,000-person movement of non-Tibetans into the birthplace of the Dalai Lama amounted to a continuation of the PRC's policies to eliminate the Tibetan culture. The U.S. Senators Mack, Helms, and Wellstone, among others, joined with House Members Gillman and Pelosi to oppose World Bank funding for this so-called "cultural genocide." President Clinton also expressed opposition to this program to World Bank President James Wolfensohn. As World Bank president, Wolfensohn was in no way legally subordinate to the U.S. president, but he still had to take this opposition seriously. According to Sebastian Mallaby:

> Confronted with the news that the Clinton administration would block the project, Wolfensohn flew into a rage. He worried about threats by the U.S. Congress to cut contributions to the bank's subsidized lending program if the project went ahead, undermining the bank's ability to help its poorest clients. He fretted that the adverse publicity might cost him a chance at winning a Nobel Peace Prize and that his Hollywood connections would turn on him.[2]

Under Wolfensohn's leadership, the World Bank created a mechanism for a special commission to monitor this project for cultural and environmental compliance. This went a long way to appease President Clinton and his administration's stated concerns, but the U.S. Congress proceeded to vote to cut U.S. funding to the World Bank. The World Bank continued to fight for the program but never attained the support of the Tibetan community in exile and the human rights advocates in the U.S. Congress. *De jure*, the United States cannot unilaterally kill a World Bank program. *De facto*, however, that is exactly what happened. The executive branch of the U.S. government has a seat at the World Bank table and can voice objections and vote against projects. Members of the U.S. Congress do not even have seats at the table. This loan, however, was stopped. The PRC withdrew its application for subsidies and began to work with its own funds. The concerns of the human rights groups may or may not have been adequately addressed by the PRC leadership. Two years of highly public debate, however, over the internal policies of the PRC toward the Tibetan minorities in China ensued. To the extent that approbation mattered in the utility functions of the autocrats in Beijing, then the policies may have been altered, thus delivering some measure of success to the advocates. This may be an unprovable victory (or defeat). In the end, however, if the behavior of the PRC leadership did not change as a result of the high-profile debate and criticisms, any damage done to the ethnic Tibetans took place without U.S. and world community subsidy.

SOVEREIGN LENDING AND FOREIGN DIRECT INVESTMENT

As with all voluntary exchanges, for voluntary foreign capital flows to occur they must make all parties involved in the transaction better off. The enrichment could be in the form of economic growth and consumption-smoothing on the part of the debtor, or a superior return on capital for the lender/investor. In this section we explore the nature of capital flows and sovereign lending, then drill deeper into the subject of foreign direct investment, specifically. Again, we will be exploring potential policy tools for security policy makers.

Financial Flows in Context

It may be obvious, given the proliferation of writing on economic growth since the mid-1980s, that under the appropriate conditions, foreign direct investment (FDI) can play a significant role in economic development. And we observe empirically and anecdotally that the economic performance of dictatorships significantly lags that of open and free market economies. Would it be easy to conclude that dictators might be better off by inviting foreign investment and technologies into their countries? Or, policy makers might ask, should external policies, such as sanctions by the United States or United Nations, prevent the inflow of investment that would be otherwise welcomed by the dictator?

To understand the importance of FDI, we will introduce the idea of economic growth and cover the topic in more depth in the next chapter. Many scholars focus on so-called *new growth* theories that capture externalities, forces not captured adequately in neoclassical growth models.[3] Training and education, best practices in management, rule of law, and contract sanctity are some of the issues that people know to be important to growth *a priori*. Empirically, however, the literature points to more questions than answers, and *new growth* remains to be proven.

Critical to improved understanding of the theories of growth and the role of externalities is the literature on the flows of financing and foreign direct investment. The next section will address misunderstandings and theoretical bright spots in this literature, and provide some insights for understanding the relationships between growth, investment, and the dictator's incentives and constraints.

The Long View: History of Capital Flows

Capital flows can take several forms, including sovereign lending, private lending, and direct investment.[4] The nature of international capital flows has evolved over the past 100 years. Prior to World War I, private investment had been expanding into the then-developing countries of the United States, Canada, Australia, Argentina, Brazil, Mexico, and India. The capital flows took the form of public government bond issues and foreign direct investment. London served as the main financial center. This international market addressed defaults with "gunboat diplomacy" and also achieved dramatic successes supported by large-scale international lending and migration. It was during this time that the market learned of the risks and lucrative rewards from investing in developing countries.[5]

During the interwar period, the United States became a large-scale lender. Money went to Europe to pay for reparations and to Latin America for development investment. With the drop in commodity prices in 1929, however, lending halted and credit rationing began. Terms of trade deteriorated, and price deflation increased the real value of debt service payments. Many countries implemented moratoria on debt payments or opted for outright debt default. Recovery did not begin in the international finance market until World War II, and full recovery was not achieved until 1960. The international flows of money changed dramatically during this time.

From the late 1940s through the late 1950s, most capital flows to developing countries took the form of direct investment or loans from multilateral institutions—no significant borrowing in the capital markets occurred.[6] Official lending and investment provided for a market cleaning in the form of buybacks of debt and write-downs of principal by the lending institutions. The transition from default back to borrowing progressed through intermediate steps of official lending, private sources, portfolio investment, and then bank lending.[7] The cleanup succeeded in allowing developing countries back into the capital markets by the 1960s.

In August 1982, however, the capital markets again suffered a dramatic challenge. Mexico led many other countries in declaring a debt moratorium. Due in part to poor financial management, increases in the values of the U.S. dollar and other OECD currencies, and deteriorating world economic conditions, debtor countries needed additional funds to make debt service payments and faced a dire liquidity problem.

We saw further crises in the early and late 1990s, and the literature on the decade of the 1990s is vast and expanding. The deep global recession of 2008–09, which seems to be coming to an end as we write this edition, could bring about additional crises. Patterns of capital flow have changed and will continue to change; history is not over.

Foreign Direct Investment as a Tool

Voluntary foreign capital flows should make all parties to the transaction better off, and the evidence makes a strong case for a positive relationship between FDI and growth in a developing country, under certain circumstances. Wealth-improving behavior explains why investments benefit the private investor. Sovereign lending may occur for the expected return on capital, or may take place for an expected social benefit.

Economic growth from capital inflow produces a greater impact on an economy with a smaller ratio of capital to labor factors of production than in countries with a larger share of capital. Capital inflows also affect: the output potential of an economy; the effect of intertemporal consumption-smoothing; the distribution of gains; foreign exchange and inflation policies; and the ability to address economic "disturbances." In the context of developing countries, however, market failures and distortions must be taken into consideration.

Much can be learned about the benefits of FDI and the role it plays in the process of technological diffusion in developing countries.[8] Some research suggests that FDI provides a vehicle for the diffusion of technology into a developing economy. There is also evidence of a *crowding in* effect: one dollar coming into a country in the form of FDI is associated with a greater than one dollar increase in total investment within that country.[9] One general understanding is that FDI has a positive overall effect on economic growth, but the magnitude of the effect depends upon the availability of human capital— the absorptive capacity of the country for the new technology. The nature of this relationship is such that, for very low levels of human capital, the introduction of FDI appears to be negative.[10] However, for above-minimum levels of human capital, the relationship between FDI and human capital is generally positive.

This is consistent with the hypothesis that it is the interaction of technology and human capital that provides growth. This effect is more important than the increase in capital stock itself. "While the imports of machinery and equipment may be one channel for the international transmission of technological advances, FDI has probably an even larger role, as it alone allows the transmission of knowledge on business practices, management techniques, etc."[11]

Studies on the impact of FDI for growth in East Asia and Latin America identify the prerequisites for FDI to promote growth, and the mechanisms through which this growth occurs.[12] They also look to *new growth* for theoretical guidance because "many of the growth promoting factors, such as human capital and externalities, have long been recognized to be the main ingredients of FDI."[13] Some important components of FDI include its nature as a composite bundle of capital and technology; its ability to contribute to growth through technology transfer and skill diffusion; its ability to promote growth and its relationship to the type of trade regime in place (protectionist vs. liberal); and the propensity for foreign-owned firms to exhibit superior productive efficiency relative to those locally owned.[14]

Some controversy remains, however, regarding the so-called *social rate of return* on FDI—the broader public benefit gained from FDI that may be difficult to measure directly in dollars alone. Endogenous growth theories maintain that increasing returns to scale, imperfect competition, human capital accumulation, and secondary or spillover effects can prevent a decline in the marginal product of capital. While some studies find that private rates of return to investment may decline over time, the social rate of return does not necessarily need to do so. Therefore, the high social rate of return hypothesized can provide the "floor to the decline in the marginal product of capital in the aggregate."[15] Therefore, evidence suggests that FDI is positively correlated to GDP, and this relationship is greater in export-oriented countries. There also appears to be a threshold amount of human capital required for FDI to increase growth.[16]

Research using data to measure effects over time and across the globe to look at the relationship between FDI and growth reveal the problematic nature of empirical work on growth because of the absence of unconditional convergence across countries.[17] In fact, for most of the countries in this sample, "It seems that the growth-FDI nexus is sensitive to country-specific factors that are unobservable in time series analysis."[18] This again leads to arguments associated with endogenous growth theories. If, in fact, growth rates can be modified endogenously, then long-run growth need not converge.

Through the transfer of *advanced* capital stocks and knowledge, it appears likely that FDI is growth-enhancing in the long run. The impact, however, seems to depend inversely on the existing level of technology. This suggests that the growth from FDI increases at a decreasing rate. Moreover, the gap between technology leaders and followers may be a product of country-specific factors such as institutions, trade regimes, political factors, domestic policies, and laws. This, in fact, provides the difficulty in the empirical study of growth. Since most FDI occurs between technologically advanced economies, it appears that FDI is sensitive to balance of payments constraints in the developing economy. These country-specific factors include: openness, trade regime, political instability, government intervention, property rights laws, and law enforcement institutions.[19]

To obtain another picture of the impact of FDI it is useful to look at the foreign-direct-investment-to-GDP ratio (FDI:GDP) on economic growth.[20] It appears that the mean GDP growth rate in Latin American countries is higher than in East Asian countries, although the FDI to GDP ratio is much lower in Latin American countries. This discrepancy suggests that FDI-induced GDP growth increases as FDI increases, but at a decreasing rate.

It is also useful to look at capital flows from the perspective of the firm in order to understand their occurrence.[21] Using industrial organization (IO) theory to analyze foreign direct investment, it becomes apparent that the traditional explanation—the search for arbitrage opportunities—is inadequate. The traditional explanation leads to the conclusion that benefits to the host country from FDI "are most likely to stem from a large capital stock, increased tax revenues, increased labor income, and favorable externalities, particularly from technological diffusion and training."[22]

Since FDI is typically found in industries characterized by oligopoly it is useful to apply what is known about IO theories. Thinking of a transnational corporation (TNC) as a firm that conducts operations in multiple countries, one can see why firms would choose to operate in a foreign country instead of "selling their 'advantage' to local firms."[23] For example, overcoming the advantages of a local firm can be accomplished through the provision of some firm-specific asset such as a special technology or management technique. These intangibles can explain the foreign firm's presence in the local market.

In addition, "[FDI] occurs in consequence of transactions costs, risks and uncertainties in arms-length markets, and the potential for increased control, improved deployment of market power, reduced uncertainty, scale and scope economies, and as a means of overcoming market imperfections generated by national boundaries, information deficiencies, and the like—and via the creation of 'internal markets,' as an important contributor to worldwide (Pareto) efficiency."[24]

TNCs, therefore, offset imperfections as opposed to creating them through oligopoly power.

Therefore, the relationship fundamentals must be looked at in a game-theoretic context. Bargaining between the TNC, the host nation, and the recipient nation can explain much of the behavior of FDI, and indeed reveals more insights than the traditional return-on-investment mentality. Advances in IO theory, focusing on transactions costs, barriers to entry, and market imperfections, explain the actions of a firm that invests in a developing country.[25]

Understanding the critical nature of FDI for economic growth impacts security policy focused on the relationship between the ruler and the ruled. To the extent that the leader has legitimacy issues and must expend resources in order to stay in power, the economic development of the general population, in many instances, will increase his cost of staying in power (S). Recall that $Y = T - C - S$; the dictator's income equals tax revenue minus the costs of running the government minus the costs associated with staying in power. If economic growth among the general population can increase S more than T, then FDI, critical to the economic growth of some countries, must be considered in the arsenal of economic tools of security policy.

While FDI enhances economic performance, can it present a security risk for the leader of a democracy, as well as the dictator? The Committee on Foreign Investment in the United States (CFIUS), made up of representatives from a group of government agencies, reviews investment from abroad for national security risks. CFIUS approval is required whenever a foreign company proposes to acquire a U.S. asset that may have national security implications. For example, certain companies or technologies are deemed to be important to the military or to U.S. critical infrastructure. The CFIUS process is a narrow exception to the longstanding "open investment" policy of the United States and can be thought of as a means to protect our national security interests while enjoying the benefits of FDI. The vast majority of CFIUS reviews have involved private companies abroad seeking to acquire or merge with a U.S. firm. Is the national security risk enhanced when the foreign investor is a sovereign nation instead of a private investor?

Case Study: Sovereign Wealth Funds

Some institutions exist neither to lend money, like the IMF, nor to insure loans and investments, like OPIC, MIGA, and AIG, but rather to acquire international financial assets for the macroeconomic gain of a sovereign. These institutions, called sovereign wealth funds (SWFs), typically take the form of large, state-owned investment portfolios that are commonly invested in more diverse and riskier assets than traditional national reserves. Whereas reserves are usually maintained and invested for liquidity so that a country has quick and easy access to money, there are a myriad of reasons to maintain and invest capital in a SWF. We will examine two cases here—Arab oil-exporting countries and Asian economies benefitting from a trade surplus—that demonstrate the primary reasons for creating SWFs. Both cases examine commodity-exporting countries, which comprised nearly two-thirds of all SWF assets in 2008. Then we will discuss some of the security implications of these sovereign economic investors.

Arab Oil Exporters

There are two reasons for oil exporters to create and maintain SWFs. First, these economies want *stabilization funds*, where the primary objective is to create assets to cushion budgets and economies against oil price swings. Daniel W. Drezner notes, "these countries are simply converting assets extracted from the earth into a more liquid form."[26] As highlighted in our discussion on trade, it is easier to walk around with dollars and cents in your pockets than it is with barrels of oil.

Second, oil exporters may also create *savings funds*. The incentives to save are twofold. In the short run, oil exporters save to sterilize revenues, that is, to avoid oil revenues being rapidly brought into the country. Although a surge of revenue may sound appealing to you and me, it can quickly lead to economic volatility and become a country's own undoing. The effect—that commodities such as oil can boom while other aspects of an economy are harmed—is called "Dutch disease," and some SWFs seek to counter it with savings. In the long run, oil exporters are motivated to save for the day when oil supplies are exhausted. In this sense, they are converting nonrenewable assets into a portfolio of assets that can be new drivers for economic growth.

Asian Exporters

China, Singapore, Korea, and Taiwan benefit from a trade surplus and use SWFs to leverage this advantage. Specifically, these Asian exporters create and maintain *reserve investment corporations*, which seek to increase the return on reserve assets. Recall that the PRC leadership pegs the renminbi at an artificially low exchange rate with the U.S dollar to keep Chinese exports competitive. To do this, China maintains a large foreign asset reserve, which reached nearly $2.4 trillion at the end of 2009. There are significant opportunity costs to maintaining such a large foreign reserve.[27] Specifically, for every $1 of reserve assets a country accumulates, the home economy pays a cost equal to the difference between the private sector's cost of short-term borrowing abroad and the yield that the central bank earns on its foreign assets. Because interest rates on short-term borrowing are typically greater than returns on reserves, which are held in very low-risk investments, there is a cost to holding foreign reserves. Consequently, China's leadership created the China Investment Corporation (CIC) in 2007 to diversify investments in both domestic and global capital markets and increase the rate of return on its foreign reserve assets. After its first complete accounting year since inception, the fund reported a 6.8 percent return on capital investments in 2008. Moreover, at the end of 2009, CIC reported to the Securities and Exchange Commission holding nearly $10 billion in U.S. equities.

Implications for National Security Policy

With increasing wealth flowing into U.S. equities from SWFs in countries benefitting from vast oil and foreign exchange reserves, some economic observers have questioned the wisdom of allowing foreign sovereigns to take ownership in large U.S. corporations and financial institutions, particularly given that many SWFs lack transparency. Could SWFs become, in effect, a new tool to conduct foreign policy? Benjamin Cohen highlights some of the possibilities: "SWFs could be used instrumentally to seek control of strategically important industries, to extract technology or other proprietary knowledge, or to achieve a degree of direct or indirect influence over host governments. Such possibilities raise legitimate concerns about national security, which in an insecure world cannot be easily discounted."[28]

While Congress has taken some measures to protect certain industries vital to national security against foreign influence—President George W. Bush signed into law an amendment to the CFIUS process known as the Foreign Investment and National Security Act (FINSA), which gives the president the authority to "prohibit any covered transactions" by foreign governments "that threatens to impair the national security of the United States"—the risks that SWFs will mix business and politics remains.[29] By threatening to withdraw investments in a large American bank, for example, a SWF could exert influence over U.S. policy makers to meet the demands of its home sovereign. Less nefarious is the possibility that, like U.S. investment institutions during the economic crisis from 2008 to 2009, a SWF could collapse, creating economic instability as its subsidiaries are forced into bankruptcy.

Sovereign wealth funds illustrate some of the perils of the movement of money across borders. Leaders must carefully balance the benefits of the exchange of currency, debt, and equities in the international monetary and financial systems against threats to national security.

DEBT DYNAMICS AND DEBATES

Capital flows also commonly take the form of loans. Private commercial banks lend to developing countries for commercial reasons. Sovereigns and multinational institutions also lend to developing countries—often motivated by some social good such as the elimination of poverty, the improvement of education or sanitation, or some other cause deemed to be worthy of the investment. In these cases, the short-term return is often justified as purely social, while in the long run it can be to provide some commercial benefit to the lending state/institution.

As described earlier, the global flow of capital has at different times in history been comprised of sovereign lending, private lending, or foreign direct investment. Prior to World War I, public bonds and FDI characterized international monetary flows. Following the defaults resulting from the Great Depression, multinational institutional lending and FDI comprised the capital flows. After the 1960s, bank lending became the dominant form. In addition, the benefits of FDI have been described as providing incentives for both the investing firm as well as the recipient country. In the case of lending, however, sovereign involvement introduces externalities that impede efficient operation of the market. This leads to problems.

The Problems with Debt

The problems and misunderstandings associated with the debt taken on by sovereign states deserve special treatment.[30] Sovereign debt is characterized typically by minimal collateral and an inability to legally enforce repayment. The days of gunboat diplomacy are gone—how does a lender get back what it loaned? The easy answer lies in the desire of the debtor country to smooth consumption. The need to do so fuels incentive for the debtor country to maintain access to the credit market, and therefore incentive to maintain good credit. This answer, therefore, also requires that a country that defaults on debt will be unable to reenter the credit market. As will be shown, however, these two conditions often do not exist, and therefore the dynamics of debt and repayment are more complex.

A country that can enter and exit the debt market regardless of its commitment to its obligations faces no threat of exclusion from future borrowing.[31] In fact, the value of the debtor country's burden can get so high as to increase its incentive to default to overwhelmingly high levels—and thus raise its chances of default to near certainty. The intuition here is that once the value of the future payments reaches a certain high level, the country is better off investing or consuming domestically and defaulting on its debt. As long as the gains from cooperating with the credit market exceed the gains from defaulting, however, the debtor country will seek to maintain access. Reputation costs can work as an effective deterrent to default.

We know from a review of the history of international capital markets that sovereigns on occasion choose to default. This results in sanctions and the associated deadweight costs of unexploited gains from trade, as well as distortions of government policies and resulting capital flight and further abandonment of otherwise profitable market actions.[32] Beyond simple enforcement problems, the market also suffers from imperfect information to the extent that a creditor may not know the full extent of debt taken on by the borrowing country.

DEBT LAFFER CURVE

Perhaps the most interesting concept in the literature is the *Laffer curve* for debt.[33] Consider this scenario: at a moment in time, a developing country has a large debt, the service of which would consume a large percentage of GDP if the country opted to pay. A secondary market for debt would likely scale down its expectations on servicing payments based upon this debt-to-GDP ratio, and lenders would accept smaller payments in order to avoid forcing the debtor country into default. If, however, the debtor country increases domestic investment and therefore improves its ability to service existing debts, then the lenders will expect higher payments. In this sense, debt serves as a marginal tax on investment. The net result of this tax is to encourage consumption and *not* investment within the debtor country.

It is interesting to note that prior to the terms of the debt being finalized, the debtor country has an incentive to increase its ability to repay the debt. Once the contract is signed, however, the incentives are reversed and the debtor then has an incentive to reduce its ability to repay.

The Laffer curve for debt, as shown in figure 8.3, captures this relationship between the amount of debt and the expectation of the creditor. On the secondary market for debt, according to Daniel Cohen, the market price and the nominal price of debt can be plotted to show a Laffer-curve relationship.[34] There is a point at which an additional unit of nominal debt would decrease the market price of the total debt. According to Michael Dooley, forgiveness of debt is in the interest of the creditor group when the debtor is on a downward sloping portion of the Laffer curve for debt.[35]

The theory holds that debt distorts decisions in debtor countries so much that a reduction in contractual debt—nominal debt—can actually increase the expected return of creditors. They base their argument on work by Cohen, who uses the secondary market price of debt to estimate the relationship between the market value and the face value of debt for sixteen highly indebted countries.[36] A debt curve would imply that there exists a point at which an increase in the nominal value of total debt would actually decrease the market value

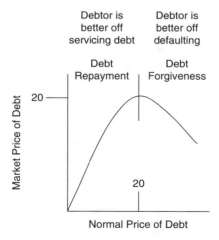

Figure 8.3

of the debt. Eaton and Fernandez argue that poor enforcement in commercial loans to sovereigns led to government participation in the primary debt market, resulting in excessive lending and the associated marginal tax on domestic investment in the developing countries. This led to delay, rescheduling, default, and capital flight.[37]

Government debt can discourage private investment and cause capital flight.[38] Government guarantees on loans also lead to over-borrowing and capital flight. The 1982 debt crisis can be attributed to the breakdown in the (implicit) guarantees of governments to their domestic commercial lending institutions that provided credit to developing countries.[39] Dooley argues that the failure of the governments to bail out banks that had extended significant credit to Mexico caused the banks to tighten lending policies and, therefore, caused additional defaults. He asserts that it was the policy decisions of the governments not to "back up" the loans of the banks that caused the debt crisis.[40]

Understanding the dynamics of government involvement in debt, we can now look for policy options to add to the list of economic tools of security. Debt relief or forgiveness provides one such policy option. It can be an incentive to use when engaging a world leader, as well as a way to boost a struggling economy so that economic benefits can get to the people of a target country.

CASE STUDY: DEBT FORGIVENESS— REPUBLIC OF CONGO

Returning to the example of the Republic of Congo from chapter 5, we can see how debt forgiveness can be used as a tool to influence the behaviors of world leaders or the people of autocratic regimes— such as Sassou-Nguesso, the president of the Republic of Congo (Brazzaville), to promote freedom, democracy, and economic growth in his country, regionally, and throughout Africa. With $9.2 billion owed to foreign creditors in 2004, Congo was one of the world's most indebted developing countries on a per capita basis. In 2006, the World Bank and International Monetary Fund determined that Congo qualified for debt forgiveness by reaching the "decision point" under the Heavily Indebted Poor Countries (HIPC) initiative, which requires a proven track record of macroeconomic stability and the preparation of a Poverty Reduction Strategy in conjunction with international financial institutions (IFIs). Although Congo began receiving interim debt forgiveness immediately, to qualify for irrevocable debt relief at the completion point, Congolese authorities were required to address World Bank concerns regarding governance and financial transparency. Pedro Alba, the World Bank Country Director for the Republic of Congo, the Democratic Republic of Congo, Burundi, and Rwanda, explained in the 2006 announcement, "The objective of debt relief is to free up resources to improve the lot of the poor. But sustained improvements in governance are necessary for these resources not to be hijacked by vested interests and used effectively and efficiently to improve the delivery of education, health and other essential services."[41]

Less than four years later, the World Bank and the IMF announced that Congo had met the completion point requirements, and agreed to support $1.9 billion in irrevocable debt forgiveness. In creating an incentive—debt forgiveness—international leaders were able to positively influence the behavior of an authoritarian regime, and, taking the broad view, improve regional stability and security.

While World Bank–type programs have the potential to offer numerous benefits to leaders and/or the people of targeted countries, as we saw in the previous example, there is also the prospect that problems will arise, which we consider here. In the context of the debate over the World Bank—criticized by the left for being too oppressive and by the right as being inefficient and ineffective—the debt vs. grants debate stands front and center. The World Bank and other IFIs provided loans to the HIPC countries. The argument against these loans is as follows:

- Transparency. The IFIs make loans to the poorest countries at such discounted rates that one could argue that they are, in fact, grants. For example, some argue a loan with a maturity in excess of thirty years with no interest and only a processing fee made to a country that will likely get the loan terms renegotiated is not a loan but a grant.
- Piling on. The IFIs are making loans to countries with high degrees of debt. They eventually get written down through the HIPC program. These loans simply pile on to the already significant debt of the poor countries. Critics say let's just give them the money and save a step.
- Accountability and Incentives. Grants should be tied to some measurable performance. The discussion of the Millennium Challenge Account in the next chapter captures some aspects of this argument.

There are those, however, who oppose grants and favor loans. They argue that the loans, if repaid, can then be loaned out to another poor country. So by giving grants, the total pool of available dollars to help the poorest people in the world is diminished. Stated another way, however, the money reflowing to another poor country is coming from a poor country. So there is no real diminishment of dollars, only a transfer from poor to poor.

The conclusion here is that marginal analysis of decision making must be considered. The debtor can be either dictator or democrat. On the credit side of the equation, think of the many players involved. Think of a marketplace for debt—a vibrant market with primary and secondary agents. Starting with the debtor, sovereigns have an incentive to repay their debts because access to future credit can prove useful. Even a responsible and law-abiding leader may want to borrow money to fund the annual budget due to recession, war, or a supply shock to the domestic economy—even though this means running a budget deficit. With bad credit, however, money will be expensive or not available.

If I am a dictator and my government owes ABC Bank of New York US$1 million per month in principal and interest, I want to service this debt. If I default, I will likely find getting another loan difficult and expensive. Now assume that I cannot generate enough government revenues and find myself illiquid. Or worse, I cannot sell enough assets of any type and find myself insolvent. No matter what I do, I cannot service my loan.

Where will my incentives lie, and what decision am I likely to make? When making a loan, the goal of international financial institutions and governments should be to make sure the debt burden is such that gains from cooperation with international financial markets exceed the benefits of defaulting. An excellent example when this did not happen is the 1980s debt crisis, where the debt to developing countries came from private institutions, but the private loaners believed in an implicit guarantee of bailout from the U.S. government in the case of default. In effect, these loans otherwise would not have happened because the commercial justification wasn't there. In the absence of a government guarantee, the marketplace would not make the loan. When the developing countries defaulted, the U.S. government made it clear that it would not guarantee the loans. Now the private sector found itself with a lot of junk.

Assuming there is a maximum amount of debt beyond which a country will prefer defaulting over servicing its loans, it is critical to understand the debtor's place along this curve to evaluate the debtor's incentive to service the debt. Creditors need to ensure that the total debt for a given leader does not exceed this critical point. Refer to figure 8.3, the Debt Laffer Curve.

Information holds tremendous value. The key here, of course, is to know where along the debt curve a country is at any time. And for the highly indebted kleptocrat, honesty endangers his access to credit. Information, which in this example is the total amount of debt and the ability to service that debt, proves critical to the debt market. It is a number that can be difficult to know. But if you assume that the theoretical point exists, then you can see the important analysis for determining the optimum level, if any, for debt reduction and relief.

Perhaps the most interesting conclusion of this research is that for a country beyond the critical debt level, total debt forgiveness is the only way to help the country. Debt relief short of total forgiveness benefits the creditors, but the real value of the debt, if actively traded on the secondary market for debt, will adjust so as to keep the real debt servicing payment of the debtor country constant.

For debtors beyond the critical point, critics argue, debt relief short of total forgiveness creates benefits that flow to creditors and investors, not to the poor people of the poor countries. U.S. taxpayers, for example, could forgive a portion of a country's debt for a public-good reason, but see the benefit go to the creditors (likely in the U.S. financial sector); the expenditure will not advance U.S. national security and stability in the area.

It is important to understand that no matter how well-intentioned our debt relief policies, the dictator running the highly indebted poor country may funnel the funds into private bank accounts. In this case, debt relief may strengthen and reinforce the practices of the dictator, even promoting behavior contrary to the stated policy goals and interests. Some of these risks may be ameliorated when the lender country has a strong relationship with the receiving country. Where the countries are geographically close to their lenders, such as Mexico's and Haiti's proximity to the United States, the lender must exercise more caution because economic conditions and migration flows have a great impact on neighbors in the region during a time of crisis. When a lending country has a weak relationship with the recipient country, it is crucial that the lending country apply caution. This is especially the case in Africa, where any country's neighbors are likely to be aid or loan recipients from similar sources, which creates a competitive rather than a cooperative environment.

CASE STUDY: DID THE GREAT RECESSION CHANGE THE COMPETITIVE EQUATION?

To date, the economic literature on the perils of unsound money or high indebtedness has focused primarily on developing countries. The West (particularly the United States, it is thought) holds the tools to capitalize on the economic misfortunes of others and influence their behavior. Do the events surrounding the deep economic turn-down that began in 2007 alter this conventional way of looking at the world? Do the United States and European nations now face threats from others, due to rapidly increasing debt and risky monetary policy? Will the Western leaders' reaction to the Great Recession permanently damage their countries' ability to project economic power?

These critical questions cannot be answered fully but there are several key data points that raise the possibility that the gradual power shift from west to east, projected by many strategists to play out over the next few decades, could be accelerated by the policies implemented by Western leaders in response to the Great Recession. In short, Western nations have taken on historically high levels of debt in attempt to spend its way out of the recession. In the United States, government spending has created budget deficits at record levels for each of 2008, 2009, and 2010, with the trend likely to continue in the future. As of this writing, total U.S. debt stands at 90 percent of GDP, the highest level of debt issued by the United States relative to the size of its economy since World War II. In Europe, debt levels are having a more immediate impact. Southern European countries such as Greece, Spain, and Portugal were either facing imminent sovereign default or seeking a bailout from the European Union or the IMF.

Nearly $900 billion of all U.S. debt is held by the Chinese government as it, along with the governments of Japan and other Asian nations, continues to finance the excess spending undertaken by the United States. Without a doubt, the United States has been a debtor nation for several decades. But as the first decade of the twenty-first century came to a close, the magnitude and holders of the debt raise new security issues for policy makers. At a minimum, it would appear that the Chinese in particular have gained a useful tool (holding of sovereign debt) against the United States. How and when they might use this tool is subject for debate. After all, as a large creditor of the United States, China has a vested interest in the success of the U.S. economy. But as China continues its rise as an economic competitor to the United States and, in the view of some, a potential military adversary, the dynamic created by China holding extensive levels of U.S. debt certainly adds a challenging wrinkle to future U.S.–Sino relations.

More broadly, do U.S. policies put in place to address the recession threaten U.S. economic dominance? Much of the spending to stimulate the U.S. economy in 2008 through 2010 appeared to be politically allocated. Large sums of government money were funneled to favored industries and nascent business ideas seemingly to further the political goals of Congress. Time will tell whether the deficit government spending during this period will have the effect of stimulating economic activity or simply adding to debt to be paid by future generations.

Summary: Money, Exchange Regimes, Debt

Sound money, safe exchange-rate regimes to safeguard a currency, and efficient debt markets dramatically impact global security issues. Foreign capital flows that arise from market incentives impelling foreign direct investment and loans into developing countries with an absorptive capacity for new technologies benefit both the investor and the recipient country. Security policy makers must understand this dynamic and the relationship between international finance and security.

Thus far, we have described the incentives facing the decision maker—the autocrat and the democrat. We have analyzed some of the conditions under which a specific policy can motivate a leader to change his behavior. We have also discussed the wealth effect. Can our policies provide resources to the people of a target political entity so they become empowered to change the institutional context in which their leaders make decisions; and can these changes advance our security policy goals?

Looking forward, *growth* literature continues to offer appealing theories. If we understand economic growth, can we in fact cure poverty? Above all, the empirical studies demonstrate the importance of country-specific factors. These must be addressed to assess the benefits of and prerequisites for investment, trade, and debt flows to a specific country. These factors include human capital and competition in the domestic market, as well as fundamentals addressed through policy prescriptions such as the rule of law, contract sanctity, bankruptcy laws, political stability, a sound financial and banking system, and sound money. The leaders make important decisions, but within the confines of institutional and resource constraints.

This chapter highlights several areas important to foreign capital flows into an autocracy, and ultimately must be understood if one believes that facilitating the growth of economies above a certain threshold supports national security goals. In the next chapter we will address the difficult question: does curing poverty promote national security by mitigating the threat from international terrorism?

Curing Poverty Helps National Security

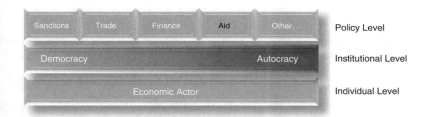

Figure 9.1

According to aid data from the Organization for Economic Co-operation and Development (OECD), during the past thirty years, often motivated by compassion, the international donor community has spent over $2 billion on development assistance for sub-Saharan Africa.[1] With this assistance, economists predicted dramatic growth for the region, which has yet to truly materialize. Do we know why? Why is Bangladesh poor while Japan is rich? Why did the Industrial Revolution occur in Europe and not China? If we understand growth, why does poverty still exist? Poverty must be the lack of understanding or the inability to implement the policies we know to be conducive to growth. While many economists continue to debate how best to spur economic growth, some policy analysts argue that despite these mediocre results, there is another, overriding reason why we must provide aid to such impoverished regions—it is a matter of national security.

Terrorism, Insurgency, and Poverty

What is the nature of the link between terrorism, insurgency, and poverty? How strong is this link? Can we fight terrorism through aid, or simply use aid for what it appears to be on its surface: a tool to alleviate suffering and feed starving children? On April 3, 2009, echoing the words of his predecessor President George W. Bush who said, "Poverty doesn't create terror—yet, terror takes root in failing nations that cannot police themselves or provide for their people," President Barack Obama described the relationship between national security interests, terrorism, and poverty in these terms:

> Over the long term...we've got to have a strategy that recognizes that the interest of the developed world in feeding the hungry, in educating children, that that's not just charity; it's in our interest. There's not a direct correlation between poverty and violence and conflict and terrorism. But I can tell you that if children have no education whatsoever, if young men are standing idle each and every day, and feel completely detached and completely removed from the modern world, they are more likely, they are more susceptible to ideologies that appeal to violence and destruction.[2]

Think about this statement. Terrorism is not caused by poverty; prosperity, however, defeats violence and destruction. If true, the battle against terrorism must include initiatives to raise living standards in impoverished nations, such as by feeding the hungry and educating children.

"Foreign Aid in the National Interest," a key document of the U.S. Agency for International Development, makes USAID's case that development and aid are intrinsically tied to security. It argues that U.S. security increasingly depends upon the prosperity of the rest of the world, and that the world is more interconnected than ever. The world remains dangerous and conventional military force cannot adequately assure national security. Economic development, and the provision of bilateral and multilateral aid necessary to spur that development, must be recognized as critical to any national security strategy. The document concludes, "For the United States to prosper and be secure, the world must prosper and be secure."

Of the nineteen suicide hijackers of September 11, 2001, most were from families in a socioeconomic category that could be considered middle class—not poor. And yet they committed suicide in order to kill nearly 3,000 people from around the world in the 9/11 terrorist attacks on the United States. What were their incentives? The theories and speculation could fill an entire book. For the purpose of this one, however, we begin with the assertion that they did not destroy themselves and others to escape poverty.

So why, then, does poverty matter in the War on Terrorism? Osama bin Laden, the recognized leader of al Qaeda, possessed exceptional wealth. He comes from one of the richest families in the world. Perhaps the poverty of other people motivates terrorists? Going back to the theory of choice, maximization and approbation, and constraints, people may be motivated to maximize for their kin, clan, or countrymen.

Perhaps poverty in the form of weak states undermines our security by providing safe havens for terrorists and insurgents? Think of Taliban fighters and al Qaeda in Afghanistan. Insurgents and terrorists have found refuge in the places on earth without a central government capable of enforcing a rule of law—thereby creating an opportunity for a terrorist's safe haven.

In some cases, violent organizations like Hezbollah have used their ability to provide basic social services that the government cannot or does not provide to gain power and support from the population. So poverty relative to the wealth of a political paramilitary organization matters. If obeying the law yields an annual income of x but supporting an outlaw—a rebel leader—yields an income of $2x$, plus safety, what will an individual choose? Most could be expected to choose $2x$, subject to institutional constraints such as rule of law and social norms.

How do we explain suicide bombings? A fascinating body of work is being developed by scholars such as Eli Berman, Larry Iannaccone, and David Laitin. If you ask why we join clubs, we gain some benefit that exceeds the cost of membership.[3] If the "club" is a terrorist organization or insurgency that offers a social safety net (health care, education, unemployment benefits, etc.) for your kin, and perhaps supernatural benefits, such as an afterlife, then one can begin to see a formula that can explain suicide attacks. We've introduced the idea of poverty's impact on the choice to commit acts of terrorist and insurgent violence. Can aid impact the decision making of the leadership of the poor country? Does development assistance provide a lever of influence over the country or the people involved?

Think of the world during the Cold War. Poor countries around the world received aid from either the United States or the Soviet Union. Often, these dictatorships led by thugs or tyrants received money based upon their actions related to communism. The United States aided dictators who opposed communist expansion; the aid, it was hoped, would encourage the leader to maintain an anti-Soviet posture. The Soviets offered aid to underwrite a pro-Soviet posture. Can we apply similar policies today to the War on Terrorism?

To immerse in the mechanics of crafting policies, we first must understand how wealth and poverty flourish. Why are some countries rich and others poor?

Growth Theory

Growth theory started with a focus on things. Some people have more things than others. Yali, the New Guinea local politician and protagonist of Jared Diamond's Pulitzer Prize–winning *Guns, Germs, and Steel: The Fates of Human Societies,* asks why developed countries have successfully manufactured and exported goods to developing countries, while places like New Guinea have failed to produce much of their own.[4]

His question centers on things: why some have more things, and are more prosperous, than other people. "Things" mean capital. The model here would read: $Y = f(K)$. Think of an equation as a recipe. Y is level of income, or GDP. $f(K)$ means a function of whatever is in the parentheses, in this case K for capital. So $Y = f(K)$ reads "income is a function of capital." Over time, the discussion included people. This meant labor: $Y = f(K, L)$. National income is some combination of things and people, capital, and labor. The frontier of the debate today includes ideas, finding the recipe or the ways of improving both capital and labor and how they are used together.

National Income Accounting

Many people recall the national income accounting equation from their introduction to economics. While not perfect, we can gain some understanding of international affairs by understanding the relationships it captures.

$$Y = C + I + G + (X - M)$$

National income (Y), also known as gross domestic product (GDP), is Consumption plus Investment plus Government spending plus net exports (eXports minus iMports). Think of a person who goes to work and produces something of value, a good or a service. In exchange for that productive work, the person receives a paycheck (money). Within an economy, what does that productive input turn into—where can that money go?

- Consumption. The person can go shopping and buy clothes, furniture, and food, for example, and consume the entire paycheck or a portion of it.

- Investment. The person can put the money into a savings account or some other form of financial account that will convert the saved dollars into money available for investment.
- Government. The government will take a portion of the paycheck and redistribute the wealth created by the person to some public good in order to, in theory, benefit many other people. A leader can build a road or fire station, for example, with tax dollars converted into government spending.
- Finally, when you open an economy, foreigners' purchases inside the domestic economy (exports) add to the gross domestic product. A domestic worker's purchase of foreign goods (imports) sends money outside of the economy.

An investment gap arises from insufficient money. When all of the value produced by all of the people engaged in the economy goes into consumption and taxes for government spending, nothing goes into investment. To grow out of poverty, people need to hold off on consumption today in hopes of greater consumption tomorrow—a goal reached through investment. But the poorest of the world need every bit of wealth just to survive the day. In this argument, therefore, the poor cannot afford investment and will not grow this wealth.

To overcome the investment gap and grow, theory states that foreign aid is needed. The aid money should be used to build roads and fire stations (infrastructure) so that the government can tax less or use the scarce revenue for highest value investments and consumption. The foreign aid dollars should be used to feed people so that they can survive the day and know that they are free to plan for tomorrow. The money should be used to develop capacity of domestic export industries; to increase national income by selling to the rest of the world. All of this makes sense, and the international donor community pursued policies informed by this theory for years. They failed. Jeff Sachs is returning to this hypotheses, however, claiming that the theory is correct, we just did not give enough money for a long enough time to make a difference. To date, this simply has not worked.[5]

THEORY OF GROWTH

To better understand this story, we return to the theory of growth itself. What do we know about economic growth, or as Stephen Haber, Douglass C. North, and Barry R. Weingast ask, "If Economists are so Smart, Why is Africa so Poor?"[6] And as Nobel Laureate Robert

Lucas commented, "Once you start to think about growth, it is hard to think about anything else."[7]

Solow's Model and the Residual

The story of growth evolves. Recall the things-and-people formulation: Income (Υ) is a function of capital (K) and labor (L).

$$\Upsilon = F(K,L)$$

This model is not a snapshot in time like the $C + I + G + (M - X)$ national income accounting framework, but rather it is dynamic, and the economy consists of two categories: things—such as capital, money, equipment, tools, and the like—and people—that is, labor.

How does this inform the poverty question? First, we convert the formula from income level to a growth rate of income over time. That is, tomorrow's income minus today's, the resulting numerical difference divided by today's income. If the income of country A—A's GDP—in year one is $100 and in year two it is $150, country A had a GDP growth rate of 50 percent. So if $\Upsilon = \$150$, and we use lowercase to denote a rate, $y = 50$ percent. Likewise, the growth rates of K and L over time are denoted as lowercase k and l.

Now, to cure poverty, simply get y greater than zero. If the world is either things or people, and population growth cannot be manipulated, then the poor simply need more things in order to grow their economies. Assuming the relationship between y and k is positive, an increase in k will increase y. This construction, therefore, supports the investment gap theory: give the poor money for them to grow.

What is the problem here? We have understood this theory since at least the 1960s, and have instituted decades of policies based upon this theory. The poorest countries in the world remain the poorest and, perhaps more significantly, they remain poor in absolute terms. As nice and simple as the formula seems, we have failed to cure poverty.

Robert M. Solow's theory, which contributed to his 1987 Nobel Prize, goes something like this. If you boil down the equation of people and things, you actually find a residual factor not explained by K or L. The Solow residual, denoted as A, suggests another factor. The growth equation becomes:

$$\Upsilon = f(K, AL)$$

This Solow residual explained growth, which "things" (K) failed to explain. You can add things, but not actually increase the rate of growth, only the level of income. Increase K and you may increase Υ, but not at the rate at which Υ increases. Once the donor community stops adding capital, the growth rate of the target country reverts to where it was. For the poor, this may mean 0 percent, or even negative growth. Give a man a fish, and soon after he eats it he will be hungry again, to borrow from the proverb. Growth depends upon fishing, not eating fish.

Augmented Labor, Human Capital, or Technology?

After Solow, we have an additional variable to consider when crafting a policy to address poverty: people, things, and some A factor. We just cannot change population levels practically, so we should keep it off the table. Adding capital can address level of income, but not the long-term growth rate of income. So clearly, we must add A. So what is it? Solow didn't tell us. He taught us to look at A, but did not tell us what it is.

Theories to explain this residual have come forward over the past decades. For example, we can think of AL as augmented labor. In an economy, you have differing levels of labor capacity. A day's work for person A and a day's work for person B will have different values depending upon the skill set of each worker and the task being performed. Some people are educated; some are trained on sophisticated machinery; some are healthy. People have different traits that help them to be productive. If not augmented labor, think instead of human capital and physical capital: $\Upsilon = f(K, L, H)$.[8]

The residual can also be thought of as technology. The quantity and quality of technology in an economy drives the GDP growth rate. Capital and labor levels define the starting point, but it is the innovation and technology that take an economy from stagnation to positive GDP growth. Correspondingly, a technological setback leads to negative growth, or contraction of the economy. Think of natural disasters or wars that wipe out electricity or telephones where the shock to technology causes a setback for the economy.

The flip side of technology is that technologies disrupt. DVDs enhance quality of life for home movie viewers, except for those who work in the VCR manufacturing industry. DVD technology disrupts existing VCR technology. Technological advancement represents improvements in the GDP growth level and perhaps even the growth rate. But the owner of the incumbent technologies may end up losing. In fact, this constituency often impedes the development and adoption of new technologies through lobbying their government officials. These vested interests can inhibit economic growth. Sometimes, the leader loses out with innovation and, therefore, works against economic growth. Theory meets the economic actor when incentives get considered; think again of the maximizing individual.

INCENTIVES AND GROWTH

Now let's marry growth theories with theories of human nature, the critical element of policy making that can no longer be overlooked. Let's say we want to promote education in a poor agricultural country because we believe education to be the critical element to growth for that country's specific circumstances. What if the parents of the children do not want their children to leave the fields to go to school? Perhaps the entire family requires all hands in the fields just for subsistence. Likewise, if a country requires a new technology and we can develop a policy to transfer it there, perhaps this technology would disrupt a domestic industry in that country and, therefore, the political leadership will resist it.

These examples demonstrate that, in spite of carefully designed theories by great economists, we must never forget the human actor who must implement the policy. Smart policies are based upon choices made by real people. People create wealth. Countries are institutions that can become wealthy with the right policies. The right policies are those that encourage people to create wealth. Why do people work? To earn a living, to maximize for self and others, and for approbation. Rich countries have institutions that encourage this behavior, and poor countries tend to have the opposite. Economic aid policies must take incentives into account to attain the goals of development and growth.

DEINDUSTRIALIZATION: WHEN COUNTRIES DO NOT INVEST IN DOMESTIC CAPACITY

Similar to sanctions, trade, and international finance, time horizons impact aid policies. Specifically, when people have income today, they may refuse structural changes that yield important benefits tomorrow. Natural resources can cause deindustrialization, for example, and stymie economic growth. For example, we see high poverty levels in Saudi Arabia and Kuwait, both of which pay royalties to citizens from oil revenues. In Colombia, farmers who grow the illicit coca plants receive significantly higher profits than farmers who grow legitimate crops. Likewise, farmers in Afghanistan face incentives to grow poppy, used for heroin production, rather than legitimate crops. In fact, both examples can be singled out as impediments to economic growth.

Recall from the previous chapter's study of sovereign wealth funds the concept of "Dutch disease," wherein the traded goods of a country can boom while other aspects of the economy are harmed in a deindustrialization of the domestic economy. Imagine a boom in the world tulip market that would cause people to move out of other Dutch industries into tulip production and export. Oil royalties make Saudi society inefficient in terms of developing other areas of their industry. Colombia constantly struggles with efforts to shift the economy from the lucrative coca to more sustainable and less harmful crops. But with the return on investment of capital and labor into coca production, the market incentives, in effect, take productive resources from transformational industries.

To create economic growth in Afghanistan, for example, and move the economy away from the drug trade, five factors must be addressed: three marginal decisions and two institutional. First, where is the best place for the individual to use the next dollar of capital? Second, how best can the individual use the next hour of labor? Third, what is the individual's time horizon? Fourth, which institutional constraints do individuals face? Finally, what are the individual's resource constraints?

If planting one acre of wheat yields a profit of x and planting one acre of coca yields a profit of $3x$, the monetary incentive for the farmer will bias him to plant coca, all other things being equal. However, the variables can be manipulated to change the farmer's behavior by considering his incentives. If the farmer maximizes for himself and his family, three variables seem important. Can he subsist today, decrease the risk of failing to subsist tomorrow, and leave something of value to his children? A government policy that guarantees an income for legal farmers and assigns a high penalty for those caught growing coca, and one that convinces farmers that the government is committed to coca eradication over the long term, can influence the farmer's decision. Under these circumstances, if convincingly implemented and meaningfully enforced, a farmer with an infinite time horizon will see guaranteed income for self and family and a decrease in the risk associated with growing illicit crops, including the risk of losing a means of future income for his children.

If the farmer, concerned for the future of his family, holds an infinite time horizon, can subsist on planting wheat, and believes there is no long-term viability in the illegal coca harvesting, his incentives will shift toward legitimate crops, as shown in figure 9.2. Profits

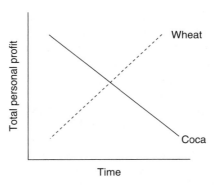

Figure 9.2

maximized this week may be higher from coca, but profits maximized over his lifetime may come from the crop with less risk and volatility. He must assume that the probability of larger coca profits decreases with increased enforcement of the prohibition by the government. Here is where good policy can make a difference. The farmer must also believe he can survive on legitimate crops, including making the transition from illicit to legitimate—from coca to wheat, for example. Finally, property rights must be strong so that he can see his children benefiting from his actions after his farming days are over and he is gone.

Under what conditions will the leader of a resource-rich country invest in the future? An incentive must exist to care about the future. As a tinpot hoping to extract as much wealth as possible until overthrown, a leader would have no incentive to invest in domestic capacity yielding returns beyond his expected term. As a democratically elected president, however, a leader would have an interest in building domestic capacity to produce wealth in sectors of the economy not related to oil. If the elected official takes the resource revenues and invests in other capacities to produce wealth when resource revenues or production declines, the economy will continue to thrive because it will have diversified. If the *tinpot* has no incentive to care about the future, then the leader will not likely take adequate actions to diversify. The market will continue to drive the economy to the immediate marginal benefits of resource revenues.

When oil was discovered in the North Sea in the 1960s, both capital and labor spending shifted in the United Kingdom.[9] Investment dollars flowed into the energy sector, and people moved into jobs in this sector. The marginal product of labor and capital in the oil industry abruptly increased, causing the shift in resources. In addition, the total income increased, since a new source of revenue became available to the economy that was not previously available. The movement of resources to the energy sector came from somewhere. People were not created coincident with the discovery of oil; workers left the manufacturing sector to work in the energy sector. Domestic income created in manufacturing, therefore, decreased while domestic income from energy increased. The question becomes: which effect had the greatest impact, the decline in manufacturing—deindustrialization—or the increase in the oil sector?

Now think of Afghanistan from the mid-1990s through 2005. The Afghan government falls to the Taliban, and the Taliban are removed by a U.S.–led international military coalition. With so much at stake for the free world, how is Afghanistan best rebuilt? What are the stabilization policies that will lead to growth in support of a democratic and free Afghanistan?

Poppy production decreased after the U.S.–led invasion in 2001, then increased dramatically in 2004 and 2005. Why? The return on investment of capital and labor so far exceeds other options that people chose the illicit production and shipment of poppies. People will maximize, but also seek approbation from and for kin and country.

Profits equal *Revenues* minus *Costs*: this is the most general formula possible. Profits will be indicated by pi, π, such that $\pi = R - C$. Decrease the revenue and increase the costs and you decrease the profits (π). Therefore, policies should do the following:

- Decrease the expected revenue from poppy production by increasing the likelihood of crops being eradicated, farmland confiscated, or other law enforcement actions;
- Increase the costs of producing poppies; and
- Provide incentives to channel economic activities to other income-producing tasks.

Recall the profit-maximizing individuals being targeted—the farmer, the smuggling syndicate, local law enforcement, the local governmental leaders and the institutions in which they operate, and the Afghan government's structure and leaders—and consider their incentives and time horizon. Only when this level of analysis has taken place can incentives be aligned to increase the likelihood of turning the economy in a direction best for long-term growth for the people of Afghanistan as well as the rest of the world. The Reconstruction

Opportunity Zones concept discussed in chapter 5 is one attempt to change the incentive structure of the Afghan people.

Deindustrialization is a distinct, complex economic factor for policy makers to incorporate into security decisions. Some market conditions will deter a leader and the population from investing in the domestic economy's future until faced with incentives to change.

CASE STUDY: THE MILLENNIUM CHALLENGE ACCOUNT

In hand are theories of growth, thirty years of lessons learned, and a sophisticated understanding of human decision making and political institutions. What policy conclusions address individual incentives? For former President George W. Bush, one answer was the Millennium Challenge Account (MCA).

Building on decades of research into economic growth and the lessons learned from failed policies, President Bush announced in March 2002 what he termed a "new compact for global development," the Millennium Challenge Account. In January 2004, with the U.S. Congress, he created the Millennium Challenge Corporation (MCC). The simple premise, as advertised, is to link "greater contributions from developed nations to greater responsibility from developing nations."[10] In short, the president acknowledged that incentives matter for economic growth.

The MCA seeks to tap into the incentives of leaders in the developing world. In the past, poor countries received aid because they were poor. Policies sought to fill the investment gap. Years later, the donor country found itself continuing to give aid to a country that was still poor. Think of the distorted incentives at work: by continuing to give aid to countries that show little improvement, such policies provide, in effect, an incentive not to improve and to remain dependent on aid.

With the MCA, aid will be linked to policy decisions by the leadership of the developing country. If the policies encourage foreign direct investment and trade, transparency, rule of law, and contract sanctity, and if they discourage corruption, then the country will be eligible for MCA assistance. If they do not adopt these pro-growth policies, then they will not be eligible for this assistance. Further, the program requires monitoring over time of the policies in the target country. If a recipient of MCA funds reverses policies, the MCC will halt the flow of aid dollars to that country. The program directly impacts the incentives of the ruler, whether autocratic or democratic.

The MCC's approach to reducing poverty through economic growth goes well beyond the investment gap theory. This is clear in several ways. First, the United States does provide capital—things. Second, however, assistance also addresses human capital. MCA focus areas include not only agriculture and trade capacity building, but also education, enterprise and private-sector development, governance, and public health.[11] Third, the MCA takes into account the critical importance of harnessing the decision-making processes of foreign leaders to spur growth. Growth-enhancing policies enacted by foreign leaders get rewarded. Fourth, the institutions in which people make decisions are addressed. The MCC partners with the recipient countries. The work plan is jointly developed, and a wide array of stakeholders is brought into the process. Transparency and buy-in in the developing country are core elements of the program.

The MCC measures results. As opposed to previous aid programs where amounts of money distributed could be confused for program success, the MCA actually required success to be defined by accomplishing growth and development goals.

So how is it working? Only in place since January 2004, this latest effort to implement the frontiers of economic thinking is probably too young to measure. However, the MCC offers the following quantitative indicators on poverty reduction:

- $7.7 billion has been approved to programs for agriculture and irrigation, transportation infrastructure, water supply and sanitation, access to health services, finance and enterprise development, anticorruption initiatives, land rights, and access to education.
- 1,200 kilometers of roads are under construction in nine countries, driving lower transport costs and better access to schools, health centers, and markets.
- Over 100,000 farmers have been trained on modern techniques for production on over 15,000 hectares of land, leading to increased productivity, higher incomes, and greater food security.

In addition, the MCC cites anecdotal evidence of early progress toward good governance:

- Bangladesh's finance minister, Saifur Rahman, while proposing a tough program targeting corruption, cited his country's

exclusion from MCA eligibility as an example of the heavy price his country was paying for being branded as a corrupt country.
- One Lesotho official said, "Even if we receive less than requested, the intangibles gained from taking control of our own development destiny are the most important part of the process."[12]

The program is not without its flaws, however. The Congressional Research Service (CRS) published an analysis of the MCC in June 2009 highlighting select issues, including:

- Grant size: The MCC has argued that to provide sufficient incentives to countries, the size of its grants must place MCC assistance among the top aid donors in a country. However, CRS research indicates that MCC grants trailed World Bank, European Commission, and bilateral U.S. aid (excluding MCC funds) in numerous recipient countries. Congressional sentiment that grants should remain manageable could hamper the MCC's ability to reach its potential as a transformational aid program.
- Speed of implementation: A recurrent criticism by Congress of MCC is the slow speed of implementation. Specifically, there is considerable lag time between appropriated funding from Congress to the MCC and disbursements from the MCC to aid recipients. In fact, as of March 2009, of the $8.3 billion appropriated for the MCC, only $1.2 billion had been disbursed. There are some good reasons for this lag, however. First, the MCC is a new aid experiment so it will take time for operational procedures to develop. Second, the recipient countries are themselves responsible for developing and submitting proposals to the MCC, and they face managerial and accountability problems common to most developing countries. Requiring them to develop proposals is part of the process for reform. Notably, the MCC announced reorganization aimed at improving implementation and expects disbursements to exceed $1 billion in 2010.[13]

CASE STUDY: THE AFRICAN GROWTH AND OPPORTUNITY ACT

If the goal of the MCC is to make aid programs more effective, the ultimate goal of the African Growth and Opportunity Act (AGOA) is to replace aid with trade. That is, change the incentive structure in a nation so that revenue is derived from markets instead of from foreign donors. The U.S. Congress approved AGOA in 2000 to expand unilateral trade benefits to the nations of sub-Saharan Africa (SSA). In exchange for making progress toward a more market-oriented economy and meeting other criteria, nearly forty SSA nations enjoy duty-free access to the U.S. market for more than 7,000 products. Soon after the institution of AGOA, textile and apparel industries developed rapidly in areas of Southern Africa. By some estimates, hundreds of thousands of jobs were created.

Stiff competition from China beginning in 2005 with the end of the Multi-Fiber Agreement, which had imposed quotas on Chinese textile imports for the past 30 years, has limited the benefit of AGOA for some nations. Nonetheless, President Bush extended AGOA through 2010 and many SSA nations have diversified their manufacturing sectors into products other than textile and apparel. The AGOA model appears to provide the right balance between incentives to trade and foreign aid. The SSA nations that made changes to their economies and governments in order to qualify for AGOA did not forego any opportunity to receive foreign aid. They did, however, provide new opportunities to raise the standard of living for their citizens by exporting products to the United States. New proposals—such as the heretofore discussed Reconstruction Opportunity Zones—are built on this successful model.

Aid, Growth, and National Security Policy

A leader like the president of the United States may support the distribution of aid in many forms and for several reasons; for instance, to alleviate poverty in the poorest places in the world, or in a poor place after a natural disaster such as a tsunami or hurricane. A person benefits from knowing that he contributed to alleviating someone else's suffering. Aid can also be a carrot to dangle in front of a foreign leader to get him to move in a desired direction. For example, it allows one leader to tell another, "Stop abusing ethnic or religious minorities in your country and we will give you foreign assistance dollars and not veto the international community's efforts to do the same." The threat of removal of ongoing aid can be a "stick" to stop a country's leader from taking particular action. For example, "Stop abusing your ethnic or religious minorities or we will cut off our millions of dollars of aid." Aid can also be a way to encourage economic growth. We want to alleviate today's poverty, but also tomorrow's with today's dollars: "Here is money, but use it to so that people in your country will build and grow the economy so that we do not need to give you more money tomorrow." And finally, we can condition aid on certain behaviors, and require that it lead to policies supportive of economic growth. So this chapter concludes where it started. If poverty is more than an issue of compassion, but also a security issue, then the developed world will opt to spend money to "cure" poverty for security reasons.

Policies that take into account human nature and the incentives and institutions that surround world leaders are the policies more likely, in theory, to succeed. The Millennium Challenge Account and the African Growth and Opportunity Act may be new ways of looking at aid that put this theory into practice with positive results. The early reports are good.

CHAPTER 10

Tools against Terrorists

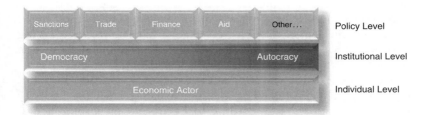

Sanctions	Trade	Finance	Aid	Other...	Policy Level

Democracy	Autocracy	Institutional Level

Economic Actor	Individual Level

Figure 10.1

September 11, 2001 demonstrated that a terrorist does not need to lead a country to have in place the institutions and resources that allow him to inflict his will on a state. Individual people make decisions, whether they are leaders of states or leaders of insurgent, drug-trafficking, or terrorist organizations. When Osama bin Laden managed to kill thousands of people inside the United States, he became every bit as relevant to national security as any state leader. In a world characterized by states—or state warfare—states matter more; when violence occurs within or across borders by substate actors, we must engage in economic analysis of the individual.

How can a policy maker influence the decisions of terrorist leaders in the context of the Global War on Terrorism? According to the U.S. Treasury Department, prior to 9/11 three systems existed to alter terrorists' behavior. First, the United States pursued efforts to change behavior through policies to "name and shame" international financial actors. Working through the Financial Action Task Force (FATF), which was established by the G-7 Summit that was held in Paris in 1989, an international coalition focused on influencing the actions of leaders in the world's financial jurisdictions that either support or allow illicit money laundering.[1] The United States also pursued these name and shame policies through the G-7 and the international financial institutions. Specifically, short of sanctioning these leaders, the policies seek to first make public the illicit activities condoned or supported within their jurisdictions. In the jurisdictions identified by the FATF, many internal reforms took place following the enactment of the policies—after 1989.[2] Second, the United States shut down terrorists' access to capital by working with finance ministries and central banks, focusing on the movement of tainted capital throughout the international financial system. These tools had been well honed through two decades of a concerted U.S. effort to clamp down on money laundering in the 1980s and 1990s. The Bank Secrecy Act provides the legal basis for the United States anti–money laundering system, explained next. Third, the United States, via the United Nations, targeted specific terrorist financing networks through the International Convention for the Suppression of the Financing of Terrorism.

Despite the existence of these systems and processes, however, combating terrorist financing was not a national security priority prior to September 11. According to Levitt and Jacobson, "Senior U.S. policymakers were not focused on issues related to terrorist financing, and to the extent that they were, reliable information was often hard to come by, particularly on al Qaeda. The U.S. intelligence community did not have a solid grasp on al Qaeda's financing. Few resources were devoted to this type of strategic intelligence collection. Compounding this, al Qaeda was a difficult collection target. International counterterrorism cooperation, critical to fighting a transnational enemy, was also often lacking."[3]

The attacks on 9/11 served as a dramatic wake-up call to interrupt the flow of cash to terrorist networks. President Bush highlighted the imperative of combating terrorist financing in his unequivocal address to Congress on September 20, 2001:

> We will starve terrorists of funding, turn them one against another, and drive them from place to place until there is no refuge or no rest. And we will pursue nations that provide aid or safe haven to terrorism. Every nation in every region now has a decision to make: Either you are with us or you are with the terrorists. From this day forward, any nation that continues to harbor or support terrorism will be regarded by the United States as a hostile regime.[4]

The United States followed the money, employed financial sanctions, began exporting these sanctions to disrupt networks and kleptocratic leaders of foreign states, and ultimately sought to change the behavior of world leaders by impacting their access to U.S. dollars.

Just weeks after the attacks on America, President Bush issued Executive Order 13224—the first policy implemented after 9/11—based upon the International Emergency Economic Powers Act (IEEPA).[5] As the first official response to terrorism by President Bush, E.O. 13224 empowered the Treasury Secretary to target the financial activities of certain individuals. Moreover, the Department of Treasury's Office of Terrorism and Financial Intelligence (OTFI) was created in 2004 to fully leverage the powers established in E.O. 13224.

In 2010, Assistant Secretary for Terrorist Financing David S. Cohen highlighted the three-pronged approach the OTFI is taking to combat terrorist financing. First, it *deters* individuals from assisting or sponsoring violent extremist groups. Second, it *disrupts* access to individuals or entities that terrorists rely on for financial support. Third, it *degrades* financial support networks.[6] How does OTFI deter, disrupt, and degrade terrorist financing?[7] Its arsenal includes directly blocking access to U.S.–held assets, identifying financial sponsors to name and shame, and, in effect, denying access to U.S. dollar accounts.

The net impact of these actions against any given individual should not be underestimated; these tools can serve as a powerful motivator. A person or entity identified under E.O. 13224 would be publicly identified and lose access to any amounts being blocked, but perhaps more noteworthy, this person would lose all access to financial transactions using U.S. dollars. For example, if he conducted a transaction with a bank under U.S. jurisdiction, the bank would be required to block the additional assets, cutting off his access to U.S. dollars. In signing the executive order, President Bush initially identified twelve individuals and fifteen entities whose assets were subject to blocking. At the end of 2009, the Office of Foreign Assets under the OTFI reported to Congress that the list had grown to 539 individuals and entities designated under E.O. 13224, and that the "Implementation of programs targeting international terrorist organizations has resulted in the blocking in the United States of more than $19 million in which there exists an interest of an international terrorist organization or other related designated party."[8]

The economic costs of losing access to U.S. financial institutions and U.S. dollars can be significant and the incentives to avoid persons or entities that may be associated with terrorism are strong. The U.S. actions, therefore, have inhibited the abilities of terrorists, state and nonstate alike, to operate internationally.

The tool is made yet more powerful through the internationalization of its enforcement. Earlier in this book we discussed the hypothesis that unilateral sanctions may not alter behavior, but making them multilateral may make a difference in a leader's behavior, using the EU–Cuba agreement as an example.

The United States worked with the United Nations to pass Security Council Resolution 1267 (UNSCR 1267) and create the al Qaeda and Taliban Sanctions Committee, or the United Nations 1267 Sanctions Committee.[9] Since many of the countries, even members of the coalition dedicated to fighting terrorism through these financial actions, do not have domestic laws in place similar to the International Emergency Economic Powers Act, many lack the domestic legal authority to block assets of terrorists and their supporters even if identified. They may, however, have domestic laws that allow the use of U.N. resolutions to empower the domestic government. So by using the United Nations, the U.S. financial restrictions become multilateral. Terrorists lose access to U.S. dollars, and also to the currencies and financial institutions of countries around the world.

In the context of name and shame, it goes without saying that condemnation by the United States means more in some corners of the world than in others, as does condemnation by the United Nations and other countries. The disapprobation tools of E.O. 13224 and UNSCR 1267 complement each other.

One final point on this tool: it can be used prophylactically. This confers tremendous power. The U.S. president and other world leaders can preemptively designate a person or entity as a terrorist or supporter and cut them off. This is a wartime power—no proof of culpability is required; no advance notice is needed.

In summary, when the United States turns its economic instruments of national security against an al Qaeda terrorist, he stands to (1) lose access to any U.S. dollar assets—dollars held in U.S. financial institutions; (2) lose the ability to conduct transactions in U.S. dollars; (3) become publicly identified as a terrorist; (4) become listed by the U.N. as a terrorist and lose corresponding access to other nations' currencies and financial institutions; and (5) lose access to many more institutions that refuse to do business with him for fear of facing U.S. and international sanctions under E.O. 13224 and UNSCR 1267.

Since the authority can be preemptive, those who have not done business with terrorists have incentive to avoid doing so.

According to the model in part I, decision makers maximize. U.S. financial initiatives have made it much more difficult for terrorists to thrive and maximize. Their costs of doing business have increased. Decision makers also seek approbation, and so will seek to avoid being placed on name and shame lists. Perhaps shame cannot work at a personal level for hardened terrorists. The policies, however, do not rely upon a terrorist with a conscience, only one who seeks to raise funds, recruit, and kill. At a minimum, these policies diminish his chances of success.

Anti-terrorism financial tools provide the freedom-loving, classical liberal leader the opportunity to prevent terrorists from using his country as a conduit for funding. Those in the middle who are indifferent may also be swayed to take action. A third-world leader, for example, who seeks to maximize resources may choose to exercise more diligence in screening business partners. The risk of working with a known or even potential terrorist supporter could have serious financial consequences for his country.

Case Study: Saudi Arabian Charities

Following 9/11, the Saudi government took action to combat terrorism and terrorist financing within the kingdom. Between 2003 and 2005, the Saudi government increased the size, training, and professionalism of its security forces, with U.S. assistance.[10] However, in a speech before the Council on Foreign Relations in 2007, Treasury Secretary Henry Paulson claimed that while the Saudis are "very effective at…countering terrorists within the kingdom," they still "need to do a better job holding people accountable who finance terrorism around the world."[11] One instance in which the Saudis are still failing to hold terrorist financiers accountable is in the country's charitable sector.

In 2002, the United States notified the Saudi leaders of U.S. intentions to employ E.O. 13224 freezing and naming actions against numerous charities it had identified as contributors to terrorism. The Saudi government responded by counterproposing joint U.S.–Saudi Arabian designation of Saudi charities and citizens, as well as the creation of the High Commission for Oversight of Charities to increase transparency of charitable giving in the kingdom. Joint efforts have resulted in moderate success. For example, in 2004 the Saudi government dissolved the Al Haramain Islamic Foundation, a large charity with links to the royal family and branches serving as front organizations for terrorist activities, after numerous joint U.S.–Saudi investigations into its alleged involvement in terrorism financing. Moreover, The U.N. 1267 Committee now receives joint designations from the United States, Saudi Arabia, and other countries. For example, the terrorist organization Jamaat Islamia was submitted to the committee by fifty-six countries.

However, efforts to establish an internal Charities Commission in Saudi Arabia have foundered. Levitt and Jacobson note that Saudi efforts to establish a Financial Intelligence Unit (FIU) have also fallen short.

In 2005, officials in Riyadh announced the opening of an FIU that was to report to the Ministry of the Interior. Then–U.S. Congresswoman Sue Kelly—one-time chair of a House Financial Services subcommittee—described what she discovered about the Saudi FIU during a 2005 trip to the country. Despite being reassured by the Saudis that the unit was operational, she found that it consisted of "an empty floor in a building under construction."[12]

In summary, the Saudi response to a fundamental problem within the kingdom regarding charities has been mixed. While internal efforts by the Saudi government have fallen short, U.S. and U.N. policy has been most effective in causing the foreign government to change its behavior when accompanied by joint enforcement programs.

CASE STUDY: IRAQ

The officials of some governments are kleptocrats: people who steal from their states for personal gain. The Iraqi government of Saddam Hussein surely contained a fair share of these criminals. President Bush's Executive Order 13315 of August 2003 empowered the secretary of the treasury to identify members of Saddam Hussein's regime and entities under his control and freeze their assets—powers similar to those of E.O. 13224. In addition, E.O. 13315 allowed for the vesting of Iraqi-blocked assets in the United States to enable their immediate return to the Development Fund for Iraq.[13]

To internationalize this policy, the UNSC proposed and evolved UNSCR 1483, in essence mimicking the international obligations of UNSCR 1267. In the Iraqi context, therefore, there exists a list of those companies, people, and entities that were part of the Iraqi regime. The list then must be acted upon by domestic governments;

they must freeze and confiscate the assets and return them to help rebuild post–Saddam Hussein Iraq.

This new economic tool of security policy has been very successful. Hundreds of people and companies have been identified by the United States and the United Nations, and billions of dollars have been frozen and returned to Iraq. The Treasury's Assistant Secretary for Terrorist Financing Patrick O'Brien highlighted the success of these specific efforts in the first U.S. government–wide, anti-kleptocracy outreach event in 2008:

> I would like to take a moment to mention Treasury and broader U.S. government efforts, domestically and internationally, to develop initiatives that identify, track, and return kleptocratic assets to those who need them most. In 2003, Treasury helped lead a focused interagency effort to find, freeze, and repatriate Iraqi assets from around the world, and to find cash and assets within Iraq that were stolen and hidden by elements of the former Hussein regime. This worldwide hunt resulted in the freezing of nearly $6 billion in Iraqi assets outside of Iraq, the return of over $2.7 billion of those monies, and the recovery of over $1 billion in cash inside Iraq.[14]

To recap, we have covered the authorities created in the immediate aftermath of the 9/11 attacks, although based upon tools already in use for combating nonterrorist activities: E.O. 13224 and UNSCR 1267. We have covered post-Saddam Iraq policies spelled out in E.O. 13315 and related U.N. resolutions. Finally, in the United States' wider War on Terrorism, the USA Patriot Act ("Uniting and Strengthening America by Providing Appropriate Tools Required to Intercept and Obstruct Terrorism"), enacted on October 25, 2001, greatly empowers U.S. leaders to go after terrorists and their financial networks. It also helped to calibrate U.S. responses. Prior to the Patriot Act, the president could freeze assets under the IEEPA or could require reporting and advisory actions under the Bank Secrecy Act. Section 311 of the Patriot Act fills in the gaps between these extremes of policy options. Section 311 allows the secretary of the treasury to designate an institution, jurisdiction, or class of transactions as a "primary money laundering concern." With this designation follows a call for disciplinary measures by the FATF.

Section 311 represents a real innovation in U.S. development of economic instruments of security policy. It gives power to implement special measures to the secretary of the treasury. These additional actions include everything from public exposure and "name and shame," to completely cutting off an entity from the U.S. dollar via official channels.

CASE STUDY: SYRIA

On May 11, 2004, the secretary of the treasury, on behalf of the president of the United States, declared the Commercial Bank of Syria a financial institution of primary money laundering concern, setting off a chain of events of considerable consequence to the Syrian leadership. Because the Commercial Bank of Syria is the primary bank of the government of Syria and its leaders, the president, in effect, cut off the Syrian government and its leadership from direct access to transactions in U.S. dollars, and therefore cut them off from most of the global financial system. Without a first-rate and globally accepted currency of its own (this is another example of the significance of having stable money, discussed previously), the Syrian government, like much of the world, conducted significant transactions in U.S. dollars. With the stroke of a pen, the U.S. president foreclosed access to U.S. dollars. In addition, at about the same time, the U.S. Congress passed the Syrian Accountability Act that allowed for additional sanctions against the Syrian government. Two years later, another series of sanctions were implemented that targeted particular individuals and institutions. Specifically, the 2006 legislation denies certain Syrian citizens and entities access to the U.S. financial system due to their participation in WMD proliferation, association with terrorist organizations, or destabilizing activities in Iraq and Lebanon.

How did Syrian leadership respond to these aggressive actions? They decided that it would be in their best interest to engage the U.S. leadership in a dialogue. In short, they wanted off the 311 list. Following diplomatic talks in Damascus in 2009—the first since 2005—President Obama announced that the United States would take steps to ease American restrictions on a case-by-case basis, while Syrian President Bashar al Assad agreed to further cooperation on securing the Syria-Iraq border against insurgent traffic to aid the U.S.–led Operation Iraqi Freedom. Using access to the U.S. dollar as a national security policy tool, the U.S. treasury secretary compelled Syrian leadership to engage in a dialogue to address a primary concern for U.S. national security—financial support for international terrorism.

Case Study: Law Enforcement
against al Qaeda

Citing a surge of public pleas from top al Qaeda leaders for financial contributions, the U.S. Treasury Assistant Secretary for Terrorist Financing told *Forbes* in 2010, "Al Qaeda is in a weaker financial state than it has been for a number of years."[15] In May 2007, for example, Shaykh Mustafa Abu al Yazid, an al Qaeda leader in Afghanistan, highlighted the group's desperate need for donations:

> As for the needs of the Jihad in Afghanistan, the first of them is financial. The Mujahideen of the Taliban number in the thousands, but they lack funds. And there are hundreds wishing to carry out martyrdom-seeking operations, but they can't find the funds to equip themselves. So funding is the mainstay of Jihad. They also need personnel from their Arab brothers and their brothers from other countries in all spheres: military, scientific, informational and otherwise....And here we would like to point out that those who perform Jihad with their wealth should be certain to only send the funds to those responsible for finances and no other party, as to do otherwise leads to disunity and differences in the ranks of the Mujahideen.[16]

How has the United States been able to stymie the flow of money to al Qaeda? While the Department of Treasury's ability to designate terrorist sponsors and enforcement mechanisms provided through the FATF remain powerful economic tools for stopping the flow of money to al Qaeda, increased interagency law enforcement efforts are also proving effective against terrorist financing—particularly in the nexus of counterterrorism and counternarcotics. Consider the multibillion dollar Afghan heroin trade, which is a critical source of funding for the Taliban. The Taliban receives revenue from taxes and toll fees related to the growth and transportation of poppy in Afghanistan. How does al Qaeda benefit from these revenues? While the link between the heroin industry and al Qaeda is disputed, the drug trade certainly empowers the Taliban, which in turn creates a safe haven for al Qaeda.

Bankrolling the Taliban and al Qaeda

Gretchen Peters notes that in 2009, "Of the State Department's forty-two designated terrorist groups, eighteen have ties to drug trafficking, according to the Drug Enforcement Administration. And thirteen of the smuggling organizations the DEA believes are primarily responsible for the United States' illegal drug supply have links to terrorist groups."[17]

Law enforcement agencies, especially the DEA, can use counternarcotics expertise to disrupt the flow of heroin money to the coffers of terrorists and those that financially support terrorism. In fact, the newly formed Afghan Threat Finance Cell, headed by the Drug Enforcement Administration, takes action against individuals and networks identified as financial supporters of terrorism by the Treasury and other agencies.

For example, the success of combined counternarcotics/ counterterrorism efforts were demonstrated in late 2009, as reported in *Forbes*:

> [T]he Drug Enforcement Administration pulled off a sting operation in Ghana, snatching three men—Oumar Issa, Harouna Touré and Idriss Abdelrahman—and shipping them to New York City to face charges of narco-terror conspiracy and providing material support to al Qaeda.
>
> According to the DEA the three men were connected to al Qaeda's most hardened criminal element, its North African affiliate. Known as al Qaeda in the Islamic Maghreb, the group appears to be involved in the trafficking of Latin American cocaine through Africa to Spain. The indictment accuses the men of agreeing to transport a series of 1,000-kilogram loads of cocaine for $2,000 a kilogram—a portion of which was to be turned over to Islamic Maghreb in return for protection along the route.[18]

The growth of the global international financial system over the past two decades has made law enforcement more complex. For this reason, terrorist organizations had little trouble finding financial contributors prior to 9/11. While financial contributions to terrorist groups have clearly not ceased, economic tools developed by the U.S. Treasury, U.N. Security Council, and other multinational organizations, as well as traditional law enforcement activities, have stymied the financing of terrorism. "There continues to exist a pool of donors who are ready, willing and able to contribute to al Qaeda," says Cohen. "We have at least temporarily disrupted some."[19]

CHAPTER 11

International Law and Courts

Figure 11.1

From the attacks on September 11, 2001, we know that targets are not always states. So should the response to protect national security be the exclusive domain of world leaders? Can they alone direct armies, impose sanctions, negotiate trade agreements, and orchestrate the other policy tools that fall easily into this domain? The fact is individual citizens can assume the role of economic actors imposing policies. Harnessing the energy and innovation of individuals toward a foreign policy can provide powerful tools to the policy maker. Leaders can choose a policy of simply getting out of the way and letting individuals take private actions; in turn, individual citizens acting in their own self-interests can advance the interests of the public.

In a secure and just world, I cannot get away with harming someone. Law-abiding states establish domestic laws, and the community of law-abiding states works together internationally to support this basic concept of law. Under the theory of a natural law—the theory that an objective standard underlies legal theories—certainly someone harmed has the right to redress. If you harm me, then I can use legal means to try to right the wrong. Beyond passing the common-sense test, the concept anchors the laws of nations around the world as well as principles of international law.

Think now about terrorism. Can private citizens seeking justice and redress under international law or internationally accepted legal standards, and for their own self-interests, advance the interests of a state? In addition to sanctions, trade, finance, and aid, what else can a policy do? It can get the government out of the way of private citizens pursuing claims against terrorists. This chapter will address the use of international law and courts as tools of security policy to impose economic costs on those who commit or support acts of terrorism, torture, or hostage-taking—gross violations of international human rights.

Up to this point, we have analyzed leaders as decision makers for states or for terrorist organizations. We have identified incentives as a driving force behind policy making. Good policies are directed toward the incentives of the leaders, as well as those of the population. This chapter is about nonelected decision makers—the individual citizen in possession of legal rights and an avenue to pursue these rights. In the scope of this book thus far we have addressed policies crafted by and directed toward leaders and people. Specifically, think of the following typology of policy, as illustrated in figure 11.2:

1. leaders craft policies aimed at other leaders—focusing on incentives, constraints, and institutions of the leaders;
2. leaders craft policies aimed at other populations—think of the wealth effect and the empowering of subjects to undermine the dictator;
3. leaders craft policies aimed at a domestic population—think of the leader, dictator, or democrat seeking legitimacy in order to stay in office;
4. individual people functioning as decision makers in an effort to influence the incentives of a leader, which is new to this chapter.

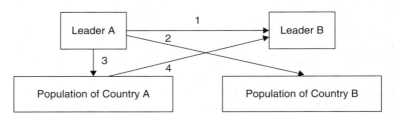

Figure 11.2

Citizens Pursuing Justice

For a victim of international state-sponsored terrorism to pursue justice under international law, the political leaders need to make a decision to get out of the way. As former President George H.W. Bush used to say, let a thousand points of light shine.

Several hurdles must be overcome before this civil-law policy can occur. First, there must be a standard of international law. Second, the law must be adjudicated somewhere. International law exists, but a permanent international court does not. Consequently international legal questions are, for all intents and purposes, decided in the sovereign courts of states. The Alien Tort Claims Act of 1787—one of the first acts passed by the U.S. Congress—allows a non–U.S. citizen to bring a civil suit against another non–U.S. citizen for an act that did not occur in the United States. This was a remarkable law for the time, and it still exists in the United States. A citizen of the PRC, for example, can bring a civil suit against a leader of the PRC in a U.S. court for acts considered gross violations of human rights that never took place in the United States. In 1787, the United States agreed to be a de facto international human rights court. Although this law was not used much over the first 200 years, it receives increasing interest today as the legal basis for victims of state-sponsored terror, torture, and hostage-taking who seek justice.

Sovereign Immunity and the Foreign Sovereign Immunities Act

After law and court, the third hurdle people must overcome is sovereign immunity. This principle of international law has been widely accepted for centuries. The overarching idea is that a citizen of one country cannot sue the leader of another country—the leader has sovereign immunity. This principle operates by mutual agreement; country A agrees not to allow its citizens to sue country B's leader, and country B likewise prevents civil suits against the leader of country A. Although people surely make mistakes—as well as choose to do bad things—the principle of sovereign immunity says that the leaders cannot be held accountable by individual citizens in the courts of another country. In effect, because they often are protected by their own courts, sovereign leaders enjoy civil immunity.

The U.S. Congress passed, and the president signed, the Foreign Sovereign Immunities Act (FSIA) in 1976, codifying the already accepted principle of sovereign immunity in U.S. law. It had been recognized previously and actively debated since the 1950s in the United States. While codifying sovereign immunity, it also spelled out some exceptions.

Foreign states and foreign leaders cannot claim immunity in U.S. courts for primarily commercial transactions. For example, if a foreign state–owned company breeches a contract with a privately owned U.S. company, the U.S. owner can sue the foreign sovereign. Another exception to sovereign immunity under U.S. law included damages occurring in the United States caused by an official or employee of the foreign state while acting in the scope of employment. A foreign state enjoyed immunity under U.S. law for everything else—including acts of state-sponsored terrorism against American citizens.

In the modern era of international terrorism, does state sovereign immunity make sense for state-sponsored acts? Beginning in the early 1990s, the members of the U.S. Congress increasingly began to think about the issue of sovereign immunity and gross violations of international law. Why should a foreign government be afforded immunity for actions violating international legal standards? Initial efforts to amend the U.S. Foreign Sovereign Immunities Act began in the early 1990s but failed to pass year after year.

Opposition existed in the executive branch based in large part on a concern for possible diminution of executive branch powers should individuals be allowed to get involved in international affairs. Without regard to the specific issue of terrorism, the State Department closely guards its prerogative in executing foreign policy. The FSIA protects a good deal of that authority. Some members of Congress, however, sought to change that power—allowing individual citizens to pursue foreign sovereigns in the name of truth, justice, and national security. Allowing private right of action costs less in monetary terms, but leaders give up power reluctantly.

CASE STUDY: BROTHERS TO THE RESCUE AND THE ANTI-TERRORISM AMENDMENT TO THE FSIA

Fidel Castro helped to resolve this issue in 1996. The Brothers to the Rescue organization patrols the Florida Straits, providing humanitarian support to people fleeing Cuba in rafts or other makeshift flotation devices. In March 1996, two Brothers to the Rescue aircraft flying humanitarian missions in international waters off the coast of Florida were shot down by Cuba's air force. By sending Soviet-made MiG fighter jets into the Florida Straits and killing four Americans—three U.S. citizens, Armando Alejandre, Carlos Costa, Mario de la Peña, and one lawful permanent resident, Pablo Morales—the imperative to take action gathered momentum, and no bureaucratic obstruction could prevent passage of the seventh exception to FSIA. President Bill Clinton, addressing the nation, called on the U.S. Congress to pass legislation to allow the victims—the family members of the Brothers to the Rescue pilots—to receive compensation directly from Castro's blocked assets held in the United States.

Congress acted by passing a version of the legislation that had been pending for several years. By April 1996, the president had signed into law the Anti-Terrorism and Effective Death Penalty Act of 1996.[1] This law created, among other things, the terrorism, torture, and hostage-taking exception to sovereign immunity.[2]

The "Anti-Terrorism Amendment," as it is commonly called, reflected a negotiation between the families of terrorism victims, Congressional leaders, and the State Department. The ability to sue foreign sovereigns in U.S. courts for the purposes of this amendment is limited in three ways. First, it is a remedy available only to U.S. citizens, though a 2008 decision by the D.C. Circuit Court broadened the scope of who can make a claim. Specifically, the court ruled in *La Réunion Aérienne v. Socialist People's Libyan Arab Jamahiriya* that the terrorism exception provides jurisdiction not only for victims but also for third-party claimants, such as an insurer suing to recover insurance payments.

Second, the terrorism exception is limited to acts of terror, torture, and hostage-taking, and only to acts taking place outside the United States. Finally, and this reflects the grand compromise with the secretary of state, only designated terrorist states lose sovereign immunity for acts of terrorism. With the conclusion of this negotiation supported by the president in 1996, the policy seemed locked in place.

The secretary of state possesses the authority, delegated by the president, to designate a state as a terrorist state. At the time of enactment of this new exception to sovereign immunity, seven states had the dubious distinction of membership on the roster: Iraq, Iran, Syria, Libya, Sudan, North Korea, and Cuba. While the secretary of state lost some authority, it was only limited to these seven states and the secretary retained the authority to add and remove states from this list. Indeed, the secretary of state exercised this authority recently. At the time of this book's publishing, there are only four terrorist-designated states, as Iraq, Libya, and North Korea were removed by the Department of State under the Bush administration in 2004, 2006, and 2008, respectively. The removal of these states from the terrorist list had little to do with the FSIA exception.

In exchange for these limits (only U.S. citizens, only victims of *international* terror, torture, or hostage-taking, and only by a secretary of state–designated state-sponsor of terror), State Department leaders supported the law that Congress was inclined to pass. It was not until President Clinton responded to the Brothers to the Rescue incident and asked Congress to pass a law that Congressional advocates of victims' rights were able to overcome the State Department's objections.

Shortly after enactment of this FSIA amendment, the families of three of the four pilots killed by the Cuban Air Force brought a civil suit in U.S. federal court against Fidel Castro, the government of Cuba, and the Cuban Air Force. *Alejandre vs. the Republic of Cuba* proceeded as follows. Castro personally ordered the shoot-down of the aircraft, according to evidence produced in the trial. At the time of the incident, Cuba had been under embargo by the United States under the Trading with the Enemy Act since 1963. During those decades, the United States also held assets of the government of Cuba; the United States blocked or froze accounts in the United States from the time of implementation of the policy, shortly after the Cuban revolution in which Castro took power. These Cuban assets, denominated in U.S. dollars, sat in whatever U.S. bank they may have been in at the time of the blocking order.

Blocking authority, not delineated in the Constitution and therefore residing with the legislative branch, is delegated to the president under existing U.S. laws. U.S. presidents have blocked assets using the Trading with the Enemy Act, which dates back to 1917, as well as the International Economic Emergency Powers Act (IEEPA) enacted in 1977. Cuba's assets are blocked under TWEA authority.

Castro ordered the Cuban Air Force to kill these Americans, and the president wanted to respond. In a White House meeting with senior advisors, he asked for his policy options. The responses ranged from military action to taking no action. The president decided that he wanted the families to receive compensation from Cuba's blocked assets. Shortly afterward he publicly called on the Congress to pass a law allowing for this. In addition, he made an *ex gratia* payment to the families from Cuba's accounts.

An *ex gratia* payment connotes no guilt or innocence; he could not do more without additional legal authority, according to his advisors. So he moved forward with an immediate symbolic payment to the families from Castro's accounts. By the time these payments were made, he had signed into law the Anti-Terrorism Act with its amendment to the FSIA allowing the families to sue Castro and Cuba in U.S. courts. The president assured the families that the *ex gratia* payment did not satisfy the debt Castro owed to them, and officials of the U.S. government encouraged the families to exercise the authority provided to individual U.S. citizens under the new law.

The president has delegated his authority to block assets to various agencies. The State Department exercises policy authority over the money, but the Treasury Department, specifically the Office of Foreign Assets Control (OFAC), actually blocks the funds. According to OFAC reports at the time, the United States was blocking approximately $180 million of Cuban assets.

After a long trial in which the plaintiffs were required to put on an extensive case regarding both liability and damages (despite the fact that the Cuban government defaulted by initially showing up to defend itself, and then after a while stopping its defense at the trial), a federal judge entered judgment against Castro and his government: compensatory damages for the lives of the three U.S. citizens at $50 million. Then, during the enforcement phase, the court imposed a sanction of $37 million against the Cuban agencies that appeared and defaulted. The sanction arose from the disruptive behavior of the Cuban government's attorneys during the trial: appearing, making statements, and then disappearing when the validity of those statements was called into question.

Under the FSIA, a judge cannot enter a simple default judgment when the defendant does not appear or leaves the trial early. Because of the international legal standards implicit in the FSIA, the plaintiff must prove a *prima facie* case. In effect, the judge must sit in the place of the defendant when the defendant does not show. Unlike an auto accident, for example, where if the defendant does not appear the judge can simply make an award to the plaintiff, under the FSIA, victims must prove to the court that rules of evidence, procedure, and standards of international law are met in order to reach a conclusion of culpability. Judges in the sovereign courts of states decide international law.

The families received their legal judgments from the court, and in 1997 came to Washington, D.C., calling on the Treasury Department's OFAC. They sought access to Castro's assets that the president had talked about in the previous year, just after the incident. They came to

OFAC in search of a U.S. Treasury Department license to satisfy their judgment from Cuba's $180 million in blocked accounts.

OFAC and the State Department opposed satisfaction of this judgment, and Congressional leaders again took up the issue. Two years later, the families successfully received satisfaction of the judgments, receiving almost $100 million from Castro for the murder of their family members.

What did Castro do? Along with rhetorical attacks, he tried to play U.S. politics to his benefit. Since several large multinational telecommunications companies provided telephone service between the United States and Cuba, Castro threatened to cut off the service. The telecommunications companies then contacted congressional advocates to complain about the threatened loss of revenue. Castro knew that if politicians did not listen to him, they might listen to major U.S. and international corporations.

It is interesting to note that since the United States did not have a trading relationship with Cuba, Castro's leverage over the United States was greatly limited. Had more U.S. businesses been dependent on Cuba for significant revenues, Castro might have been able to threaten more potent economic repercussions to U.S. businesses and citizens. More U.S. trade with Cuba would have made the dictator more powerful in this aspect.

Castro's threats to cut off the phone lines, however, did not derail the payment from his accounts. After the families received the payments, the lines were indeed shut down. Given the sophistication of the international telecommunications network, however, his actions had no real impact. It turns out that phone service from Miami to Cuba continued uninterrupted; the calls were automatically routed via Mexico. Castro's threat had no impact on the United States. Most significantly, he paid $100 million for his decision to shoot down the unarmed planes.

The precedent had been set. The brothers' families successfully met the legal standard to prove complicity by the Cuban government in the murders of Armando Alejandre, Jr., Carlos Costa, Mario de la Peña, and Pablo Morales.[3] They received judgments in U.S. federal courts and received payment on those judgments.

Case Study: Alisa Flatow and the Flatow Amendment to the FSIA

The second suit under the Anti-Terrorism Amendment was brought by Steven Flatow, who sought to hold the government of Iran accountable under the new law. His daughter, 20-year-old Alisa Flatow, was killed in 1995 by Iranian-backed terrorists in Israel. She was a Brandeis University student studying in Israel. She was on a bus headed to the beach when a suicide bomber blew up the bus.

In his pursuit for justice for victims of state-sponsored terrorism, Steven Flatow lobbied Congress to pass legislation that would allow punitive damages, which were previously unavailable under the statutory scheme of the FSIA. Five months after the passage of the terrorism exception to the FSIA, Congress passed an additional amendment, often called the "Flatow Amendment," that provides punitive damages.

To understand the theory of this policy, an overview of damage awards is helpful. Judges assign compensatory damage amounts on a daily basis. Placing a value on the life of a person is something that nobody should take lightly; it is something that politicians and bureaucrats do not do. Judges have this responsibility. When it comes to setting a damage award, therefore, the actuarial calculation of the value of a life can be best determined in a courtroom.

Punitive damages regarding violations of law also are set by judges. When it comes to punishing foreign sovereigns, however, some argue that judges should not be empowered to do so. In *Flatow vs. Islamic Republic of Iran*, for example, the judge awarded $22.5 million compensatory judgment and $225 million punitive damages against the government of Iran. The Flatow family collected the compensatory amount only. Specifically, the $400 million held in Iran's subaccount of the U.S. Foreign Military Sales (FMS) trust fund was used to secure a $20 million compensatory damage award to the Flatow family. Compensatory damages, as the name indicates, compensate the family for the loss. Money can never replace a daughter, but the judge has the job of assigning a value to her life anyway. The judge takes several factors into consideration such as the deceased's age, level of education, marriage and children if any, and life expectancy, among other things.

Nowhere in these cases is a payment to a victim guaranteed. A civil judgment, however, accomplishes a few things. The successful plaintiff receives a public acknowledgment of the loss and assignment of blame on the perpetrator, a judgment and assignment of value from a U.S. federal judge, and an opportunity to pursue satisfaction of that judgment. The truth becomes public and certified, and a right to pursue the awarded amount is created. Notice, however, that the guarantee of collection is not assured.[4]

CASE STUDY: LIBYA AND AN
INCENTIVE FOR REFORM

The families of victims of the 1988 Pan Am flight 103 international terrorist incident wanted to hold Libya and Muammar al Qadhafi accountable for killing their family and kin. Observing the actions toward Cuban and Iranian money, Qadhafi was given reason to believe Libya's approximate $1 billion blocked in the United States was in jeopardy. Following the enactment and actual implementation of the amendments to the FSIA in the late-1990s, Qadhafi's behavior changed. Immediately following the incident, Qadhafi denied Libyan involvement. But in 1999, Qadhafi played a role in securing the capture of two Libyans suspected of the bombing, and handed them to UN authorities for prosecution. Nobody can say for sure what caused this change, or the relative value of the FSIA amendments compared to all the other policies directed at him, though it certainly seems reasonable that the FSIA policy gave him additional incentives to reform. In return, Libya was removed from the list of State Sponsors of Terrorism in 2006. Two years later the executive branch, in an effort to renew economic ties with Libya, extinguished all pending terrorism-related claims against the country. This was preceded by Libya taking steps to resolve outstanding judgments awarded to victims of Libyan terrorist attacks. Libya's willingness, however, stemmed from a $6 billion judgment against it by a Washington, D.C. federal district court in *Pugh v. Socialist People's Libyan Arab Jamahiriya*. We don't know his thoughts, but see his preferences in the context of constraints and goals. The United States took part in a series of policy exchanges advancing national security.

LIMITATIONS OF THE FSIA
TERRORISM EXCEPTION

American citizens held hostage by Saddam Hussein as human shields during the Gulf War of 1990–91 sought compensation from $2 billion of Saddam Hussein's money that was held in blocked accounts in the United States. Shortly after invading Kuwait in 1990, Hussein rounded up Americans in Iraq and Kuwait and held them hostage in Iraq. Many were held hostage at key strategic sites in and around Iraq, such as radar sites and power plants. Because the American hostages were there, U.S. military aircraft were unable to bomb the facilities containing them—thus the name "human shield."

In *Acree v. Republic of Iraq*, seventeen American prisoners of war (POWs) during the first Gulf War received a judgment of $959 million in July 2003. Meanwhile, as the United States led the invasion of Iraq in March 2003, President Bush argued that under a provision of the Emergency Wartime Supplemental Appropriations Act, the remaining assets could be used for assisting Iraqis during the war. Presidential Determination 2003–23 made Iraq's blocked assets unavailable to pay subsequently awarded judgments under the FSIA. The POWs challenged whether the president had the legal authority to effectively restore a terrorist state's sovereign immunity and make its assets unavailable to victims of terrorism who had obtained judgments against Iraq. In June 2009, the Supreme Court held that a presidential waiver of the applicability of the FSIA terrorism exception acts prospectively as well as retrospectively to all suits involving the country, effectively reinstating Iraq's sovereign immunity and denying POWs the ability to seek compensation from the frozen Iraqi assets. Ultimately, however, about $100 million was paid out of Iraq's accounts by the president to satisfy the earlier FSIA judgments.

This case illustrates the often competing interests at the intersection of economics and national security. On the one hand, the U.S. government created an economic instrument to change the behavior of leaders in states that sponsor terrorism and provide monetary relief for victims of terrorism. On the other hand, these useful economic instruments can work contrary to other diplomatic or military stability goals. Other limitations of this policy are as obvious as the simple clarity of the benefits. A terrorist doing a cost-benefit analysis may choose to kill despite the price. There may not be enough money at stake in the world for a state sponsor of terrorism to alter the leader's behavior. Perhaps the support for international terrorist groups provides domestic legitimacy to the regime; it may factor into a dictator's oppression and loyalty equations. At a minimum, however, one conclusion from this policy seems clear: the FSIA exemption passes the common-sense test and increases the international cost of terror, torture, and hostage-taking of American citizens. When cost goes up, quantity demanded decreases; the U.S. policy aligns incentives consistent with security.

Given the limitations highlighted in this discussion, however, some have criticized the efficacy of this approach to providing relief for victims of terrorism. In fact, Judge Royce Lamberth of the U.S. District Court for the District of Columbia wrote a 191-page opinion in 2009 that concluded that the FSIA exception, in general, has not provided relief for most victims and could potentially interfere with broader national security goals:

> [T]he reforms implemented as part of § 1083 of the 2008 NDAA last year—which are just now being implemented in individual cases here today—will not, in this Court's humble opinion, lend much support to the cause of these victims or their long march toward justice. These most recent reforms, like others before them, are premised on the same failed private-litigation model that has, in effect, doomed these actions from the start. These terrorism cases...are likely to face the same obstacles discussed in this opinion, such as...limited assets to satisfy judgments, conflicting laws and regulations, and the President's foreign policy prerogative, among others.
>
> These are intractable problems that are more often political, rather than jurisprudential, and so it seems that the new § 1605A, although well intentioned, is destined to prolong and perhaps aggravate the ways in which the same intractable issues have continuously foiled plaintiffs in these cases time and again. Today, more than a decade after these suits began—and with the majority of Iran's blocked assets depleted to pay for earlier judgments—the hope for justice under the terrorism exception is growing increasingly distant and unobtainable.[5]

Since 1996, however, U.S. courts have awarded more than $19 billion under the FSIA terrorism exception to American victims of state-sponsored terror, torture, and hostage-taking. The judgments in themselves serve as a symbolic public acknowledgment of the loss and assignment of blame on the perpetrator. Moreover, they give the victims of state-sponsored terror, torture, and hostage-taking a right to pursue the awarded amount.

Conclusion

What motivates a leader to act? When a policy maker can answer that question she can design an effective policy. Although a policy maker will never have perfect information about the incentives of another leader, one can enhance the probability of a new policy's success by using knowledge of human nature.

We began our study of economic analysis by considering moral philosophy and fundamental human nature. Some human traits apply to people throughout the world and throughout history, and provide a constant variable for modeling and a framework for evaluating and crafting security policies. Second, this theory—based upon observations of human interaction—allowed us to pursue empirical work and case studies to explore the power of the theory. We looked at economic theories and economic tools, all related to security.

Several hundred years of study of how people make decisions has evolved based upon these theories and observations, giving us economic science as it exists today. The reader, armed with these analytical tools, can better understand and predict human behavior.

Building on this knowledge, we studied specific economic instruments. Opening one's market to a foreign leader consistent with the principles of free trade can be a tool to influence a leader's behavior. Free trade can build powerful constituencies on each side of the trading relationship, and these constituencies—manufacturers, exporters, consumers—in turn can impact their leaders' behavior. In this way, free trade can advance our own national security agenda. Conversely, restricting trade with another country through instruments such as sanctions, export controls, and import restrictions can be powerful levers to force a leader to act, especially when the tools are targeted for specific behavioral purposes.

As the global economy struggles to emerge from the Great Recession that began in 2008, old issues have taken on greater importance and opportunities to employ a variety of new instruments have emerged. The level of debt issued by sovereigns and the fact that much of that debt is held by foreign leaders is a dominant policy debate in many world capitals. Choices of monetary policies, exchange rate regimes, and policies impacting access to international financial institutions have become more important as some countries teeter on the edge of insolvency while others continue to grow. Any serious national security debate now encompasses the limits of foreign investment by private companies as well as sovereign wealth funds. As the global financial landscape has changed, so have the economic instruments of advancing a country's interests.

The case studies included in each chapter bring the use of these instruments to life. The reader can judge whether the policies highlighted in the case studies were effective, and evaluate the causes of success or failure using the economic principles outlined in the book. Could one have predicted the results we discussed? Were the policies employed doomed to fail because economic rules were violated?

The authors have had the privilege of working with some of the leading policy makers of the last two decades. During that time, the world has remained dangerous while becoming more complex. We have gone from the Cold War state-on-state conflict to one with innumerable substate actors capable of incredible violence for political ends. Terrorists have struck mighty blows and continue to seek the weapons to create even more widespread harm. Insurgencies continue to stifle our security goals in regions around the world. As analysis evolves from state-level to group-level to individual-level, economic analysis provides powerful insights. Much work remains, but by understanding the man we can indeed better understand the world.

Appendix

In order to look for internal policy cues, we surveyed the *Miami Herald*'s Spanish language newspaper, *El Nuevo Herald*, which provides a close watch on the events taking place inside Cuba for the exile community in South Florida. Following are selected headlines that may explain the positive economic performance in Cuba.

1. August 1994 to October 1994

August 24, 1994 *Zozobra Bonanza De Negocios Con Cuba* (Bonanza of Business with Cuba Failing)

August 30, 1994 *Cuba Suaviza Las Restricciones Para Viajar* (Cuba Eases Travel Restrictions)

September 9, 1994 *Cuba Ha Dado 'Enormes Muestras De Flexibilidad', Segun Alarcon* (Cuba Has Given "Enormous Demonstrations of Flexibility," According to Alarcon)

September 18, 1994 *Cuba Permite El Libre Mercado Agropecuario* (Cuba Permits Agriculture and Fishing Free Market)

September 22, 1994 *Mercado Libre Agricola Regresa A Cuba En Medio De Crisis Total* (Agricultural Free Market Returns to Cuba in Middle of Total Crisis)

October 4, 1994 *Cuba Desea Dirimir Diferencias Con Eu* (Cuba Would Like to Settle Differences with U.S.)

October 6, 1994 *Aprueban Servicio Telefonico Directo Entre Cuba Y Eu* (Direct Telephone Service between Cuba and U.S. Approved)

2. Spring 1995 to Summer 1995

April 11, 1995 *Alarcon: Es 'Idiota' Quien Crea Que Cuba Va Al Capitalismo* (Alarcon: Anyone Who Believes That Cuba Is Moving toward Capitalism Is an "Idiot")

May 2, 1995 *Asedio A Turistas En Cuba* (Tourists Blockaded in Cuba)

May 19, 1995 *Arrestados 14 En Cuba En Batida A Disidentes* (14 Arrested in Cuba in Raid on Dissidents)

May 25, 1995 *Cuba Cobrara 100% De Impuestos A Viajeros* (Cuba Will Charge 100% Tax on Travelers)

June 2, 1995 *Cuba Indica Que Ampliara Permisos Para Empleos Privados* (Cuba Indicates that Permits for Private Employment Will Be Increased)

June 19, 1995 *No Hay Voluntad De Cambio En Cuba, Dice Oscar Arias* (There Is No Will for Change in Cuba, Says Oscar Arias)

June 19, 1995 *Zafra De Cuba Es La Mas Baja En 50 Anos, Segun Cifra Oficial* (Sugar Harvest Is Lowest in over 50 Years, According to Official Statistics)

July 4, 1995 *Cuba Multa A Trabajadores Por Cuenta Propia* (Cuba Fines Self-Employed Workers)

July 8, 1995 *Cuba Prepara Elecciones Con Alabanzas Al Unico Partido* (Cuba Prepares Elections with Praise for Sole Party)

3. SUMMER 1995 TO FALL 1995

August 28, 1995 *Economia De Cuba Urge Alzar La Produccion Del Azucar, Dice Ministro* (Cuban Economy Urges Raising Sugar Production, Says Minister)

September 5, 1995 *Castro Dice Que Los Exiliados Deberian Poder Invertir En Cuba* (Castro Says Exiles Should Be Able to Invest in Cuba)

September 6, 1995 *Cuba Abre La Puerta Financiera Al Exilio* (Cuba Opens the Financial Door to Exiles)

September 10, 1995 *Cuba Permitira Cuentas En Divisas A Ciudadanos De La Isla Y De Fuera* (Cuba Will Permit Exchange Accounts for Citizens in the Island and Outside)

September 13, 1995 *Pacto Amplia El Comercio Con Cuba* (Pact Increases Commerce with Cuba)

September 18, 1995 *Capitalistas Alteran Faz De La Cuba Socialista* (Capitalists Alter Face of Socialist Cuba)

September 24, 1995 *Inversionistas Le Apuestan A Cambios En Cuba* (Investors Bet on Changes in Cuba)

October 17, 1995 *Cuba Y Rusia Firman Acuerdos Comerciales* (Cuba and Russia Sign Commercial Accords)

November 21, 1995 *Cuba Pacta Creditos Para Producir Alimentos* (Cuba Agrees on Credits to Produce Food)

November 23, 1995 *Plan Telefonico Abriria La Via Para Invertir En Cuba* (Telephone Plan Would Open Path for Investment in Cuba)

4. SPRING 1998

March 20, 1998 *Eu Suaviza Postura Con Cuba Permitiren Vuelos Directos Y Remesas* (U.S. Softens Stance on Cuba, Will Allow Direct Flights and Remittances)

April 5, 1998 *Lage Asegura Cuba Continuare Siendo Un País Socialista* (Lage Assures Cuba Will Continue Being Socialist Country)

April 11, 1998 *Cuba No Paga Deuda Dice El Gobierno Hóngaro* (Cuba Doesn't Pay Debt Says Hungarian Government)

April 18, 1998 *Opositores Honran En Cuba A Exiliados Caódos* (Dissidents in Cuba Honor Exiles from Shootdown)

May 13, 1998 *Alarcón: Cuba No Daró Nada A Cambio De Suspensión De Embargo* (Alarcon: Cuba Will Not Give Anything in Return for Suspension of Embargo)

5. Winter 1998 (down market)

November 24, 1998 *Cuba Espera Aumentar Producción De Azúcar* (Cuba Expects to Increase Sugar Production)

December 3, 1998 *Cuba Pide Apoyo Para Economías Díbiles* (Cuba Asks for Support for Weak Economies)

6. Fall 2000

October 17, 2000 *Cuba Resucita El Estribillo De La Agresión De Eu* (Cuba Resuscitates Chorus of U.S. Aggression)

October 20, 2000 *Denuncian Nueva Oleada De Represión En Cuba* (New Wave of Repression in Cuba Denounced)

October 24, 2000 *Amenaza Cuba Con Cortar Las Llamadas* (Cuba Threatens to Cut Calls)

November 3, 2000 *Represent Los Homenajes A Biscet En Cuba* (Tribute to Biscet in Cuba Repressed)

November 4, 2000 *Se Reúnen Decenas De Opositores En Cuba Y Piden Libertad Para Biscet* (Dozens of Dissidents Get Together in Cuba and Ask for Freedom for Biscet)

November 7, 2000 Cuba Pierde Millones En El Sector Hotelero (Cuba Loses Millions in Hotel Sector)

November 16, 2000 *Cuba A La Espera De Un 'Socialismo Más' Eficiente' Para Salir De La Crisis* (Cuba Hoping for a "More Efficient Socialism" to Get Out of Crisis)

Notes

1 States Don't Make Decisions; People Do

1. Adam Smith and R. H. Campbell, *An Inquiry into the Nature and Causes of the Wealth of Nations.* Oxford: Clarendon Press, 1976: IV, VII, III; IV, IX.
2. Joseph Cropsey, *Polity and Economy: An Interpretation of the Principles of Adam Smith.* The Hague: M. Nijhoff, 1957.
3. Adam Smith, *The Theory of Moral Sentiments.* Oxford; New York: Clarendon Press; Oxford University Press, 1976: Section 3, Chapter 3, 10.
4. Ibid., Section 3, Introduction.
5. Cropsey, *Polity and Economy.*
6. Smith, *The Theory of Moral Sentiments*: Section 1, Chapter 1.
7. Ibid. For instance, see Section 3, Chapter 2, 115; and Section 3, 3, 125.
8. Ibid., Section 2, Chapter 2.
9. In particular, Daniel Kahneman, "Maps of Bounded Rationality: Psychology for Behavioral Economics." *American Economic Review* 93, no. 5 (2003): 1449–75; and Daniel Kahneman, Barbara L. Fredrickson, Charles A. Schreiber, and Donald A. Redelmeier. "When More Pain Is Preferred to Less: Adding a Better End." *Psychological Science* 4, no. 6 (1993), 401–5.
10. Douglass C. North, "Economic Performance through Time." *American Economic Review* 84, no. 3 (1994), 359–68. This is from his lecture delivered December 9, 1993, when receiving the Nobel Memorial Prize in Economic Science.
11. Ibid.
12. Ibid.
13. Ibid.
14. Ibid.
15. Vernon L. Smith, "Governing the Commons." *Forbes* (October 12, 2009): http://www.forbes.com/2009/10/12/elinor-ostrom-commons-nobel-economics-opinions-contributors-vernon-l-smith.html.

2 The Economics of Autocracies

1. See http://www.jstor.org for more information on this database. For this study, the database was searched in 2010.

2. Gordon Tullock, *Autocracy*. Dordrecht; Boston: Kluwer Academic Publishers, 1987.
3. Ronald Wintrobe, *The Political Economy of Dictatorship*. Cambridge; New York: Cambridge University Press, 1998.
4. Mancur Olson, "Dictatorship, Democracy, and Development." *The American Political Science Review* 87, no. 3 (1993), 567–76.
5. In particular, see Mancur Olson, *The Logic of Collective Action; Public Goods and the Theory of Groups*. Cambridge, MA: Harvard University Press, 1965.
6. Olson, "Dictatorship, Democracy, and Development," 568.
7. If an autocrat received one-third of any increase in the income of his domain in increased tax collections, he would then get one-third of the benefits of the public goods he provided. He would then have an incentive to provide public goods up to the point where the national income rose by the reciprocal of one-third, or three, from his last unit of public good expenditure. Olson, "Dictatorship, Democracy, and Development," 569.
8. Ibid.
9. Hannah Arendt, *The Origins of Totalitarianism*. New York: Harcourt, Brace, 1951.
10. Carl J. Friedrich and Zbigniew Brzezinski. *Totalitarian Dictatorship and Autocracy*. 2nd ed. rev. by Carl J. Friedrich. Cambridge, MA: Harvard University Press, 1965.
11. Jeane J. Kirkpatrick, *Dictatorships and Double Standards: A Critique of U.S. Policy*. Washington, DC: Ethics and Public Policy Center, Georgetown University, 1979.
12. Wintrobe, *The Political Economy of Dictatorship*.
13. See Wintrobe's discussion of the dictator's dilemma. See also James E. Rauch, "Leadership Selection, Internal Promotion, and Bureaucratic Corruption in Less Developed Polities." *The Canadian Journal of Economics / Revue canadienne d'Economique* 34, no. 1 (2001), 240–58.
14. The significant distinction between this model and Olson's is the presence of the cost associated with security in this model, which represents a concave function and, therefore, after some given level of Y begins to diminish net income.

3 Principles for Policy Makers

1. Adam Smith and R. H. Campbell. *An Inquiry into the Nature and Causes of the Wealth of Nations*. Oxford: Clarendon Press, 1976; IV, VII and III.
2. Ibid., II,i,1.
3. Ibid., I,i,3.
4. Ibid., I,ii,2.
5. Ibid., I,ii,2.

6. We are indebted to Jim Gwartney for the inspiration for this section. See James D. Gwartney, Richard L. Stroup, Russell S. Sobel, and David Macpherson. *Economics: Private and Public Choice*. Australia; Mason, Ohio: Thomson South-Western, 2003.

7. W. Enders and T. Sandler. *The Political Economy of Terrorism*. Cambridge: Cambridge University Press, 2006.

8. George A. Akerlof, co-winner of the Nobel Prize in Economic Sciences in 2001, developed theories regarding asymmetric information and used the used car market as an example. His work is often referred to as "Akerlof's lemons" problem where good cars eventually disappear from used car lots. A salesman wants to sell a used car for the highest price, and knows the real value of the car. The prospective purchaser of a used car knows very little about the used car. There exists an information asymmetry: buyers and sellers using different information. This asymmetry drives down the quality of used cars, leading to the sale of "lemons." The salesman, seeking to maximize the sale price, will take advantage of the information advantage, and overstate the car's actual value. The buyer, unaware of the real value of the car but aware of the salesman's incentives, will assume the salesman overstates the value. The information asymmetry leads the salesman to overprice and the purchaser to underbid. Over time, if unable to further increase the sales price of the car, the salesman will lead the customer to a lower quality car while seeking to keep the price constant. For example, if I as a salesman think I can get $10,000 from you for a used car, I may overstate the qualities of an $8,000 car as opposed to a $9,000 car. Over time, the purchaser will expect this lowering of quality, and further depress his offer price. In order to make a profit, the salesman will bring continually lower quality cars to the original price point; customers will begin to assume this is happening, further lowering the price they are willing to pay. Eventually, this drives the salesman to bring the lowest value cars to the market. Akerlof's work has applications far beyond the lemon lot in its interpretations of market behavior when principals have different information about the commodity being traded. The more informed the buyer and seller and the more symmetrical their information, the more efficient the market. Efficient markets assume perfect information. Information is a good of value in decision making. See George Akerlof, "Behavioral Macroeconomics and Macroeconomic Behavior." Prize Lecture (December 8, 2001).

4 Castro's Cuba and U.S. Sanctions

1. Jorge Pérez-López, "Foreign Direct Investment in the Cuban Economy: A Critical Look." Paper prepared for presentation at the First International Meeting of the Latin American and Caribbean Association, Mexico City (October 17–19, 1996).

2. The CDRs were formed on September 28, 1960, inaugurated by Castro in a speech given at the Plaza of the Revolution.

3. Kanan Makiya, *Republic of Fear: The Inside Story of Saddam's Iraq*. New York: Pantheon Books, 1989.
4. Decree Law 50.
5. Pérez-López, "Foreign Direct Investment."
6. Stated in an interview to a reporter with *The Chicago Tribune*. Laurie Goering, "The Revolution Will Live Beyond Me—Durable Leader Shows Wit, Grasp of Details." *The Chicago Tribune* (March 18, 2001), 1.
7. Later in this study, the infinite time horizon assumption will be relaxed to assess the implications for the model.
8. For instance, see Horowitz, Irving Louis, and Jaime Suchlicki. *Cuban Communism*. 10th ed. New Brunswick: Transaction, 2003.
9. From Cuba in Transition: Papers and Proceedings of the Annual Meeting of the Association for the Study of the Cuban Economy (ASCE), see Roger R Betancourt, "Cuba's Economic 'Reforms': Waiting for Fidel on the Eve of the Twenty-First Century," 1996; Hernández-Catá Ernesto, "The Fall and Recovery of the Cuban Economy in the 1990s: Mirage or Reality," 2000; Gary H. Maybarduk, "The State of the Cuban Economy 1998–1999," 1999; Carmelo Mesa-Lago, "The Cuban Economy in 1997–1998: Performance and Policies," 1998; and Jorge Pérez-López, "The Cuban Economic Crisis of the 1990s and the External Sector," 1998. See also Jaime Suchlicki, *Cuba: From Columbus to Castro and Beyond*. Washington, DC: Brassey's, 1997.
10. Subsidies averaged $4.3 billion per year from 1986–90, or 15 percent of Cuba's GDP at official exchange rates. This number would be much higher if converted at market exchange rates.
11. Pérez-López, "Foreign Direct Investment."
12. Ibid.
13. Ibid.
14. Hernández-Catá "The Fall and Recovery."
15. Ibid.
16. Stephen J. Kimmerling, "A Survey of Significant Legal Changes During Cuba's Special Period: Setting Parameters for Change." Cuba in Transition, Papers and Proceedings of the Tenth Annual Meeting of the Association for the Study of the Cuban Economy (ASCE). Miami, FL: Florida International University, 2000.
17. Paraphrased from Thomas T. Vogel, Jr. "Socialists Flirt with Profits." *The Wall Street Journal* (August 5, 1995), as quoted in Pérez-López, "Foreign Direct Investment in the Cuban Economy: A Critical Look": "And this is Cuba, land of vast possibilities and murky probabilities. Money managers who visited Cuba for three days earlier this summer with LatInvest Securities Ltd., a London-based investment bank, found themselves in an economic twilight zone. They discovered a country that wants capitalists, but not capitalism."
18. Kimmerling, "A Survey of Significant Legal Changes," 455.

19. The significance of this law was captured in the September 6, 1995, *San Francisco Chronicle*: "[It] allow[s] creation of free-trade zones.... [It] opens the way for foreigners to wholly own business and property and allows foreign investment in every sector of the economy except the 'strategic' areas of education, health and national defense. It also guarantees that foreign properties cannot be expropriated without compensation and speeds the process of approving proposed investments."
20. Hernández-Catá. "The Fall and Recovery."
21. Matías F. Travieso-Díaz and Alejandro Ferraté. "Recommended Features of a Foreign Investment Code for Cuba's Free-Market Transition." Cuba in Transition, Papers and Proceedings of the Fifth Annual Meeting of the Association for the Study of the Cuban Economy (ASCE). Miami, FL: Florida International University, 1995, 9.
22. Pérez-López, "Foreign Direct Investment."
23. Specifically 1994 to 2000.
24. B. Dan Wood, "Weak Theories and Parameter Instability: Using Flexible Least Squares to Take Time Varying Relationships Seriously." *American Journal of Political Science* 44, no. 3 (2000), 603–18.
25. This criterion comes from the literature on recursive regression, see William H. Greene, *Econometric Analysis*. Upper Saddle River, NJ: Prentice Hall, 2003, and the E Views software package and users guide.
26. Kimmerling, "A Survey of Significant Legal Changes."
27. Suchlicki, *Cuba: From Columbus to Castro and Beyond.*
28. We searched *The Asian Wall Street Journal, Atlanta Journal and Constitution, The Baltimore Sun, The Boston Globe, The Boston Herald, The Buffalo News, The Chicago Sun-Times, Christian Science Monitor, The Columbus Dispatch, The Daily News* (New York), *Daily Yomiuri* (Tokyo), *The Daily/Sunday Telegraph* (London), *The Denver Post, The Dominion* (Wellington), *The Evening Post* (Wellington), *The Financial Times* (London), *Gazeta Mercantil Online Gazette* (Montreal), *The Guardian* (London), *The Herald* (Glasgow), *The Houston Chronicle, The Independent* and *Independent on Sunday* (London), *The Irish Times, The Jerusalem Post, The Journal of Commerce, Kansas City Star, The Los Angeles Times, Miami Herald, New Straits Times* (Malaysia), *New York Times, The Observer, The Omaha World Herald, Ottawa Citizen, Plain Dealer, The San Diego Union-Tribune, San Francisco Chronicle, The Scotsman* & *Scotland on Sunday, The Seattle Times, The South China Morning Post, Southland Times* (New Zealand), *The St. Louis Post-Dispatch, St. Petersburg Times, Star Tribune* (Minneapolis MN), *Straits Times* (Singapore), *The Tampa Tribune, The Times* and *Sunday Times* (London), *The Times-Picayune, The Toronto Star, The Toronto Sun, USA Today, The Wall Street Journal,* and *The Washington Post.*
29. We know that some of the most democratic and egalitarian constitutions in the world are and were those of the People's Republic of China and

the Soviet Union. The implementation of these documents, however, was far from rigorous and the world understood the governments based upon their deeds.

30. D. Ignatius, "Putting the Squeeze on Iran." *The Washington Post* (March 7, 2010), A17.

31. These include: *Economic Sanctions Reconsidered*, 2nd Edition by Gary Clyde Hufbauer, Jeffrey J. Schott, and Kimberly Ann Elliott, December 1990; *Economic Sanctions Reconsidered*, 3rd edition by Kimberly Ann Elliott, Jeffrey J. Schott, Gary Clyde Hufbauer, and Barbara Oegg, June 2009; and "A Short Survey of Economic Sanctions: Case Study on Economic Sanctions," Columbia International Affairs Online, by Gary Hufbauer and Barbara Oegg, June 2001.

32. Gary Hufbauer and Barbara Oegg. "A Short Survey of Economic Sanctions." Columbia International Affairs Online (June 2001).

33. One of the authors, Gary M Shiffman, reviewed the earlier version of what was eventually published as Kimberly Ann Elliott, "Trends in Economic Sanctions Policy: Challenges to Conventional Wisdom" in Peter Wallensteen and Carina Staibano. *International Sanctions: Between Words and Wars in the Global System.* London; New York: Frank Cass, 2005.

34. Jesse Helms, "What Sanctions Epidemic?" *Foreign Affairs* 78, no. 1 (1999), 2–8.

5   DEMOCRACIES AND THE POLITICS OF TRADE

1. Michael D Bordo, Barry Eichengreen, and Douglas Irwin. "Is Globalization Today Really Different than Globalization a Hundred Years Ago?" in *Brookings Trade Forum 1999*, ed. Susan M. Collins and Robert Z. Lawrence. Washington, D.C.: Brookings Institution Press, 1999, 1–72.

2. Alexander Hamilton, James Madison, John Jay, and Michael A. Genovese. *The Federalist Papers.* New York: Palgrave Macmillan, 2010, Federalist No. 10.

3. According to calculations by the Center for Responsive Politics based on data from the Senate Office of Public Records, as of April 25, 2010, there are 10,578 unique, registered lobbyists who have actively lobbied.

4. Robert A. Manning, "Reality Check: From the MFN Debate to a Tough, But Smart, China Policy." Progressive Policy Institute (May 27, 1997): http://www.ppionline.org/ppi_ci.cfm?knlgAreaID=108&subsecID=1 27&contentID=256.

5. See http://www.ned.org/events/democracy-award/1998 for more information on Wei Jingsheng and Wang Dan.

6. From the State Department's 2004 report: "Although the Government respected human rights in some areas, its overall record continued to reflect many problems. Reported continuing abuses included police abuse and mistreatment of detainees, allegations of torture, arbitrary

arrest and detention, lack of transparent investigations and of accountability within the security services resulting in a climate of impunity, denial of due process of law stemming from the expanded authority of the State Security Court and interference in the judicial process, infringements on citizens' privacy rights, harassment of members of opposition political parties, and significant restrictions on freedom of speech, press, assembly, and association. Citizens did not have the right to change their government. Citizens may participate in the political system through their elected representatives to Parliament; however, the King has discretionary authority to appoint and dismiss the Prime Minister, members of the cabinet and upper house of Parliament, to dissolve Parliament, and to establish public policy. The Government imposed some limits on freedom of religion, and there was official and societal discrimination against adherents of unrecognized religions. There were some restrictions on freedom of movement. Violence against women, restrictions on women's rights, and societal discrimination against women persisted. "Honor" crimes continued. Child abuse remained a problem, and discrimination against Palestinians persisted. Abuse of foreign domestics was a problem." Available: http://www.state.gov/g/drl/rls/hrrpt/2004/41724.htm.

7. Meghan L. O'Sullivan,. *Shrewd Sanctions: Statecraft and State Sponsors of Terrorism.* Washington, DC: Brookings Institute, 2003, 293.

8. United States Government Accountability Office, GAO-08–58: Report to the Ranking Member, Subcommittee on National Security and Foreign Affairs, House Committee on Oversight and Government Reform, "Iran Sanctions: Impact in Furthering U.S. Objectives is Unclear and Should Be Reviewed." Washington, DC: GAO, 2007, 35.

9. From the biography of Secretary Gutierrez "... oversees a diverse Cabinet agency with some 38,000 workers and a $6.5 billion budget focused on promoting American business at home and abroad. His Department gathers vast quantities of economic and demographic data to measure the health and vitality of the economy, promotes U.S. exports, enforces international trade agreements, regulates the export of sensitive goods and technologies, issues patents and trademarks, protects intellectual property, forecasts the weather, conducts oceanic and atmospheric research, provides stewardship over living marine resources, develops and applies technology, measurements and standards, formulates telecommunications and technology policy, fosters minority business development and promotes economic growth in distressed communities." Available at http://www.commerce.gov.

10. P.L. 110–369 (H.R. 7081, S. 3548), which was signed into law on October 8, 2008, contains two certification requirements that must be met before the law can enter into force. It requires that the president certifies to Congress that the agreement is consistent with aspects of the Nonproliferation Treaty (NPT) and that it is U.S. policy to work with the multinational Nuclear Suppliers Group "to agree to further restrict

the transfers of equipment and technology related to the enrichment of uranium and reprocessing of spent nuclear fuel." Although President Barack Obama certified in February 2010 that certain nuclear safeguards required under the NPT have been met, hurdles remain for India before both requirements can be met.

6 Money and Finance as Security Tools

1. Paul Cashin, Luis Céspedes, and Ratna Sahay. "Commodity Currencies." *Finance & Development* 40, no. 1 (March 2003): http://www.imf.org/external/pubs/ft/fandd/2003/03/cash.htm.
2. Mervyn King, "The Institutions of Monetary Policy." *American Economic Review* 94, no. 2 (May 2004), 1–13.
3. Ibid.
4. For instance, Justin Wolfers, and Eric Zitzewitz. "Prediction Markets." *Journal of Economic Perspectives* 18, no. 2 (2004): 107–26; and Paul W. Rhode and Koleman S. Strumpf. "Historical Presidential Betting Markets." *Journal of Economic Perspectives* 18, no. 2 (2004), 127–41.
5. University of Iowa News Release, November 24, 2008, "IEM within less than half percentage point in presidential race prediction." For more information see: http://www.biz.uiowa.edu/iem.
6. Robin Hanson, "Designing Real Terrorism Futures." *Public Choice*, vol. 128, no. 1/2, The Political Economy of Terrorism (July 2006), 257–74.
7. As reported by Mike Allen, "Ukraine, Nauru Face U.S. Sanctions; Countries' Banks Target in Terror War." *Washington Post* (December 20, 2002), A06.

7 Exchange Rate Choices and National Security

1. The Federal Open Market Committee. "Frequently Asked Questions." The Federal Reserve Board: http://www.federalreserve.gov/generalinfo/faq/faqfomc.htm.
2. Robert E. Lucas, "Expectations and the Neutrality of Money." *Journal of Economic Theory* 4, no. 2 (1972), 103–24.
3. See World Annual Exchange Rates (IFS).
4. Jim Saxton, Congressman (R-NJ), Vice Chairman, Joint Economic Committee, International Dimensions to U.S. Monetary Policies, Joint Economic Committee, United States Congress (August 2000).
5. Kurt Schuler, "Features and Policy Implications of Recent Currency Crises." Joint Economic Committee, U.S. Congress. Washington, DC: Government Printing Office, 2001. Kurt Schuler, "Basics of Dollarization." Joint Economic Committee, U.S. Congress. Washington, DC: Government Printing Office, 2000.

6. The *renminbi* is the name of China's currency, though the *yuan* is the unit of denomination. The economist Paul Krugman explains that Chinese currency is somewhat analogous to Britain's currency, which is sterling and is measured in pounds. When discussing the exchange rate between the United States and the UK, we typically discuss the dollar exchange rate with the British pound. Throughout this discussion and others in the book, however, we will use renminbi and yuan interchangeably.

7. Robert E. Scott, "The China Trade Toll: Widespread wage suppression, 2 million jobs lost in the U.S." Washington, DC: Economic Policy Institute (July 30, 2008): http://www.epi.org/publications/entry/bp219//.

8. For an interesting discussion on the weaponization of money, see Jodi Liss, "Making Monetary Mischief." *World Policy Journal* 24, no. 4 (2007), 29–38.

8   Maximizing over Time through Lending and Borrowing

1. According to a 2009 MIGA report: "The private underwriting market includes about 18 Lloyd's syndicates and about 10 private insurance companies. The majority of private insurers are based in three insurance centers—London, Bermuda, and the United States (primarily New York)—and several of the larger insurers have offices in Singapore. The private PRI market forms part of a wider insurance market that offers protection from political perils either as 'stand-alone' cover, or in combination with commercial credit risk cover. Due to the complex nature of the private market, brokers play an important role in promoting and sourcing PRI. Chartis Insurance (USA), Zurich (USA), Sovereign Risk Insurance Ltd. (Bermuda) and Chubb (USA) account for about 43 percent of the market share..." See Multilateral Investment Agency. *World Investment and Political Risk*. Washington, DC: The World Bank (2010), 49.

2. Sebastian Mallaby, "NGOs: Fighting Poverty, Hurting the Poor." *Foreign Policy* no. 144 (2004), 50–58. Although advocating a certain view on the efficacy of the incident described in this book, his account provides great detail and is worth reading.

3. For a discussion on new growth see, for example, Paul M. Romer, "Endogenous Technological Change." *Journal of Political Economy* 98, no. 5, Part 2: The Problem of Development: A Conference of the Institute for the Study of Free Enterprise Systems (1990), S71–S102.

4. These terms in this book mean lending by a state, lending by private individuals, and investment, respectively. See Eliana Cardoso and R. Dornbusch. "Foreign Private Capital Flows," in Chenery, Hollis Burnley, T. N. Srinivasan, Jere R. Behrman, Dani Rodrik, and Mark R. Rosenzweig. *Handbook of Development Economics* [vol 2]. Amsterdam; New York: North-Holland (Elsevier Science Pub. Co.), 1988.

5. Ibid.

6. "Immediately after the war and through the 1950s, there was virtually no borrowing by developing countries in the world capital markets. Most took the form of direct investment as well as loans from the IBRD and the EX-IM bank." (Cardoso and Dornbusch 1989); also see http://www.worldbank.org/prospects/gdf2000/CH6--118-139.pdf.

7. International Monetary Fund at International Monetary Fund: *Balance of Payments Statistics Yearbook*, p. 456 (2006) "Portfolio investment: Prior to 1997, transactions in equity, appropriate to portfolio investment were classified as direct investment capital. From 1997 onwards, equity transactions pertaining to an ownership of less than 50 percent are classified as portfolio investment. From September 1999 onwards, the 50 percent ratio changed to 10 percent." See also http://www.aph.gov.au/library/pubs/rn/2001–02/02RN08.htm: "Direct investment is where an investor's interest in an enterprise exceeds 10 per cent. Ten per cent is the level at which an investor is deemed to have acquired a significant influence in an enterprise. This category can be further subdivided into those enterprises where an investor holds 10–50 per cent of the equity and 50–100 per cent of the equity. In terms of control the second sub-category would give an investor a controlling influence in an enterprise. Portfolio investment is where an investor has less than a 10 per cent stake in an enterprise. This type of investment is regarded as not substantial enough to give an investor a significant influence over the management of an enterprise."

8. When focusing on FDI, Cardoso and Dornbusch emphasize the benefit from technology accompanying capital. Several empirical studies have looked at this relationship. Eduardo Borensztein, Jose De Gregorio, and Jong-Wha Lee conduct an empirical investigation into the role of FDI on growth. E. Borensztein, J. De Gregorio, and J-W Lee. "How Does Foreign Direct Investment Affect Economic Growth?" *Journal of International Economics* 45, no. 1 (1998), 115–35.

9. Ibid.

10. Ibid. While this does not make sense a priori, the empirical study could be trying to measure a linear relationship where one does not exist.

11. Borensztein, De Gregorio, and Lee, "How Does Foreign Direct Investment Affect Economic Growth?"

12. V. N. Balasubramanyam, M. Salisu, and David Sapsford. "Foreign Direct Investment as an Engine of Growth." *Journal of International Trade & Economic Development: An International and Comparative Review* 8, no. 1 (1998), 27–40.

13. Ibid., 27.

14. Ibid., 27–29.

15. Ibid., 29.

16. Ibid.

17. Luiz R. de Mello, Jr. "Foreign Direct Investment-Led Growth: Evidence from Time Series and Panel Data." *Oxford Economic Papers* 51, no. 1, Symposium on Trade, Technology, and Growth (1999), 133–51.

18. Ibid., 148.
19. Ibid.
20. Mohammad N. Elahee and Jose A. Pagan. "Foreign Direct Investment and Economic Growth in East Asia and Latin America." *Journal of Emerging Markets* 4, no. 1 (1999), 59–67.
21. Gerald Helleiner, "Transnational Corporations and Direct Foreign Investment," in Chenery, Hollis Burnley, T. N. Srinivasan, Jere R. Behrman, Dani Rodrik, and Mark R. Rosenzweig. *Handbook of Development Economics* [vol 2]. Amsterdam; New York: North-Holland (Elsevier Science Pub. Co.), 1988.
22. Ibid.
23. Ibid.
24. Ibid.
25. Ibid.
26. Daniel W. Drezner, "Sovereign Wealth Funds and the (in)Security of Global Finance." *Journal of International Affairs* 62, no. 1 (2008), 117.
27. See Dani Rodrik, "The Social Cost of Foreign Exchange Reserves." *International Economic Journal* 20, no. 3 (2006), 253–66.
28. Benjamin J. Cohen, "Sovereign Wealth Funds and National Security: The Great Tradeoff." *International Affairs* 85, no. 4 (2009), 719.
29. H.R. 556—110th Congress: Foreign Investment and National Security Act of 2007. (2007).
30. Jonathan Eaton and Raquel Fernandez. "Sovereign Debt," in Chenery, Hollis Burnley, T. N. Srinivasan, Jere R. Behrman, Dani Rodrik, and Mark R. Rosenzweig. *Handbook of Development Economics* [vol 2]. Amsterdam; New York: North-Holland (Elsevier Science Pub. Co.), 1988.
31. Jeremy Bulow, and Kenneth Rogoff. "Cleaning Up Third World Debt without Getting Taken to the Cleaners." *Journal of Economic Perspectives* 4, no. 1 (1990), 31–42.
32. Eaton and Fernandez, "Sovereign Debt."
33. Daniel Cohen, "Debt Relief: Implications of Secondary Market Discounts and Debt Overhangs." *World Bank Economic Review* 4, no. 1 (1990), 43–53.
34. Ibid.
35. Michael P. Dooley, "A Retrospective on the Debt Crisis." NBER Working Paper #4963 (1995).
36. Cohen, "Debt Relief."
37. Eaton and Fernandez, "Sovereign Debt."
38. See Jonathan Eaton and Mark Gersovitz. "Country Risk and the Organization of International Capital Transfer," in Jorge B. deMacedo and Ronald Findlay, editors, *Debt Growth, and Stabilization: Essays in Memory of Carlos F. Diaz Alejandro.* Oxford: Blackwell (1988); Jonathan Eaton and Mark Gersovitz. "A Theory of Expropriation and Deviations from Perfect Capital Mobility." *Economic Journal* 94, no. 373 (1984),

16–40; and Jonathan Eaton and Mark Gersovitz, "Debt with Potential Repudiation: Theoretical and Empirical Analysis." *Review of Economic Studies* 48, no. 2 (1981), 289–309.

39. Dooley, "A Retrospective on the Debt Crisis."

40. Ibid.

41. Pedro Alba, 2006. "Republic of Congo Reaches Decision Point Under the Enhanced HIPC Debt Relief Initiative." Press Release No.: 2006/301/AFR. The World Bank. http://web.worldbank.org/WBSITE/EXTERNAL/TOPICS/EXTDEBTDEPT/0,,contentMDK:20847652~menuPK:64166657~pagePK:64166689~piPK:64166646~theSitePK:469043,00.html.

9 CURING POVERTY HELPS NATIONAL SECURITY

1. Data gathered through the OECD's Query Wizard for International Development Statistics (QWIDS) for Africa's South of Sahara aid recipients from Development Assistance Committee countries between 1980 and 2008.

2. Remarks by President Obama at Strasbourg Town Hall (April 3, 2009): http://www.whitehouse.gov/the_press_office/Remarks-by-President-Obama-at-Strasbourg-Town-Hall/.

3. See Eli Berman, *Radical, Religious, and Violent: The New Economics of Terrorism.* Cambridge, MA: MIT Press, 2009; Laurence R. Iannaccone and Eli Berman. "Religious Extremism: The Good, the Bad, and the Deadly." *Public Choice* 128 (July 2006); and Eli Berman, David D. Laitin, "Religion, Terrorism and Public Goods: Testing the Club Model," *Journal of Public Economics*, 2008.

4. Jared M. Diamond, *Guns, Germs, and Steel: The Fates of Human Societies.* New York: Norton, 2005.

5. Jeffrey Sachs, *The End of Poverty: Economic Possibilities for Our Time.* New York: Penguin Press, 2005.

6. Stephen Haber, Douglass C. North, and Barry R. Weingast. "If Economists Are so Smart, Why Is Africa so Poor?" *Wall Street Journal* (July 30, 2003).

7. Robert E. Lucas, "On the Mechanics of Economic Development." NBER Working Paper No. R1176 (May 1989): http://ssrn.com/abstract=227120.

8. N. Gregory Mankiw, David Romer, and David N. Weil. "A Contribution to the Empirics of Economic Growth." *Quarterly Journal of Economics* 107, no. 2 (1992), 407–37.

9. Max Corden and J. Peter Neary. "Booming Sector and De-Industrialization in a Small Open Economy." *Economic Journal* 92 (December 1982), 825–48.

10. "The Millennium Challenge Account," Background paper, at http://www.mcc.gov.

11. See fact sheet at http://www.mcc.gov.

12. "Millennium Challenge Account: Already Paying Dividends," April 2005 at http://www.mcc.gov.

13. Curt Turnoff, "Millennium Challenge Corporation." Congressional Research Service (June 26, 2009).

10 TOOLS AGAINST TERRORISTS

1. See http://www.fatf-gafi.org/.

2. See U.S. Department of Treasury information at http://www.treasury.gov.

3. Matthew Levitt and Michael Jacobson. "The U.S. Campaign to Squeeze Terrorists' Financing." *Journal of International Affairs* 62, no. 1 (2008), 67–85.

4. President George W. Bush's address to a joint session of Congress on September 20, 2001: http://www.september11news.com/PresidentBushSpeech.htm.

5. See http://www.treas.gov/offices/enforcement/ofac/legal/statutes/ieepa.pdf.

6. See http://www.treas.gov/press/releases/tg515.htm.

7. Under E.O. 13224, individuals and entities can be designated if they meet one of five sets of criteria, summarized as follows: foreign individuals or entities listed in the Annex to E.O. 13224 (E.O. 13224, 1(a)); foreign individuals or entities that "have committed or ... pose a significant risk of committing acts of terrorism that threaten the security of U.S. nationals or the national security, foreign policy, or economy" of the United States (E.O. 13224, 1(b)); individuals or entities that either are "owned or controlled by" or "act for or on behalf of" those parties already designated under subsections 1(a), 1(b), 1(c), or 1(d)(i) of E.O. 13224 (E.O. 13224, 1(c)); individuals or entities that "assist in, sponsor, or provide financial, material, or technological support for, or financial or other services to or in support of" such acts of terrorism or those parties already designated under E.O. 13224 (E.O. 13224, 1(d)(i)); individuals or entities that are "otherwise associated" with those parties already designated under subsections 1(a), 1(b), 1(c), or 1(d)(i), of E.O. 13224 (E.O. 1 3224, 1(d)(ii)). See http://www.treasury.gov/offices/enforcement/designations.

8. Office of Foreign Assets Control. "Terrorist Assets Report: Calendar Year 2009 Eighteenth Annual Report to the Congress on Assets in the United States of Terrorist Countries and International Terrorism Program Designees." U.S. Department of Treasury: http://www.treasury.gov/offices/enforcement/ofac/programs/terror/terror.shtml.

9. See http://www.fatf-gafi.org/TFInterpnotes_en.htm.

10. Government Accountability Office. "Combating Terrorism: U.S. Agencies Report Progress Countering Terrorism and Its Financing in

Saudi Arabia, but Continue Focus on Countering Terrorism Financing Efforts Needed." Report to Congress Requesters, GAO-09-883 (September 2009).

11. Henry M. Paulson, "Targeted Financial Measures to Protect Our National Security" (June 14, 2007): http://www.ustreas.gov/press/releases/hp458.htm.

12. Levitt and Jacobson, "The U.S. Campaign to Squeeze Terrorist Financing."

13. See http://www.cpa-iraq.org/budget/DFI_intro1.html.

14. Patrick O'Brien, "Treasury's Approach Toward Combating Kleptocracy" (December 1, 2008): http://www.ustreas.gov/press/releases/hp1300.htm.

15. Nathan Vardi, "Al Qaeda's New Business Model?" *Forbes* 185, no. 3 (March 1, 2010), 60–65.

16. Evan Kohlmann, "Al Qaida Leader in Afghanistan Begs for Cash Donations." Counterterrorism Blog (May 25, 2007): http://counterterrorismblog.org/2007/05/alqaida_leader_in_afghanistan.php.

17. Gretchen Peters, *Seeds of Terror: How Heroin Is Bankrolling the Taliban and Al Qaeda*. New York: Thomas Dunne Books, 2009, 10.

18. Vardi, "Al Qaeda's New Business Model?"

19. Ibid.

11   International Law and Courts

1. See P.L. No. 104–132, codified at 28 U.S.C. § 1605.

2. An excellent database of legal resources used for reference in writing this chapter can be found at http://www.law.cornell.edu/

3. Pablo Morales was not a U.S. citizen at the time and therefore not eligible under the FSIA to seek justice against Fidel Castro. His family was not a party to the suit.

4. In January 2008, President Bush signed the National Defense Authorization Act for FY 2008 (NDAA) replacing Section 1605(a)(7) with a new terrorism exception, codified as Section 1605A, further enhancing victims' abilities to seek punitive damages.

5. In re: Islamic Republic of Iran Terrorism Litigation, _F. Supp. 2d_, 2009 WL 3112136 (D.D.C. 2009).

Index